HAROLD GATTY
(Walter Bird photo)

Finding Your Way Without Map or Compass

Harold Gatty

Foreword by
Lt. Gen. James H. Doolittle

DOVER PUBLICATIONS, INC.
Mineola, New York

Copyright

Bibliographical Note

This Dover edition, first published in 1999, is an unabridged reprint of *Nature Is Your Guide: How to Find Your Way on Land and Sea by Observing Nature,* originally published in 1958 by William Collins Sons & Co in the United Kingdom and E. P. Dutton & Co. in the United States. In this Dover edition the two color plates have been moved to the inside front and back covers.

Library of Congress Cataloging-in-Publication Data

Gatty, Harold, 1903–1957
    Finding your way without map or compass / Harold Gatty ;
    foreword by James H. Doolittle.
        p. cm.
    Originally published: Nature is your guide. 1st ed. New York : Dutton 1958.
    Includes index.
    ISBN-13: 978-0-486-40613-8
    ISBN-10: 0-486-40613-X
    1. Orientation. 2. Wilderness survival. 3. Navigation.
    I. Gatty, Harold, 1903–1957. Nature is your guide. II. Title.

GV200.5.G38 1999
796.58—dc21

                           98–55117
                             CIP

Manufactured in the United States by Courier Corporation
40613X07
www.doverpublications.com

Contents

Acknowledgments

I wish to extend my grateful thanks to Dr. Robert Cushman Murphy, eminent ornithologist and leading authority on oceanic birds, whose advice and assistance in the chapter on the habits of sea birds have been most valuable; and also to James Fisher, the distinguished English naturalist, for his valuable editorial assistance in this chapter and elsewhere in the book, and for contributing a number of original facts, useful criticism and suggestions. I owe much also to my wife, without whose aid in the translating of research materials from other languages, and in the testing of methods and theories of pathfinding in the field in various parts of the world, this book would not have been possible. For all her help and encouragement over the years I am deeply grateful.

HAROLD GATTY

Illustrations

Harold Gatty   *Frontispiece*

COLOR PLATES

MONOCHROME PLATES

LINE DRAWINGS, DIAGRAMS AND MAPS

Sea bird plates by Francis Lee Jaques
Color plates and drawing on page 151 by Robert Graves
Other line drawings by Douglas Woodall

Foreword

LIEUTENANT GENERAL J. H. DOOLITTLE

U. S. AIR FORCE, RESERVE

FUTURE GENERATIONS will have reason to be grateful that Harold
Gatty, during the latter years of his life, recorded with painstak-
ing care his immense and unique fund of knowledge in the realm
of pathfinding by natural methods on sea and land. Even in
these days of highly advanced technical aids, situations can arise
when it is vital for us to be able to find our way by observing the
signs of nature. In this field Harold Gatty was uniquely qualified.
During World War II, *The Raft Book*, his first work on the subject, was standard equipment in U. S. Army Air Force life rafts.
Written to help men who were adrift at sea, it proved of great
value. In *Nature Is Your Guide*,° Harold Gatty has vastly expanded his treatment of the topic. The present book covers
much of the marine material in the earlier work, and also deals
with pathfinding on land—in the wilderness, in the desert, in
snow-covered areas, and under other conditions, in most parts
of the world. Drawing on years of study and observation, the
author has provided illuminating accounts of the methods by
which early explorers and primitive peoples found their way on
their long journeys by observing nature. In fascinating detail,
he records ways in which we also can profit from their methods
simply through greater knowledge and observation of such phenomena as birds, animal life, weather, vegetation, the shifting of
sands and patterns of snow fields, and of course the position of
the sun, moon and stars.

Harold Gatty was born at Campbelltown, Tasmania, January
5, 1903, and educated at the Royal Australian Naval College.
Thereafter he served for several years as a ship's officer in the

°Title under which this book was originally published.

merchant marine, and undertook special research in air navigation. My own friendship with him started in 1931 when he won
worldwide fame as an air navigator through his record-breaking
eight-day flight around the world with Wiley Post in the *Winnie
Mae*. For this achievement, our country, by special Act of
Congress, awarded him the Distinguished Flying Cross.

That same year, the U. S. Army Air Corps embarked on its
first specialized courses in air navigation, and Harold Gatty was
placed in charge of Air Navigation Research and Training. The
military regulation normally restricting such a post with our
armed forces to American citizens was waived in his case to
enable him, as an Australian, to accept this position, which he
filled with distinction for several years. Among his students were
many officers who have since held prominent commands in our
Air Force.

During World War II, he served with the rank of Group Captain in the Royal Australian Air Force. In this capacity, his excellent work as Director of Air Transport for the Allied Air
Forces, first in Java and later at General MacArthur's headquarters in Australia and New Guinea, contributed to the final
victory.

After the war Harold Gatty settled in the Fiji Islands, where
he established and operated the Fiji Airways. He also conducted
a coconut plantation on his beautiful island, Katafanga, in the
South Pacific.

In the course of my own early experiments in instrument flying, I learned that there is, among humans, no such thing as an
innate or intuitive sense of direction or balance, and that maintaining altitude and course depends upon observation, either of
instruments or of natural things.

Through long and patient research which led him on special
journeys to many parts of the world, Harold Gatty gathered and
tested in the field the wealth of pathfinding secrets presented in
the following pages. His book is a treasury of practical and little
known lore, most of it given in no other volume. Clearly and
graphically, it tells exactly what natural indications to look for
in finding your way, and how to interpret them.

Shortly after finishing this book, Harold Gatty died suddenly at his home in the Fiji Islands. It is fortunate that this work will remain as a monument to his boundless interest in the natural world around us and to the precision of observation and thought which made him the foremost navigator of his time. To many readers everywhere it will be a rare and valuable experience to share in this life work of research and observation, which included also a great love of nature and all outdoor life. To a unique degree, Harold Gatty has given us a work which can serve as a companion, illuminating and expanding our pleasure in the outdoors, and at the same time minimize its dangers. The reader will not only gain confidence; he will also discover a more intimate appreciation and understanding of the world of nature. And I feel sure that that is what Harold Gatty, himself, hoped to accomplish in writing this book.

J. H. DOOLITTLE
Lieutenant General
U. S. Air Force, Reserve

Preface

THIS IS a new sort of outdoor book. In it I have attempted to bring together in a single volume the natural methods which can be used as practical aids in pathfinding. The book's aim is to enable the reader to find his way, on land or at sea, if necessary without map or compass, by using his own powers of observation and knowing how to interpret the signs of nature.

The countless clues and guideposts which nature places at our disposal as aids in natural navigation are for the most part little recognized or known today. With the invention of such technical devices as the chronometer and gyrocompass, radar and the automatic pilot, modern man tends to forget that earlier and more primitive peoples have had little difficulty in finding their routes through the wilderness and across the wide deserts and oceans completely without the aid of any such devices. My hope is that this book may help to revive this all but vanished art, and that it will enable the reader to acquire a practical and dependable knowledge of pathfinding by natural means.

In the course of my regular work I have been engaged for the past thirty-five years in research in navigation, including not only modern methods but also those used by early and primitive peoples. This latter phase of the work soon made it clear to me that the early explorers, lacking modern aids in navigation, relied in large part on observing and interpreting the natural things around them. This has been true not only of Occidental explorers but also of pioneers of other races such as the Polynesians, the American Indians, and the aborigines of Australia. These and many other peoples unversed in modern science have amply demonstrated their remarkable skill in traversing long distances through the wilderness or across the oceans, aided only by natural signs and their own skill in observing and interpreting them.

Today, these same methods of pathfinding can be used equally effectively by those who know what to look for and how to read the signs correctly.

In the course of my own work as a navigator, and on other occasions, the methods described in this book have been tested and found practical. The various chapters have been designed to cover the many differing types of conditions encountered over a large part of the world. Most of the methods described will not be found in the usual outdoor books, and it is hoped that they will be useful to readers engaged in many different outdoor pursuits.

In order to use the book most effectively, a few general considerations should be borne in mind. Although it embraces many diverse parts of the world, it is obvious that no one book could possibly hope to cover every locality in detail. The examples given apply in some cases to particular areas, but are also meant to illustrate the type of thing which every reader can learn about his own locality. Many of the general suggestions given in the book can thus be adapted to local conditions and applied in your own region.

In using these methods of observing and interpreting the evidence of the natural things about us, it is important to remember that under difficult conditions too much reliance should never be placed on any one observation since it may perhaps be an exception to the general rule. It is the combined evidence of a number of different indications which strengthens and confirms the conclusions to be drawn from them individually.

It should also be emphasized that the methods of pathfinding described in this book are intended not to replace the use of map and compass, if these are available, but rather to supplement them. Map and compass techniques are dealt with in many readily available outdoor books and manuals and are beyond the scope of the present volume. Nor is the book intended to cover methods of obtaining food, water and shelter in order to sustain life in the wilderness, or in case of distress at sea, subjects which have already been adequately covered by publications of the armed forces.

Compact tables for telling directions from the sun, at all times of year and in all latitudes from the equator to 60 degrees north and 50 degrees south, will be found at the back of the book. These tables have been especially prepared for the book, to fill the need for such data in compact form, practical for the use of the average outdoorsman. The professional sun tables hitherto in print are so detailed and voluminous that only a trained navigator or surveyor has the specialized knowledge needed to use them.

May I add that this book is not only intended to help the traveler who is seriously concerned with finding his way in the outdoors. In my experience, a knowledge of natural methods of pathfinding and orientation adds a great deal to the pleasure of even an otherwise uneventful walk in the country or cruise on waters near home or in the world's far places. Whatever the reader's individual circumstances in this respect, therefore, it is my hope that this book will add to his enjoyment by helping him to understand and interpret the natural world around him.

HAROLD GATTY

Katafanga Island
Fiji Islands
August 1957

Chapter 1

Nature Is Your Guide

"HE MUST have a wonderful sense of direction." I must have
heard this expression in everyday use by honest people hundreds,
perhaps even thousands of times—used by them, in all innocence
and sincerity, to convey the idea of a mysterious ability, somewhat vague and quite indefinable in its nature and operation.
Some people, with a knowing nod, will even go further and imply
that the sense of direction is a sixth sense, a quite special sense to
be added to the five senses with which the ordinary man or wo-
man (and many another animal) is born.

I do not believe that there is any such sixth sense. A man with
a good sense of direction is, to me, quite simply an able pathfinder—a natural navigator—somebody who can find his way by
the use of the five senses (sight, hearing, taste, smell and touch—
the senses he was born with) developed by the blessing of experience and the use of intelligence. All that the pathfinder needs is
his senses and knowledge of how to interpret nature's signs.

There is a whole world of these natural signs and guideposts
for us to observe and interpret. By means of them we can find
our way in remote and lonely places, on land or sea, if need be
without map or compass. Nature always has a reason, and the
chief purpose of this book is to help you interpret those reasons
and apply them in pathfinding.

A good pathfinder can become so proficient that he can amaze
the average person. If he likes to be mysterious he can easily
persuade his friends that he has a sixth sense; but if he wants to
be honest he must admit that he has nothing of the kind.

Nearly everybody is born with eyes, ears, a nose, taste buds and a sensitive skin. Some, of course, are born with sense organs more sensitive than those of others. All of us use our sense organs instinctively; that is, we do not have to be taught to use them, but inherit the ability to do so along with the organs themselves. But some use them better than others; and all of us are given the power of improving the use of our senses, by experience, by practice. Much of the use that we make of our senses depends on our early environment. Many city dwellers do not seriously have to consider the necessity of pathfinding once they have learned to talk and read, but for their own self-preservation the country dweller, the forester, the fisherman, the sailor and many others of us have to become thoroughly familiar with the natural things around them.

In our increasingly urban civilization the necessity of observing and interpreting nature's signs is, I suppose, slowly disappearing. By this I mean it is no longer often a matter of life and death: but because it is no longer a vital necessity there is no reason why it should decay, any more than music, painting, bird watching, tobogganing or any other form of pure art, science or sport should decay. I think that the interpretation of the signs of nature can and should be taught to children in schools at the same level as geography, mathematics. I think it is still tremendously important for everybody to be able to find his way by the use of nature's signs; and I think it is even more important that, trained in the use of nature's signs, all should be able to gain a wide appreciation of the natural things around them even if they are not likely to have to navigate. The habit of natural observation, of noticing natural details, natural features, is one that can easily be developed with proper training and practice—developed to such a pitch that astonishing feats can be performed without conscious mental effort.

There is something which all the greatest artists and writers, naturalists and scientists, voyagers and explorers, poets and pioneers, share. It is an interest in the external world and the ability to contribute something creative to human life in this world by means of taking parts of the world to pieces and putting them all together again. The ability to observe, and the ability to see the little things that seem trivial at first, may become amazingly important and meaningful. Out of little observations huge ideas may grow; and if a mind, made receptive by training in the use of the senses, can store away a mass of observations, the time will come when the whole collection can be unrolled, connected together as a great novel is planned, in a compelling pattern that tells us something *new*.

Many of our greatest naturalists, like Gilbert White and Charles Darwin, spent many years of their youth pottering around, in activities which must have seemed aimless to many of their friends. Darwin's parents and teachers, indeed, got very anxious because they thought he was lazy, when all the time he was quietly storing up observations which many years later came spinning forth, all welded together as the greatest scientific idea of the nineteenth century. Not all of us can be Darwins, but all of us can be constructive potterers, all of us can go for walks with no purpose in view but that of watching, of observation, of developing the use of the senses we are born with, of arousing thought and stimulating the imagination, of awakening the creative faculties. Everything becomes more meaningful to him who watches and listens without too much thought to the value of his time.

One man, Lord Baden-Powell, the first Chief Scout, built a whole movement on watching and listening. He called it "Scouting" and the movement swept the world. I have met many natural scouts in a life of much travel and in a long search for material for this book. I have rubbed my own theories and knowledge of pathfinding against those of others and often I have come across many surprising examples of people who have developed keen faculties of observation. I have only space to devote to three of them here, three very different people. What they can do shows how striking are the results of training, of natural interest, of long experience and practice.

In the summer of 1949, I was visited in Fiji by Dr. Robert Cushman Murphy, the eminent American ornithologist. He is certainly the world's greatest authority on sea birds: but my first taste of his ornithological ability came when he and his charming wife motored four miles with me, mainly through the town of Suva, from their ship to my Fiji home. Now Fiji has not got a very large variety of birds. There is no recent published list of the birds of Fiji but if you study Dr. Ernst Mayr's *Birds of the South-West Pacific* you will find that you could spend a whole season in the gardens and country around Suva without seeing more than about thirty-three different kinds of birds, although you will pick up a few more if you go farther inland into the dense forests or up to the hills. On our way to my house we talked, quite busily, but when we arrived there Dr. Murphy remarked, "I've seen eleven different kinds of birds since we left the ship." That was about a third of all those he could have seen if he'd stayed there a year. This great scientist had so trained himself that he could observe birds and identify the species all the while talking of other things.

My second example shows what an interest in nature can unveil to the untrained observer. My wife was brought up in Holland and has lived in cities most of her life, and in them has had no very great need to navigate by nature's ways. She traveled with me all over Europe and North America to further the research for this book, and took such a great interest in the subject I was working on at one time—directions from plants and trees—that when we reached San Francisco after a tour of two months she could tell north, south, east and west just by looking out of her hotel window.

This window looked out onto Union Square. In this square there was a tree surrounded on four sides by a border of pansies. My wife had quickly noticed that the yellow pansies were in bloom on the east, south and west sides, but were not yet out on the north side—which was sheltered from the sun by the tree.

And now for the results of practice. Colonel Richard I. Dodge, the well-known author and authority on the American Indian, wrote a passage in his book *Our Wild Indians* which well shows the peak of practice that necessity brings to the pathfinder:

Ask an Indian how to go to a point at a distance, one mile or a hundred miles, and he will simply point out the direction. Press him closely and if he has been to that point, he will by his minute descrip-

tion disclose another of his remarkable traits, his wonderful memory
of landmarks.

Similar and monotonous as they appear to the uneducated eye, each
hill and valley, each rock and clump of bushes, has for him its distinguishing features, which, once seen, he knows forever after, and care-
less as he appears when traveling, not one of these distinguishing
features escapes him. . . . If going on a journey into a country unknown to him, he consults with some warrior who has visited it; and it
is simply astonishing how clearly the one describes and the other
comprehends all that is necessary to make the journey a success.

I should explain at this early stage of my book that I have had
thirty-five years' experience, first as a marine navigator and later
as an air navigator. For many of these years I had my own Navigation School in Los Angeles and later I taught navigation to the
United States Air Force. During all my teaching I stressed to my
students the importance of natural navigation—the kind of navigation that they did not then, and do not now, find in textbooks.
Conventional air navigation is performed, of course, by all kinds
of instruments and mechanical devices, and by maps. I tried to
show my students that they needed to use their eyes for register-
ing the details of the country below them, in addition to all the
modern mechanical aids.

After our world flight in 1931, the late Wiley Post and I spent
five months on a good-will tour, during which the *Winnie Mae*
traveled in a crisscross pattern across the United States, averaging
almost a town per day. Wiley Post was pilot, I was navigator;
and while we were in the air I used to familiarize myself with
the country below, especially with those aspects of it that were
not marked on any conventional maps or charts. Such things
were the type of vegetation, the kinds of crops, the layout of
farms and farm buildings, the architecture of the houses and
barns, the shape of the haystacks and grain stacks, the type of
fencing and field boundaries.

Many things told me which way the wind was blowing on the
ground, the smoke of houses, the bending of trees, the silvery
undersides of their leaves. I found that it was much easier to
tell the wind direction on Mondays than on any other day by

watching the clotheslines, for Monday is wash day the world over. And by watching for the odd details I discovered that certain regions had their own peculiarities, almost their signatures. Throughout the farming areas of Ohio, for instance, almost every little barn and building had an elaborate lightning conductor; there was an amazing number of these rods bristling on buildings throughout the state. Now, compared with any of the other neighboring states, Ohio is not more subject to lightning: it seemed to me that the enterprise of some persuasive salesman had left its mark.

Of course, not everybody is lucky enough to be able to see the country from the air and follow its changing personality over a great continent. Certainly my early North American flights taught me much of the value of exercising my awareness. Indeed, after practicing observations such as those I have described, I found that in quite a short time I had become able to recognize a locality almost anywhere in the United States without consulting my map.

To read the personality of a countryside like this, it is not invariably necessary to leave the comfort of one's own home. If you cannot for the time being study scenery from the air, from a railroad train or car, you must study photographs. It is great fun to observe the details in a scenic illustration whose caption is covered up. After some practice, the careful observer of detail can often tell a great deal from a photograph of an area with which he is personally quite unfamiliar. The amateur indoor nature detective can occupy himself for many profitable hours with a collection of air photographs, such as is published (under the auspices of the British Institute of Sociology) in E. A. Gutkind's *Our World from the Air*. The accompanying drawing, based on a photograph, depicts a scene somewhere in the British Isles. Supposing that we know no more than this, what can we further deduce by studying it closely?

From the general nature of the hillside country it is clear that the picture cannot have been taken anywhere in central, southern or eastern England.

An analysis of this picture can indicate the general region, the time of the year, the time of the day, and the direction in which the house is facing. (*After a photograph from* Coming Events in Britain, *courtesy British Travel & Holidays Association*)

From the architecture of the building it seems very likely that the place is in northern England.

From the state of the vegetation, the season appears to be early spring.

The main part of the house probably faces south to get the greatest warmth in the living rooms; from this we can make a first deduction of the orientation of the picture.

From the length and direction of the shadows, we can further deduce that the picture was taken around noon and that the shadows point towards the north. Thus the road must run roughly east and west with its eastern end in the foreground.

The shape of the trees confirms the north-south direction of the shadows and of the south-facing building, for the southern branches of trees tend to be more horizontal because they secure full sunlight, whereas the northern branches tend to be more vertical as they reach up to obtain more light. There is also a greater branch foliage on the southern side.

Needless to say, the presence of Shetland ponies is no indicator of place. There are far more Shetland ponies outside Shetland than in it, and the picture could not possibly have been made in Shetland, where few trees grow and those seldom more than twenty or thirty feet high, and where the architecture and general physiognomy of the countryside are quite different.

I often play the photograph analysis game. It is amazing how much the problem of identifying a photograph without captions adds to its interest and improves one's own powers of perception and deduction. The photograph ceases to be a photograph and becomes, instead, a story.

We may play this photo-navigation game in fun and may make a sport out of pathfinding. Sometimes we may forget that to our own ancestors these affairs were no game but a dire necessity. Actually, the primitive ancestors of most humans in our western civilization, though pretty good navigators, were by no means the best of all the primitives. Undoubtedly those primitives who have made history as pathfinders, by living with and by nature, were the Polynesians, the Australian aborigines and the American Indians. More often than others, these races have been accredited with the mysterious "sixth sense" I wrote of earlier in this chapter, with a mysterious "bump of locality," with a magical "sense of direction." At the risk of making a point more than once (and I shall make it again) I must repeat that these primitives, or indeed any human navigators, and as far as we know any animal navigators, have used and use no more than the five senses of conventional literature and philosophy, namely, sight, hearing, smell, taste and touch. If they use a sixth sense, which may be different from or at least partly independent of any of the conventional five, then that sense is a time sense, an ability to perceive accurately the passage of time which may be dependent on "internal rhythm" and at least partly independent of the observation of the movement of the sun. I shall have more to say of time sense later.

The great primitive navigators, then, simply used nature as their guide, and no better example of their keenly developed powers of observation can be given than that of their ancient art of tracking. Of course tracking does not consist of navigation and orienting of oneself. It consists of the reconstruction of a journey made by man or beast from the marks and signs left behind on that journey's path. It is universally acknowledged that of all the primitives the most skilled native trackers are Australian aborigines. An "abo" tracker's ability is not simply due to his great personal acuity of vision and other senses. Undoubtedly the instinctive senses of the aborigine are very highly developed, but his incredible skill lies as much in his training and in his intelligence and reasoning capacity. A good aboriginal tracker has a thorough knowledge of bush craft, animal lore and the habits of human beings; and a brilliant faculty of putting a mosaic of observations together and making deductions therefrom. He can locate his quarry with the least possible effort and with an almost unerring success.

The following account of the remarkable training process of the aborigines was given in a paper by A. T. Magarey in 1897:

No sooner does the dusky child of the sparse wilds of Australia begin to leave his mother's head-borne cradle, than he is set to chase and capture some living thing. Step by step the youngster rises in proficiency until beetles, spiders, ants and such like fairy track-makers are followed over the telltale ground. Such training is continued until manhood is reached; until of gliding snake, bounding wallaby or the crafty dangerous lurking foeman, all the earth signs are seen, noted, interpreted, followed or avoided as the circumstances may demand. To his vigilant eye the fresh sharp-cut imprint, the up-springing grass blade, but newly bent by the swiftly passing foot tread, each tells in its own way its own story.

It is true to say that all the aboriginal natives of those vast, arid regions in the continent of Australia can follow tracks imperceptible to the average European. But even though each aborigine is trained from childhood and is constantly practicing his art, there is always a difference between the ability of one individual and another. Only a few aborigines of fantastic skill know how to follow really obscure tracks.

This difference in navigating and tracking ability between individuals is, of course, just as likely to occur among any group of humans as it is among the aborigines. In our Western civilization, pathfinding and natural tracking are so little developed (except perhaps in some well trained fighting services and the Boy Scout movement) that notwithstanding all differences of innate ability, the man who has learned the simplest secrets of reading nature's signs is bound to outstrip the inexperienced observer, however intelligent he may be, and can not only outstrip him, but frequently amaze him. Nature's signs can be read with a little practice by the average intelligent Western man just as clearly as if they were street signs.

The drill for proficiency is fairly simple; the beginner must walk, and preferably walk alone, for talk distracts the beginner and prevents concentration; the seasoned pathfinder thinks only of the job on hand. He must think purely of the external world. The man who walks to solve an internal problem on his mind, or to daydream, is going to learn nothing about natural navigation. I would never advise any beginner to overstrain his memory in the early stages of improving his powers of observation by practice. The quick tracker and fine natural navigator has developed his powers of memory through years of practice; the beginner has to carry a pencil and notebook to list features, landmarks, associations. It is extraordinary how the novice forgets colors. I would almost go so far as to say that most people have a black and white mind, unless they have seriously cultivated painting or color photography. The average person is much more sensitive to shape than to color. He is more inclined to note a misshapen rock, or a twisted tree trunk, than a tree of a distinctive color, and as often as not the beginner, too, will rely more purely on sight than on any other of his senses, forgetting that places have their own characteristic sounds and their own characteristic smells. Oddly enough (at least as far as my own experience is concerned), sounds and smells often stick faster in the unconscious memory than in the conscious memory.

Often the beginner in natural navigation fails to see his journey in reverse, as he must do if he is successfully to retrace his steps. I would advise him to practice sketch maps and sketches of the relative positions of landmarks seen from time to time "over his shoulder" on the outward journey. I call this exploring with one eye on the return journey, "maintaining the thread." All primitive pathfinders and trackers use the method, which largely accounts for their success. To them, it is quite natural to remember detours around obstructions, zigzags and turns, and file them away in their memory in such a way that they can be followed in reverse.

The primitive natural navigator almost invariably measures his distance between landmarks by time rather than by space. So accustomed is the Western man, however, to judging distances and measuring spaces on maps, and so greatly has he lost his natural sense of time, that he chooses to think in terms of distance. Navigating by nature, the careful traveler chooses, if he can, a high point near his starting place and looks all around the horizon, estimating the distance to the natural features, taking in the detailed picture in each cardinal direction, noting, remembering (and if he cannot remember, sketching) the general outline and profile of mountains or any other silhouettes on the horizon, then switching his attention to the foreground in each of the cardinal directions, north, south, east and west, noting the type of country, the dominant vegetation, the configuration of hills, the direction of valleys and streams, the architecture of buildings and the relationship of all these features to each other and to the point of observation. The habit of mental map-making thus developed tends, as it improves, to become progressively free of the notebook. Eventually small hills, stones, trees, bushes, are mentally recalled with very great ease, and in their proper succession, and become bound in the observer's memory as the links of a chain.

To conclude my remarks on the use of powers of observation, here is a remarkable example of a person finding his way in extreme circumstances.

About fifty years ago, Enos Mills, a mountain guide, became snow-blind and found himself lost when he was on the summit of the Continental Divide in the Rocky Mountains, 12,000 feet above sea level with the nearest house many miles away across rough mountain ridges. His factual story of how he successfully found his way by the intelligent application and observation of natural things is recounted in his book, *Adventures of a Nature Guide*, written some thirty-six years ago.

It is an excellent illustration of how the practice of noticing nature's signs can be developed by learning to interpret them. Mills was an unusually keen observer of nature and he managed to remain calm and confident of finding his way back when he found himself lost. He said of the incident: "My faculties were intensely awake. The possibility of a fatal ending never occurred to me." His matter-of-fact attitude coupled with his ability to interpret the natural signs of that particular region—e.g., certain pine trees growing on a slope, the bark of trees, trail blaze marks on trees, echoes and aspen smoke—enabled him to survive.

Mills was confident of his ability to get out of the predicament in which he found himself. He could not use trails because of the extreme depth of snow, but in his mind he had a clear mental map of the slope down which he had to travel. It was made up of the impressions he had gathered before the darkness of snow-blindness settled over him.

Carrying a long staff, he set out on snowshoes to find the blaze marks on the trees which he had made on his forward journey. Making his way from tree to tree he thrust an arm into the snow, feeling the bark of the trees until he discovered the mark of the blaze. He resorted to the trees for the points of the compass. In his study of tree distribution he had learned that, in this locality, canyons running east and west carried limber pines on the wall that faced south and Engelmann spruce on the wall that faced north. With limber pines on his left and Engelmann spruces on his right he was now satisfied that he was traveling eastward and should be on the eastern side of the range. To check this, he examined the lichen growth of low-lying boulders and the moss which encircled the trunks of trees, concluding that the surrounding area must be such as to admit light freely from all quarters.

To get an idea of the topography of the canyon he shouted, noting from which direction the echoes came, their intensity and the cross replies—concluding from these that he was going into the head of a deep forest-walled canyon.

In the night a snowslide almost smothered him as he made his way and progress was made more difficult by the enormous rock masses and entanglements of fallen branches and leaves.

Suddenly he caught the scent of smoke, which he recognized as that of aspen, a wood burned in the cookstoves of the mountain people. Under favorable conditions a person with a keen sense of smell can detect aspen wood smoke for a distance of two or three miles. Going forward in the direction from which the wind was blowing, he emerged from the woods where the smoke was strongest and knew that human habitation was near. In fear of passing it, he stopped to use his ears. As he stood listening, a little girl gently, curiously asked: "Are you going to stay here tonight?"

Chapter 2

How Early Man Found His Way

"FOR TWENTY-FOUR HOURS there have passed by the ship a great many pieces of wood and fruits that we do not know; the sea is calmed down in spite of the strong wind from the south-east and these circumstances combine to convince us that there is land close by to the south-east of us."

In those words Louis de Bougainville told, nearly two hundred years ago, how he knew that he was near the coast of Australia (although it was out of sight) on his famous voyage round the world. De Bougainville, like all great early explorers, kept a log, and like nearly all the logs of his contemporaries, his account often shows how necessity forced him to use his powers of observation, to use natural navigation in the absence of the full repertoire of mechanical aids and charts that the navigators of today enjoy.

Nowadays navigators rely so closely on technical aids that they find it much harder than the Western explorers of a couple of centuries ago to believe in primitive navigation. It is the very technical advancement in scientific navigation which has made the scientific navigators of today only too prone to build a wall of mystery, fable and myth around the natural navigators of the past. So used are we to navigating by the compass, the chronometer, the sextant, the radio, radar and echo sounder, that some of us just cannot believe that early peoples could make long journeys in unknown areas, and find their way through unexplored wilds and across uncharted seas, with only their normal senses and traditional wisdom to guide them. It is an interesting fact that the whole myth of the mysterious sixth sense of direction of the

34

primitive human or animal navigator has come into prominence only in this latest era of scientific and electronic navigation. With these fantastic devices around us, many of us have lost sight of the truth, that the native, the perceptive savage, the "uncivilized" primitive, has or had keener perceptions and more highly developed powers of observation than most of us, and used these powers to perform almost incredible feats of pathfinding on land and landfinding at sea.

One of the greatest barriers to a public understanding of the navigating abilities of primitive races is the conventional history book, which gives us a picture of the world inhabited by "natives." These natives, in the islands and countries where they lived, were "discovered" by the great explorers of the West. Somehow the fact that the "natives" had in nearly every case "discovered" their homes by their own much earlier and unaided exploration gets left out of the books. The books forget to make a point of the astounding fact that at the time of the first great Western opening of the undiscovered world, practically every part of the land surface, including such remotest oceanic islands as were habitable, was already occupied by humans, usually by dark-skinned humans.

These people themselves had made long migrations overland or oversea from their original homelands. Unblessed with the written record, they left but verbal legend or traditional tale to explain how they got there. Such legends, such tales, are often garbled and unreliable. It is only when we look into the methods of navigation which were found to be still in use by some of these primitive but undoubtedly civilized peoples in fairly recent times, that we get some idea of the ways in which the ancient human migrants navigated.

One thing becomes immediately clear if we study the navigation of primitives and early Western man—exploration was seldom, if ever, at random. Few, if any, primitive explorers appear to have led a voyage or expedition haphazardly into the unknown. Almost invariably they had some goal, even if that goal was a fabled goal and not an actual one. The history and folklore of Western Europe, especially Ireland and Portugal, is full of mythical islands which supposedly lay to the West in the Atlantic Ocean and which were the cause of many voyages of search. My own belief is that the visible tracks of bird migration were also a powerful influence in the opening up of the world. Some of even the greatest of our Western naturalists were arguing as late as the eighteenth century whether birds migrated or not, but for thousands of years the primitives have certainly known better than this. They knew that birds migrated, all right. They saw the land birds setting off across the seas on their annual migration. They surmised that these birds could not survive if they alighted on the ocean and they concluded by the simplest common sense that another land lay in the direction of their flight.

Most people may think that bird migrations occur only in a north and south direction, but this is by no means universally the case. Ornithologists are beginning to map a clear network of migratory routes or "flyways" over the surface of the earth. Not all birds migrate on restricted flyways; many species pass on their journeys across land and even across great oceans on what is known as a broad front. But perhaps the majority of species and individuals of all migrant birds, use flyways. By no means all of these flyways run simply north and south; some run east and west, others up and down river valleys, others along coasts; some skirt mountain ranges or find their way through them by well-marked through-passes; others (and particularly birds of prey) choose migratory routes where abundant thermals provide risings of hot air on which they can soar their way to their goal without using up muscular energy; many of these thermal flyways pass or skirt sun-warmed deserts. Some of the spring flyways differ from the autumn flyways, mostly because of prevailing winds; thus several species of birds from South Greenland may cross direct to Europe in the autumn on the prevalent westerlies but island-hop *via* Britain, the Faeroes and Iceland on their way back in spring, assisted by the then prevalent southerlies. The migratory routes of birds are probably very ancient; though some may well have been modified, even in historical times, with the changes in the distribution of the species and in climatic conditions.

A score or more species of birds use, in spring, the Scotland-Faeroes-Iceland steppingstone migration route, with sufficient predictability to have assisted the Scandinavian ships which, sailing westwards from Norway, could pick up the avian pilots. The first settlers in Iceland were probably Culdee priests from Ireland and they probably found their way there in their open currachs in the spring by the route Ireland-Hebrides-perhaps Shetland-Faeroes-Iceland; which is a route used by many species of ducks that nest all over Iceland, especially in that wildfowl oasis, Lake Mývatn in the north-central part of that great island, and by at least one Irish goose, the yellow-billed race of the white-fronted goose that summers and nests in West Greenland and that almost certainly flies back to Greenland in spring by the Iceland route.

Some of the migratory routes of birds should probably be described as emergency routes. It would seem, for instance, that the bulk of the spring and autumn passage of Western European migratory birds runs along the Continental coast of Norway and the North Sea; but when easterly winds prevail (as they often do because of the standing anticyclone over Scandinavia) many birds get deflected from this route and use instead the eastern coast of the British Isles, joining up with the Continental coastal route again by the shortest sea gap between Scotland and mainland Europe, which lies between Shetland and the westernmost point of Norway. Although this may be a secondary route and is not used by quite such a dense or regular stream of birds as the Continental coastal route, it is probably sufficiently reliable to have helped a human passage across this same sea gap. In any case, once the help of migrant birds has demonstrated to humans that a route is possible, future navigators on the same route can to a certain extent dispense with the birds' guidance—particularly if a group of vessels sail in company with the ships arranged on an extended front after the habit of the old-time Polynesian voyagers.

It seems certain that the Polynesian voyagers (who seem to have been greater and even more daring explorers of the sea than the early Irish and the early Vikings) must, like the Irish and the Vikings, have been assisted by the visible migration of

Bird migration routes in the Pacific. (*After Wells Cooke*)

birds. Just above is a chart derived from a paper written by
Wells W. Cooke illustrating the probable pattern of bird migration flyways in the Pacific Ocean. The interesting thing about this
chart is that it was prepared by someone who was concerned only
with the problems of bird migration and was (unlike myself) not
particularly interested in the movements of the Polynesians
through the area. But if we study Cooke's map, we find that the
route marked 1 coincides with the conclusions of nearly all authoritative scientists about the original path of the Polynesians
in their colonization of the Pacific.

Indeed, alone among prominent scientists Thor Heyerdahl, of *Kon-Tiki* fame, remains in unequivocal adherence to a belief in the South American origin of the Polynesians. Since the much publicized account of the daring and successful *Kon-Tiki* expedition, scientific journals have been filled with a critical discussion of Heyerdahl's theories; and universally the scientific critics agree that in his main thesis he was probably wrong and that the origin of the Polynesians was from exactly the opposite direction, that is from the Indo-Malayan area. From this region they migrated eastwards and eventually have peopled islands over the length and breadth of the Pacific. If we want to study the navigation of early man, then we need go no further than the Polynesians, the only truly oceanic people in the world.

Polynesia's vast extent in the world's greatest ocean can scarcely be exaggerated. It comprises a fantastic scatter of islands, occupying a triangular area of the great ocean with sides of four thousand miles. One apex lies at the Hawaiian Islands, another on Easter Island, two thousand miles west of the coast of Chile, the third at New Zealand. And the whole of this vast triangle was settled by one people, of one culture and language. Within the great triangle it is certain that this people could make back-and-forth voyages over distances of two thousand, five hundred miles and more; that is, for instance, between Tahiti and New Zealand and between Tahiti and Hawaii. A century after the *last* of the great Polynesian colonizing migrations, Western Europeans were still afraid to venture out beyond the Pillars of Hercules into the green sea of darkness, the Atlantic. The Pacific Ocean islands had been discovered and happily settled long before the birth of Christopher Columbus.

The Polynesians were the greatest pathfinders in history. Who knows why they first started to explore? Pressure, perhaps, of overpopulation in southeast Asia, tribal differences and wars, maybe. Whatever the cause of the start of their great wanderings, they were the first of the world's peoples to become truly seafaring. Colonizing, trading in semiprecious greenstone, or simply visiting friends and relations, they maintained frequent intercourse be-

The departure of six Maori canoes from Rarotonga for New Zealand, about 1350 A.D.

tween groups of islands thousands of miles apart, in an ocean that belies its name.

The Pacific Ocean, of course, is far from calm, and the Polynesians never sailed great distances upon it in vessels which could reasonably be described as "canoes," although they often have been so described. In fact, when Captain Cook sailed into the Pacific in the 98-foot *Endeavour*, he was surprised to find that these ingenious islanders traversed the vast and often rough stretches of the Pacific Ocean in doubled-hulled vessels—catamarans—110 feet long, with two masts and mat sails, a small cabin on deck, and capable of carrying one hundred and forty people. Once the Polynesians reached Tahiti, it became an important headquarters and dispersal point for these people, for from Tahiti they colonized north to the Hawaiian Islands and south to New Zealand. Their voyage from Tahiti to the Hawaiian Islands was on the same track as is used every year in spring by the Pacific golden plover, *Pluvialis dominica*, and the rare bristle-thighed curlew, *Numenius tahitiensis*. Both these species to this day fly between Alaska and the Hawaiian Islands, Tahiti and other islands of the Southwest Pacific each year.

The second Polynesian migratory track is considered to be along the route marked 2 in Cooke's map. I have added to this map a route, 6, which is the well-established track of the long-tailed cuckoo, *Eudynamis taitensis*, a brown and rufous bird spotted with white, with white underparts streaked with black, which breeds in New Zealand and on migration is found throughout Polynesia. In September this migrant cuckoo flies south to New Zealand, and it seems more than a coincidence that its flyway is the route used by the Maori fleet which colonized New Zealand from Tahiti in about 1350 A.D. The Maoris, of course, were not the first colonists in New Zealand. My own belief is that the original Polynesian inhabitants of New Zealand came from settlements in the vicinity of the Solomon Islands, also following the migratory track of birds, in this case probably the shining cuckoo, *Chalcites lucidus*, which is much commoner in the Solomon Islands than the long-tailed cuckoo and which also flies to New Zealand for the breeding season. Another bird which may have helped the first New Zealanders is the Pacific race of the bar-tailed godwit, *Limosa lapponica,* which breeds in north-eastern Siberia and Alaska and winters throughout the South-west Pacific as far as New Zealand. Unlike the cuckoos, this god-wit is a nonbreeder (i.e., a winterer) in the South, but its migra-tory flight takes place at about the same time and in the same direction.

There is no doubt whatever that, season after season, the Poly-nesians watched the bird migrations; and when they were confi-dent that they had found a consistent flyway they set out to follow it. A study of their old chants and their old legends shows most clearly the importance they attached to the direction of the flight of birds. I know of nothing else that could have led these seafaring people from Tahiti to New Zealand but the repeatedly observed migration of the long-tailed cuckoo between these two places. In such migration flights the long-tailed cuckoos do not all set out at once, but straggle over a period of two or three weeks. Once en route, the cuckoos never fly very high over the sea and the following voyager could doubtless see some part of the migratory flock nearly every day and perhaps hear them at night.

On setting out to follow a flyway, the Polynesians took careful departure by lining up range marks on the shore sighted on the ob-served bird flights. Some of these range marks, pointing to dis-tant lands, are still known in the Pacific. The Polynesians had no compass; they had no charts of the kind that we know. As I shall presently describe, they navigated, at least when in the open sea, by the stars. It would have been possible, of course, for the Polynesians to establish or check their shore marks by the stars, but it is a much more probable hypothesis that these landmarks were a line on bird flyways, bird flight lines.

When Christopher Columbus made his famous voyage in 1492, he remembered that the Portuguese had already discovered the Azores by noting the directional flight of migratory birds; and it was because he kept a sharp lookout himself that he discovered the North American avifauna before he discovered the New World. Columbus made his first landfall in America in the Bahamas—by his decision to alter course to the southwest because of the great number of small land birds which he saw flying in that direction.

The use of captive birds as an auxiliary aid to navigation is almost as old as civilized man: indeed, the method is first mentioned in the Gilgamesh epic written several thousand years B.C. This Babylonian version of the Flood describes how Noah's prototype sent forth a dove on the first occasion; it found no resting place, and returned. Next to be released was a swallow, which also returned to the vessel. Finally a third bird, a raven, was sent out; it flew away and, seeing trees emerging from the waters, did not return.

A Hindu legend of the fifth century B.C. tells how Hindu merchants, when sailing on overseas voyages, carried with them several shore-sighting birds to locate the nearest land when the ship's position was in doubt. The same custom is mentioned by Pliny as being practiced in his time—the first century A.D.—by the seamen of Ceylon on ocean voyages: they did not know how to steer by the stars.

Not unexpectedly, the captive bird method was known to the Polynesians. Most commonly they took with them one of the most agile and skillful of all the sea-bird fliers, the frigate bird or man-of-war bird. Frigate birds are plentiful in the Polynesian region and, although patrollers of the open sea, do not normally land on water—their plumage gets waterlogged if they do. With a huge wing span and large wing area the frigate bird has a vast operational range, and even in recent times has been used as a message carrier between the islands. When released, the birds fly to a height which gives them a far more distant vision than that of the crew on the deck of a ship. If and when they sight land they immediately fly in that direction. Since frigate birds are particularly disinclined to land on any water, they almost invariably return to the vessel if they do not see land.

Like other early voyagers, the Vikings used shore-sighting birds to show the direction of land. The saga tells that when Floki, the Norse navigator, left Shetland for Iceland he carried a number of birds called sea ravens, which were probably shags or cormorants. When he was a few days out from Shetland he released a bird: it circled for altitude and, seeing land astern, flew towards it, thus giving Floki a back bearing on his point of departure. Several days later Floki released a second bird: and this one took a forward course to Iceland, showing him the direction to follow.

It is probable that those hardy sea kings, the Vikings, were never able to obtain much precision in their navigation, because of the weather conditions in the North Atlantic Ocean. The skies of the North Atlantic are almost chronically overcast; and it is natural that the Vikings were never able to develop a system of navigation by the stars. They were able to make return voyages between Europe and Iceland with reasonable certainty, but navigated to and fro between Iceland and Greenland only with the greatest difficulty. Their basic directions were obtained only by the flight of birds, the direction of the wind and waves, and the sun.

It was the Polynesians—whose ocean has more stable weather —who first developed natural navigation by the stars to a fine art. But it is possible that they may have inherited certain principles of star navigation from the early Arab navigators.

We know that the Arabians in the Indian Ocean—in addition to the use of birds—navigated by the Pole Star in a very simple manner. They used the fingers of the outstretched hand to measure the height of this star above the horizon, and this angle gave them their latitude. Later, they developed a better method of obtaining latitude with a piece of string and a short stick, and from this was evolved the cross-staff, a forerunner of the sextant used by modern navigators. In their long voyages across the Indian Ocean, they also used, often as a principal method, the known direction of chronic seasonal winds such as monsoons.

On these trips they noticed that the stars rose at the same points of the sky all year round and set on the opposite horizon. Although they had no magnet, they divided the horizon into thirty-two points. These points were derived from fifteen stars which rose at approximately equally spaced points of the eastern horizon. The setting points of these stars on the western horizon gave them another fifteen points and north and south brought the total to thirty-two. The Arabs made a dial of wood with thirty-two spikes placed around its circumference representing these points. Checking the well-established prevailing wind with a star or some other sign, they steered by this device, which was in fact what is known today as a pelorus, or dummy compass—a compass dial without a magnet.

It was in about the second century A.D. that the Arabs brought the magnetic needle from China. At once they combined it with their thirty-two point division of the circle. This division of the horizon, coupled with the magnet, was first introduced into Europe at the time of the Crusades; and it is still found on many of today's marine compasses.

The first European explorers in the Pacific were amazed to find that although the Polynesians did not know the magnet, many of the peoples in the Pacific used the thirty-two point dummy compass. From my studies I consider this further proof of the Indo-Malayan origin of the Polynesians: evidence that they explored and colonized into the Pacific from the coast of India *before* the introduction of the magnet, that is, before the second century A.D.—but *after* they had learned from the early Arabs the thirty-two point dummy compass.

With this dummy compass (but without the magnet) the Polynesians, when out at sea, were able to navigate by the stars with remarkable accuracy and simplicity. They saw the heavens as the inside of a dome, across which the stars traced their courses. Each could be regarded as a moving band of light; and the Polynesians knew the stars or bands which passed over the islands in which they were interested.

These accomplished navigators had names for one hundred and fifty stars. They knew the point on the horizon where each of these rose, and the time at which it did so. They knew the islands which each passed over. Watching the heavens, night after night, they saw that the stars stayed in the same relation to one another and rotated around an imaginary axis. Month after month the same stars passed over the same islands. They saw that the stars kept to the same path; but that each night they appeared slightly earlier—earlier by about four minutes by our way of measuring time. The Polynesians had no watches or clocks, but like all sensitive primitives and many wild animals they had an amazingly accurate time sense. These island mariners could thus sail towards the star that they knew was over their destination at that particular time. Their system was amazingly simple; and needed no instruments whatsoever.

To clarify this method, let us imagine the stars stationary for a moment. Each star in the heavens will be exactly overhead at some place on the surface of the earth. If we can identify the star which at this moment is over the island of Hawaii, we have a shining beacon leading to it which can be seen thousands of miles away. Moreover, if we steer for this star, we actually follow the shortest possible course—the course which modern navigators allude to as a "great circle." Indeed, we are thus following a system more perfect in principle than our modern methods of compass navigation, for if the distance involved is fairly great the compass course is different from and necessarily longer than the great circle course to a given destination.

Not only does this star give us the direction and shortest course to our island, but also tells us when we can expect to reach it, for when we do so the star will be overhead.

Now let us start the heavens (or, more accurately, the earth) rotating again. Our star is now moving on a definite track westwards. It is no longer stationary over Hawaii: but other stars which are the same distance north of the equator will follow on exactly the same track. We can use the next one which passes over Hawaii to steer by, and then yet another in the same band, and another and another. This succession of guiding stars will continue until we make our landfall at Hawaii underneath the star which at that time of year and at that time of night is directly overhead.

If we disregard time entirely we can reach our destination from east or from west, simply by sailing along underneath this narrow band of stars that rotates year after year over our destination. From any other direction we can also steer to our island if we possess a sufficiently accurate time sense, and accept a certain margin of error—which must be corrected, in order to make the final landfall, by all the other natural means that we describe elsewhere in this book. The native navigators use this star method to bring them within a distance of, say, fifty to seventy-five miles of their island destinations. I have practiced this method myself and have by turning myself around been able to judge that a star was overhead within an accuracy of one degree, which is equivalent to an error of sixty miles at sea.

Although primitive peoples had no mechanical means of telling the time during the day or night, they had an excellent concept of time. In these days "civilized" man thinks of distance in terms of miles; our whole habit of geographical thinking is concerned with space. Nevertheless, though civilized man has very little use for his innate time sense, and takes little opportunity to improve it with practice, the presence of an innate time sense has been proved beyond question. MacLeod and Roff, for instance, confined two people in a soundproof room in which there was no possible external aid to the appreciation of the passage of time. The estimated time given by one of the subjects, who was released after eighty-six hours, was correct to within forty minutes; and that of the other, released after sixty-six hours, correct to within twenty-six minutes. The cumulative error of each subject was thus about ten minutes a day. Unquestionably the Polynesian must have added constant practice to this innate time sense and could get even better results—results as good as those attained by many different kinds of domestic and wild animals, of which there is an excellent collection in Frank W. Lane's *Animal Wonderland*. Mr. Lane shows that a sharp time sense, usually involving an accuracy at any time of day of within less than five minutes, is possessed by members of nearly all the principal orders of mammals and birds, by some fish and by a number of invertebrates, from sea anemones and worms to ants and bees. Bees not only have a time sense remarkably developed, but can communicate information about time to each other.

The Polynesian had no word for distance, no use for space. He thought only of time. Between one place and another were so many canoe-days (not so many miles); and it is clear that he thought in terms not just of canoe-days but the equivalent of canoe-hours, even of canoe-minutes. The Polynesian had the innate time sense that all animals appear to have; and this he improved with constant use and checked with precision by his stars.

When Captain Cook first encountered the Polynesians he had as navigator the advantage over them of compass, sextant and chronometer. He also had the chart, though in the parts of the Pacific that he was exploring the Western chart was not of much use to him. He found that the Polynesians had mental charts based partly on the time interval rather than space difference. A chart made by Cook and one of his assistants, Lieutenant Pickersgill, from information supplied by a native navigator led them to many islands which Cook would otherwise have overlooked. Tupaia, the famous Polynesian navigator, supplied the information for a chart to be drawn which encompassed nearly eighty islands, an amazing exhibition of the outstanding geographical knowledge of these early oceanic peoples. This chart made from Tupaia's information marked Tahiti and the Fiji Islands, which are more than 2500 miles from each other! But Cook and his companions did not know Tupaia's language well, and mistook the native's directions of north and south, and thus reversed many islands on the chart. Nevertheless half of the islands on the chart were unknown to Cook and this led him officially to "discover" many of them.

The only known cartographers of sea movement were the Micronesians of the Caroline and the Marshall Islands, who made, as an aid to their memory, wave charts and swell charts which showed a navigational technique which existed among no other native race. When the early explorers encountered these charts or wave maps they simply could not interpret them. Only later, and quite difficult, ethnological research has unlocked the secret of the Micronesian chart.

The part played by the primitive navigator in the opening up of the world is much misunderstood. In most of our books on exploration it is scarcely credited at all. Yet Captain Cook was not the only European explorer who received geographical advice from the natives of the lands which he "discovered." Nearly every Western explorer and voyager in the unmapped and uncharted (and thus, he fondly imagined, "unexplored") parts of the world encountered the native in his role of natural navigator, accurate chart and map maker—found, in fact, that the resident explorers had been there before him. Many of the early voyagers to Greenland encountered the Eskimos, who made maps for them depicting the coastline and outlying islands in a remarkably accurate manner. Often the Eskimos carved these maps on driftwood, realistically representing the natural features in three dimensions.

In the records of Beechey's voyage to the Bering Straits is clear evidence of the outstanding memory of the North Pacific Eskimo. Beechey tells how at Kotzebue Sound the Eskimos drew him a map of the countryside in the sand. "In the first place," he writes "they drew the coastal line with a stick and measured it according to day voyages. After this they erected the mountain chains with sand and stones and they represented the islands, with attention to their size and form, with heaps of gravel." After some time, when the mountains and islands were correctly placed, "they then showed the villages and fishing stations by means of a number of sticks which were placed in the ground, so that an imitation of the reality appeared." This chart, indeed, was almost a facsimile of the Western relief map.

Of course the secret of primitive chart making is the habit of making *mental* maps—maps of the outline and general shape of the homeland, of prominent landmarks and the relative positions of other people's homelands with the home village as the focal point. So keenly were these maps printed in the mind of many natives that they could at any time reproduce them from memory.

James Fisher tells me that, in 1953, when he and the American ornithologist Roger Peterson spent some days in the Yukon-Kuskokwim tundras of western Alaska they found themselves in one of the few parts of North America not yet fully surveyed from the air. The combined delta of the two great rivers is a vast wilderness of flat alluvial lands and water in which pathfinding in the absence of large-scale maps is a matter of maze-threading a mosaic of meandering lakes and rivers of fantastic complexity. To reach the present Eskimo village at New Chevak from the now deserted old village at Old Chevak, a distance of not more than eight or ten miles as the crane flies, means a day's journey along winding rivers of nearer thirty miles than twenty miles. Every bend of the river, every landmark on this journey, every warning of blind alley or dead end was carefully sketched for Peterson and Fisher on the back of an odd piece of writing paper by the young Eskimo, Jack Paniyak, in a couple of minutes. His map was far more precise than the existing small-scale published map, which contained at least one misleading and imaginary water channel which, had they attempted to follow it, would have cost them a day's journey.

Everywhere, then, and until the present day, skillful native pathfinders can lead the explorers of the West; and can do better, with their natural powers of navigation, their skill with compass, sextant and timepiece. The Australian aborigines, with their capacity to draw sketches and maps from memory, often aided white explorers. In the same way, the eastern Siberian tribes reproduced their mental maps in the form of drawings on wood, with the outline and detailed features painted with reindeer blood. These charts were accurate enough to lead explorers on to new discoveries.

Often members of native races passed geographical knowledge in this way, not to white explorers, but to each other. An extract from *Our Wild Indians* by Colonel Richard I. Dodge illustrates this point:

The old guide Espinosa, from whom I learned the rudiments of plainscraft, told me that when he was a boy-prisoner among the Comanches, and the youngsters wished to go on a raid into a country unknown to them, it was customary for the older men to assemble the boys for instruction a few days before the time fixed for starting.

All being seated in a circle, a bundle of sticks was produced, marked with notches to represent the days. Commencing with the stick with one notch, an old man drew on the ground with his finger, a rude map illustrating the journey of the first day. The rivers, streams, hills, valleys, ravines, hidden water holes, were all indicated with reference to prominent and carefully described landmarks. When this was thoroughly understood, the stick representing the next day's march was illustrated in the same way, and so on to the end. He further stated that he had known one party of young men and boys, the eldest not over nineteen, none of whom had ever been in Mexico, to start from the main camp on Brady's Creek in Texas, and make a raid into Mexico as far as the city of Monterey (a distance of over 380 miles as the crow flies), solely by memory of information represented and fixed in their minds by these sticks.

Of course the mental map, and the picture map based on it, could not solve all the problems of travel facing the native or "primitive." They could not guide him in unknown regions. When he wished to explore (and the "primitive" was as great an explorer as any hero of the West) early man devised a means of orientation which insured him against losing his way. This method seems to have been used by all primitive races alike. Its systematic nature alone is proof, if proof now be needed, that no primitive was under the illusion that he had an instinctive power, a "sixth sense" for pathfinding.

In the myths of the Greeks is the story of Theseus, to whom Ariadne gave a thread which enabled him to find his way out of the mazelike cave after he slew the monster. Theseus carried the physical means of returning to his starting point, his place of refuge in known country. It is this "home-center" system that the primitive employs. Only, in his case, the thread is an imaginary one. There can be no doubt that birds and other wild animals also employ this home-center system to an important extent, though it is certainly not the only method which they use for "homing."

As early peoples ventured forth in search of food, they maintained a constant anxiety about their homes and would often look back to see where they were in relation to their point of departure. Each time they went out more territory would become familiar to them; and they would proceed farther and farther into the mysterious unknown, never once losing the thread.

An Australian aborigine described his method of orienting himself in unknown areas in the following way: "I don't go far in the beginning; I go some distance and come back again, then, in

another direction, and come back, and then again in another
direction. Gradually I know how everything is, and then I can
go out far without losing my way."

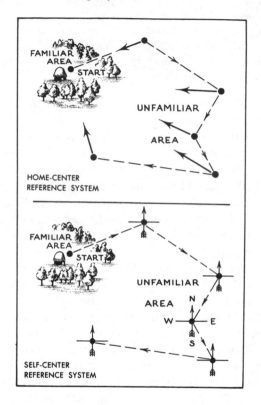

Compare this simple and practical method of orientation with
our much more complicated "self-center system." Modern man,
using this system, considers himself (wherever he is) as the center. He divides the horizon into north, south, east and west, or
even into the 360° of the full circle of the modern compass. He
involves himself in an intricate network of calculations and, even
with the aid of a compass, often loses his way. At each point
when he stops to refer to the points of the compass, he may
sever his connection with the previous place at which he did the

same thing. All too easily, in this way, can he lose the thread which tied him to his original place of departure.

A better system than the self-center system combines it with the home-center system. We may call it the "local reference system." Under this system directions are related to some local prominent feature—a range of hills, a river, a coastline, a lake front. Some primitives have used this system: it is the basis of very accurate maps by Greenland Eskimos discovered by European explorers. Rather interestingly, it is also used by New York taxi drivers when they refer to "uptown, downtown and crosstown."

From this we might conclude that the white man, the "civilized" traveler, can easily transfer to himself the "primitive's" remarkable pathfinding powers, by the simple adoption of the methods of mental map making and the use of the home-center system. But this is not so, because in the process of evolution of our civilization we have lost something which was a matter of life and death to the primitive; that is, his highly developed powers of observation. These powers were common to all early men: and I do not hesitate to repeat myself by saying that they were due not to any innate keenness of the senses of sight, smell, hearing or touch different in any essential from that which we possess ourselves; but rather to the development by practice of the use of these faculties. The primitive traveler reached a state of awareness that only a few of the civilized have ever attained. He reached it because his survival depended upon it. Present-day man can reach a similar state of keen perception only by special and unusual efforts.

There are, of course, examples of intelligent Europeans who have applied primitive systems to finding their way, and have thus become excellent pathfinders. In the journal *Nature* in 1873, A. W. Howitt expressed his opinion, based upon many years' experience among the Australian aborigines:

I have not met with aboriginal natives either as savages or as "tame blacks," who possessed any power of finding their way from place to place differing in its nature, though perhaps its degree, from that to be found in every good "bushman" among the whites. Their knowl-edge of country is entirely local—special as regards the district be-longing to their tribes or family—general as regards the country of the neighboring tribes. They know it thoroughly because they have been born in it and have roamed over it ever since.

As Howitt claims, the white man can equal, if not better, the primitive at his own pathfinding. It is my hope that I may rid the reader of any illusion he may have of the existence of a "sense of direction"—a mysterious sixth sense—and to this subject I devote the next chapter.

Chapter 3

Is There a Sixth Sense?

IF WE DELVE into the preserved and written records of antiquity, we discover that older civilizations than our own had no special idea of a "mysterious sense of direction." They were not prone, as only too many of us are today, to attribute magical powers to humans or even to animals. On the contrary, in the ancient writings of the Orient and the West, there is a most realistic appreciation of the ease with which man can get lost on both land and sea.

It seems that the prevalent misconception about the pathfinding ability of native peoples began only in the middle of the last century, and it appears to derive very largely from the loose testimony of a few explorers and missionaries. Not all such travelers are to blame, of course: for instance, the Jesuit missionary Père Joseph Lafitau, in 1724, gave a clear account of how the Iroquois Indians found their way through dense country entirely by visual means. But others who were less inquiring credited them with a mysterious ability.

Another French missionary, Père François Xavier de Charlevoix, was responsible for gross exaggeration of, and absurd theories about the instinctive abilities of the Indians in finding their way. De Charlevoix spent only five months among the Indians; but his statements, published in Paris in 1744, disregard the clear explanations given earlier by Lafitau, and indeed actually distort the facts given by him.

Other explorers added to the fable by similar claims about the pathfinding abilities of native peoples in many different parts of the world. Sir H. Bartle Frere, who had been governor of the

region of Sind in India before the mutinies of 1857, read a paper
in London in 1870 to the Royal Geographical Society, of which he
was vice-president. Frere actually gave the key to the problem
of how the native inhabitants of Sind kept their direction, when
he described the interminable succession of sand dunes which
were all aligned with the direction of the prevailing wind of the
southwest monsoon. But as if not content with the most obvious
explanation, he sought to make a mystery of it by stating:

In the flat country of Sind, and especially in the great *Runn* of
Cutch, where one finds neither natural landmarks nor tracks, the best
guides seem to count entirely on a kind of instinct. They do not
affect any mysterious science but are generally altogether incapable of
giving the least reason in favor of their conclusion, which seems to
be the result of an instinct similar to that of dogs, horses and other
animals; an infallible instinct. . . .

Clearly Bartle Frere was ignorant of the discussions of the
evolutionists of the time, for already Charles Darwin and his
school had exposed the error. But Darwin *was* personally to
blame for some confusion by his misquotation from memory of
the account of von Wrangel's expedition to Siberia. In 1873 the
English scientific journal *Nature* invited correspondence on the
mysterious sense of direction of men and animals. Like Bartle
Frere, von Wrangel mentioned the true method of navigation
that he had experienced, only to "throw it away." He described
the parallel ridges of snow which were aligned with the dominant
winds, and praised his Cossack driver's ability to maintain his
direction—an ability which was shared by the other Siberians in
his party: but he then wrote: "They appeared to be guided by a
kind of unerring instinct." Darwin's misquotation was that they
were guided by a kind of instinct. Later writers took up the
testimony of de Charlevoix and Bartle Frere and the supposed
testimony of von Wrangel and enlarged upon them—to the extent
that, quite widely and generally, through Western thought during
the latter part of the nineteenth century and much of the present
century, some native peoples and even some Europeans were
endowed with the ability of instinctive direction finding. Many

people still believe in this, though I am certain that the theory can stand up to no well-designed, scientific test.

Many believers in the sixth sense, of course, also believe in natural navigation. They hold that the "homing instinct" comes to the fore only under extreme circumstances. Let us see, then, what that famous antarctic explorer, Sir Douglas Mawson, writes about navigation under extreme circumstances:

Thick drift and a fifty-mile wind on January 12 [1913] kept us confined for thirty-six hours. It was clear enough after noon on the 13th, and five miles were covered in four hours through thick surface drift. What the course was we did not care as we steered by the sastrugi [parallel ridges of snow]. If ever a man had any homing instinct it would surely show itself on such an occasion as this.[1]

Yes, Mawson steered not by his sixth sense but by the sastrugi.

Many adherents of the sixth sense theory believe implicitly that it is possessed by blind people. This delusion persists in spite of the fact that not one sightless person has been able to come forward and demonstrate this supposed ability. Yet if there was even one among all the blind, who could prove that he was guided by a sixth sense and did not use the normal senses, the whole world would know about it.

It is, of course, hard to realize that without the use of his eyes a man can avoid obstacles in his path and find his way. This problem has puzzled scientists whose experiments go back, at least, to 1749. It was in that year that D. Diderot was curious about "the amazing ability of a blind acquaintance not only to perceive the presence of objects, but to judge accurately their distance from him." Diderot's conclusion was that his subject judged the proximity of objects by the increased sensitivity of his facial nerves. This seemed to satisfy early writers, and Diderot was supported by other investigators for the next century. One of these investigators claimed that sightless people used their cheeks as "feelers," and another put a name to this ability—"*Perceptio Facialis.*"

---

[1] From *The Home of the Blizzard*, London, © 1915.

In 1905, Emile Jarval was responsible for introducing the term "sixth sense." He applied it to the blind, and supposed that it was akin to touch and was aroused by "ether waves." Others sought to explain it in terms of magnetism, electricity, vibration and the subconscious. Confusion reigned. Those who favored the mysterious sense battled with the supporters of the normal senses, and among the investigators on both sides there was also internal disagreement. Each arguer thought that he could produce experiments which proved his theory. Theories dominated, almost directed, investigations. Only when investigations direct theories can interpretations be unprejudiced. Most interpretations remained prejudiced.

From this controversy of a half century ago emerged a few who were on the right track. In 1904 T. Heller concluded from experiments that "sensations of approach do not depend upon a special touch quality nor upon a stimulation of a certain part of the skin" and he noted that "the perception of changes in the sound of his [the blind's] footsteps leads to careful attention for sensation of pressure in the forehead. If these characteristic sensations then arise he is sure that an obstacle is in his path and he turns aside in good time."

F. B. Dresslar conducted further experiments with those deprived of sight which qualified Heller's theories, stating that "the basis for judgment was due to differences in sound." Although the work of these two men did not entirely reveal the truth, their conclusions were the basis for further work which provided the logical answer to the question. In 1907, L. Truschel noted that as a man approaches an obstacle, the sounds of his footsteps rise steadily in pitch. Pierre Villey also paid attention to hearing. One of his observations involved the questioning of blinded soldiers and of these, he found 25 per cent thought they detected obstacles by ear and 25 per cent by touch, and 50 per cent by a combination of the two senses. Villey concluded that both hearing and touch were used and that a combination of the two would, indeed, increase the ability to avoid obstacles. This was the real answer: but other investigators were not prepared to believe it; and many continued experiments and produced highly fanciful and illogical theories which served to lead people away from the truth. The problem was made no easier by the difficulty that the blind themselves found in explaining what sense they used.

It was not until 1944 that three American investigators, Michael Supa, Milton Cotzin and Karl M. Dallenbach of Cornell University published the results of many experiments in *The American Journal of Psychology*. These experiments, which were very thorough and too numerous to detail here, were designed to "resolve the contradictions between theory and experimental results" in a study of the perception of obstacles by the blind. The conclusions from them have completely clarified the question and calmed the confusion.

These three scientists tested a number of completely blind students in a large hall and observed their reactions when they came to obstacles placed in their path. They also questioned the students to determine exactly at what distance they felt the presence of the objects.

In the final summary of their conclusions, they eliminated the former theories of air and sound waves and the pressure theory of "obstacle sense" as applying to the exposed areas of the skin. They confirmed the use of hearing by the simple method of blocking the ears of the students, who then invariably bumped into the obstructions. One student had previously maintained that his judgments were based on "facial pressures" and that sound was not important. But when his ears were blocked, he lost his confidence completely, and reported that he was "not getting any sensations at all." He walked forwards with his hands held apprehensively in front of him. Another student said "the curtains of facial pressures that I once reported were pure fancy."

Supa, Cotzin and Dallenbach noted that one of the students, who was particularly good in his perception of an obstruction, obtained his cues from the increased tautness of the carpet in the immediate vicinity of the obstacle; but in general they observed that touch played a small role in the avoidance of obstacles by the blind. At the end of the series of experiments, the blind students and the investigating scientists were in complete agreement.

They defined the perception of obstacles by the blind as the use of the sense of hearing aided at times by touch: and their experiments, or others very similar to them, have been repeated and confirmed many times over by scientists throughout the world.

The realization that the blind have no instinctive powers, but highly developed natural senses, has been of immense benefit to the blind themselves—for work has gone ahead on aids to help them locate obstructions. Such inventions had been long delayed by the useless controversy. In England and the United States, research workers have been recently busy developing devices that send out ultra-sonic waves ahead of the persons carrying them. Another device, made in the United States, involves a reflected light beam which is transformed into a whistling noise which sounds every second in the user's ear and relays information about the distance of the obstacle. All of these inventions are in their early stages, and will undoubtedly be perfected for everyday practical use. They are tangible proof that the blind are not guided by a "sixth sense."

Chapter 4

Walking in Circles

MANY THEORIES have been put forward to explain why lost people travel in circles. Some, less logical than others, favor a mysterious influence. There need be no mystery. There are several reasons why we walk in circles (whether we are lost or not) each of which is quite simple.

To understand the main reason we need only study the classic statue of the Venus de Milo. This traditional example of perfect human beauty is asymmetrical. She has the left half of her head more developed than the other—a characteristic she shares with nearly all right-handed people. Her right eye is lower than her left, and the dividing membrane of her nostrils is to the left of the center line of her face. There was no mistake in the sculpting of the Venus de Milo. Every human body is lopsided. Ninety-eight people out of a hundred are born right-handed; and their right arms usually become longer than their left, with greater circumference, volume and weight, and their right shoulders become from half an inch to nearly one inch lower than their left. The directing impulses for the right hand come from the left brain, and it is a rule that the left brain of right-handed people is larger than the right brain and that the left cranial cavity is consequently also larger.

With regard to our anatomy, we are all of us unbalanced.

Right- or left-handedness has a divided effect on a person's rowing or swimming. Right-armed swimmers veer to the left when they are without visual clues to guide them, for their right arm is longer and stronger. A right-armed rower when facing aft will tend to pull his boat to the right of its forward course.

Right-armed people normally have their right hands bigger than their left, as any glove manufacturer's records will show.

It is unlikely that anybody is born truly ambidextrous, although a popular theory would have it so. Ambidexterity is acquired and not innate. Many people—especially those who pursue sports and games—develop by practice the inferior arm until its dexterity almost approaches that of the dominant arm; but they still retain a preference for the use of the dominant arm —a preference which is doubtless inherited. Incidentally, apes form an exception to this rule, close though they are to humans in other physical aspects. They appear to be born ambidextrous, and can use either hand or foot with equal ease without training.

Psychologists tell us that while it is wise to encourage the naturally left-handed individual to develop the use of his or her right hand, it is unwise to compel this to the exclusion of the preferred hand, as this may even cause conflict which in some instances results in stuttering—possibly because the development of that part of the brain which directs movement may affect the speech center which lies adjacent to it.

The effects of right- or left-handedness appear to be confined entirely to the arms, shoulders and head, and are not linked, as far as we know, in any way with the lack of symmetry of the rest of the body. But that the rest of the body is asymmetrical is unquestionable, and few persons exist who have not at least a slight difference in the length of their two legs. This difference is, of course, of great importance in determining the direction in which the person will veer in walking; and generally we find that for each individual there is a constant error in the same direction. Moreover, this error may be quite independent of the person's right- or left-handedness.

The famous originator of the Scout movement, Baden Powell, warned his scouts of the dangers of walking in circles in fog. Once, in the mountains of Scotland, the Chief Scout was with a mountaineer in whom he placed considerable trust. After a time Baden Powell advised him that the wind had changed; it was on their left side when they set out: now it blew from the right. The mountaineer insisted that they were going in the correct direction, although the wind was then blowing on their backs. They soon found themselves back where they started, having gone in a complete circle. Although Baden Powell was aware of this tendency to walk in circles, he did not seem to realize the cause of it, nor the consistency with which the tendency applies to each individual one of us. This consistency appears to have been overlooked even by military authorities in field training— even though, as long ago as 1897, a German researcher, Mach, pointed out that when large numbers of troops marched at night or in a snowstorm they walked in circles and could end up at their starting point. Yet in the armed services' field training it would be quite practical to test each man to find the constant direction of his deviation, and its extent. Any man who knows his own deviation through his early training in maneuvers knows something really valuable when, in actual warfare, he is overtaken by darkness or obscurity.

A swerve pattern test is comparatively easy to make. Walk blindfold in a large open area, such as a field covered by snow, or a sandy beach on which there are no obstacles, even minor ones. The swerve pattern of your footprints will be there for you to see, measure, assess and compensate for in the future. A swerve test is even possible in a large hall, with the aid of a friend who can observe the extent and direction of your veering and prevent you from walking into obstacles.

As far as I know the first recorded tests on the constancy of circular movement were made by the Norwegian scientist F. O. Guldberg in 1896: he reported that deviation was greater when the pace was faster, and found a correlation with uneven body structure, not only among humans but also among animals.

It is curious how some scientists have passed over the natural reasons for veering, and have attached importance to the most unlikely sources and causes instead of taking into consideration the most probable hypothesis, namely the difference in leg length of the veering individual. A much quoted authority, Professor L. Schaeffer of the University of Kansas (author of *Spiral Movement in Man*), believed that there was a spiraling influence centered in the brain of all living creatures and that this, and not a structural difference, was the cause of veering. He stuck to this theory even though the relationship between the clear difference in leg lengths and veering should have been evident to him.

It was Professor Frederick H. Lund of Bucknell University who put the whole question to the most exhaustive tests. In 3542 trials of 125 students he found that the greater the difference in leg length in each individual, the greater was the degree of deflection. A good correlation between the difference in leg length on the one hand, and the direction and extent of veering in walking on the other, was noted in 80 per cent of a group of students. His tests also showed the consistency of veering in a number of trials of the same students; and the consistency of the reversal of veering when the same students walked backwards. The 20 per cent of cases which did not fit involved students who deliberately gave great impetus to the short leg, which resulted in compensating changes in their direction of deviation. Perhaps the most interesting of Lund's discoveries was that approximately 55 per cent of his students consistently veered to the right and 45 per cent to the left: a sure sign that veering may have little or nothing to do with right- or left-handedness, since only 2 per cent of people are left-handed.

Further evidence showed that the greater the actual difference in leg length, the greater the amount of veering. Curiously, we learn from many tests conducted in 1913 on blindfolded boys and girls that the extent of deviation was 5.7° for boys as against 10.8° for girls. This has been confirmed by the work of Carl Sandstrom in 1951.

Practically everybody deviates. Among the majority of people, the full blindfold deviation circle is formed in about half an hour. Others become displaced more slowly and may take from one to six hours to complete a circle. Practically nobody continues in a straight line. Deviation is increased when the subject's head is bent forward. If the subject walks forward and turns his head to one side, he will deviate to the opposite side. If he walks backwards with his head turned to one side, he will deviate to the same side. If the subject leans his head towards one shoulder, he will deviate in the direction in which he leans his head.

The physical difference in leg length is in most cases the primary cause of deviation from a straight path; but there are at least two other causes, one physical, the other psychological. To appreciate the second physical cause a simple test can be made.

Keep both your eyes open and hold a forefinger up right at arm's length so that it is centered on some object ahead of you. Close your left eye. If your finger is still in line with the object your right eye is your dominant and sighting eye (though not necessarily your "better" eye). Now close your right eye. Your finger will appear to jump to the right of the object, if you are right-eyed; but will remain aligned with it, if you are left-eyed.

Everyone has a dominant eye, though few people realize it. In the field you may line up two nearby objects in order to preserve a straight path, but although you keep both eyes open the two objects will be aligned with only one of them. This produces another—though minor—source of error in preserving a straight path.

Among other minor sources of error can be the wrong balance of a haversack, a heavy weight or even a pick or rope held in the same hand for any length of time, and other physical factors which tend to pull an individual out of his normal balance.

A person tends to edge away from what I term the "irritant direction." Wind, rain, snow or dust storms can cause a man to deviate from his path. Of course he will lean his head away from the force and his steps will constantly deviate. Even a strong sun to the right of his path will cause a person to ease unconsciously to the left. A walker intending to take a level path along a hill may subconsciously follow the line of least resistance and gradually walk downhill.

But beyond these errors, due to structure and balance and "irritant forces" we must consider some undoubtedly due to a powerful mental influence which should not be underrated. When a subject meets an irritant force head on he will still tend to deviate, and his deviation will then be governed by what can only be identified as a psychological preference. Man has developed a preference for the right-hand side which is deep-rooted: it has been handed down to us either by inheritance or by age-old tradition (or both) and has become an influence of which few of us are aware. This preference is most clearly shown when a traveler meets a simple obstacle in his path. Each deviation then tends to be in the same direction and can result in an accumulation of edgings to the right which can reach substantial proportions on a long journey.

So powerful is this preference for right over left that, when given an otherwise uninfluenced selection, people almost invariably choose the right. Even the word "right" itself strengthens the prejudice. The right hand is the happy hand, the strong hand, the agile hand, the clever hand. Nearly all the peoples of the world, in their religions, beliefs, superstitions, laws, administrations, armies and tools have imposed the rule of the dominant "right." The honored guest is placed on the host's right as a mark of distinction, and the other guests arranged on right or left according to the rank they hold in the social scale. In ancient battles the right hand held the lance and the weaker left the defensive shield; the right became the side of honor, the left its poorer cousin. The right hand is the hand of good faith, legally qualified to take oaths, to effect treaties. The joining of right hands makes marriage sacred.

One investigator, R. Hertz, sums this influence up as follows:

So from one end of the world to the other, in the holy places where the faithful meet their god, as in the accursed places where diabolical pacts are made, on the throne as at the witness box, on the battlefield and in the peaceful workroom of the weaver, everywhere there is a fixed law governing the attributes of both hands. As the profane cannot mingle with the sacred, the left cannot encroach on the right. The predominant activity of the bad hand can only be illegal or exceptional, because it would be the end of man and of everything if the profane could ever surpass the sacred, and death over life. The supremacy of the right hand is both an effect and a necessary condition to order which rules and preserves good creation.[1]

[1] "La préeminence de la main droite," *Revue Philosophique*, II, 1909.

This preference for right over left has been particularly noted in the Swiss Alps. Here the most important of the old mountain passes are almost invariably to the right of the mountains: the St. Gotthard, the Old Grimsel, the Furka, Bernhardin, Splügen, Julier, Abula, Brenner and others. Moreover, each of the old paths on the surrounding flat country shows the same right-handed inclination, and the smaller mountain tracks also run where possible over right-handed slopes.

Charles Widmer, who wrote an interesting article in a Swiss alpine journal on this question of the selection of right over left, went so far as to state that when a person is alone and has to make a sudden decision, he will never turn left when he has a completely open choice. Widmer confirmed this peculiarity in an interesting and most practical way by the study of thousands of pictures of skiers at ski resorts. But it does not need the spectacle of a skier presented with a sudden obstacle to demonstrate this rule. Most of us can see it in operation much closer to our homes—indeed in any public place where there is an option of two entrances. So important is the operation of the rule, indeed, that its study has led to special arrangements in the design of display sequences in museum halls. At the entrance to any display chamber or art gallery the public chooses to turn right rather than left. For instance, when thousands of people were observed at the New York World's Fair, the majority were found to turn right when they had the alternative of two directions.

The moral to the traveler of this clear tendency to deviate to the right when irritated by some force or obstacle in his direct path is a simple one. Consciously he should keep this influence in mind and deliberately alternate to the right and to the left in passing obstacles.

To sum up then, in trying to follow a straight line without landmarks, the following principal sources of deviation must be guarded against, and the consequent errors anticipated and corrected:

1. In swimming a right-handed person will veer to the left, in rowing to the right, because of the different length and strength of his dominant arm.

2. In walking almost every person tends to veer in one direction or another in a consistent way. The chances of the deviation being to the right or to the left are approximately equal (55 per cent tend to veer to the right, 45 per cent to the left). This error is due in most cases to the difference in length of any individual's two legs. The tendency can only be measured, and therefore corrected, after personal experiment.

3. Irritant forces, such as wind, rain, or even sunlight, tend to deflect a person from his intended path.

4. In meeting obstacles, or irritant forces head on, on the intended path, the traveler nearly always prefers to pass on the right side.

Chapter 5

Walking in a Straight Line

THE DEFINITION of a straight line is the shortest distance between two points. It is true enough in terms of space: but there must be few cross-country journeys (except in some plains and deserts) on which the shortest distance between two points is the quickest or the easiest. Seldom does the desired path run in a direct line between starting place and objective. Normally the economical path involves detours which must be appraised and coldly calculated. Each detour must be estimated in length, and related in direction to both origin and objective; and these calculations must be committed to paper if the mind is not trained enough to store them. Each intentional detour should be kept as much as possible on a straight line. As every marine navigator knows, and every land navigator soon learns, curves are very hard to record.

Every region has its own anatomy and topography. Snow-covered mountainous country has its own constant natural signs of direction just as has a dense forest or an alluvial flood plain. A stranger with keen powers of observation and particular experience in the *sort* of country he is traveling through can do much to help himself in maintaining a straight line when walking. He must be careful not to generalize from a particular tree, a particular rock, a particular hillside or stream course. It is the average (or, if you like, the consensus) of the local characteristics which enables him to sense the "grain" of the country, to plan his detours to find his way to his goal.

First of course—and this specially goes for treeless open country—the traveler must pick out distant landmarks and work to them or by them. It is elementary practice to find two landmarks ahead and line them up, and to do the same thing looking back. Back marks are just as important as, if not more important than, fore marks; and, in the absence of natural back marks, you can make your own. During Scott's expedition to the South Pole, T. Griffith Taylor, in a difficult country where there were few natural landmarks, resorted to the broken end of a signal pole. He tied a piece of sealskin to the top for a flag and painted it with black blubber soot. His resourcefulness was rewarded; he could see this artificial landmark for miles back and could line it up with a natural one, a large crack in a granite cliff. This proved most helpful on his return journey, when he found it an excellent landmark, the stake lying directly in line with the crack in the cliff five miles off across the bay.

Less easy is it to make long distance landmarks in forests; but all primitive woodsmen follow the old and tried method of trail blazing, breaking branches and hacking marks on trees with hatchet or knife. The best blaze mark for a forest trail is one gash on the front of a tree and two on the back. The back marks again are the most important, if the traveler intends to return home by the same route. The fore marks help the rescue party if you become lost: and their job will be the easier if the traveler practices the old dodge of breaking a branch in the direction of a turn.

The Indians of the eastern United States devised a very practical method of marking their trails, by deforming the trees in the direction of the trail. By one method they pulled a branch away from a sapling for a few feet in a horizontal position and tied it down with vines. In time the branch grew vertically from the place where it was tied. By another method they bent the top of a sapling over until it was buried in the ground, when a new shoot from it would sprout up vertically. (See cut, page 71.) Many of these permanent living road signs, marking nodal positions and important detours on the Indians' regular routes, exist to this day. In Highland Park, Illinois; in the Mississippi Valley; and at Kregeville in Pennsylvania they are preserved as historic landmarks.

Forest trail blazing should of course be used with discretion. Nobody wants to inflict unnecessary scarring or permanent damage to trees. It would certainly be wrong to use this form of marking in national parks; but in dense forests where route finding may be a matter of life and death accurate blazing is very necessary. Often the trail blazer in really dense forest must check his blaze line from time to time by climbing a high tree to pick up the distant landmarks.

Two types of American Indian trail markers

A method of trail blazing which damages no living thing is the method of the paper chase. When I was a boy in Tasmania the cross-country trail was a popular sport. The boy who was "hare" carried a sack of paper over his shoulder, and dropped a handful here and there along his tracks for the "hounds" to follow. In serious travel it is of course as often as not the hare who wants to follow his own trail home. Travelers in difficult country where few landmarks could be used or trees blazed, have used pebbles and red paper on snow, pebbles and black paper on sand. The paper chase method even works on calm waters; in the sheltered inlets of the coast of British Columbia the Indians on fishing trips

Camel caravan in Australia keeping the smoke from three fires in line used cedar chips dropped from their boat to mark their route in times of thick fog.

There is scope for much originality and invention with self-made trail marks. In Australia the aborigines light fires of Spinifex plant in open country and keep the smoke from these fires in line. As they progress beyond the fires they take a back line now and then to check their course. Spinifex, which will burn when it is green, is found in the sparse open country of central Australia. It must be used with circumspection and never if there is danger of fires spreading. The traveler wants smoke and not flames and no one wants to destroy cover in semiarid country.

One of the simplest of trail markers and back liners is the cairn. The traveler must survey the surrounding country and take care to heap his rocks up in a pattern sufficiently distinctive from any local natural formation. There are parts of the world where a cairn is the only means of establishing direction, and very few parts where it is not of some use. Cairns, of course, can be made of snow or ice; and in the vast expanses of the antarctic, where monotonous weeks' journeys can be devoid of any landmark, such cairns have been indispensable to history-making explorers. In the journal of his last tragic expedition to the South Pole, Captain R. F. Scott writes: "Had we been dependent on landmarks we should have fared ill. Evidently a good system of cairns is the best possible traveling arrangement on this great snow plain."

And Scott's further accounts relate how the sight of these man-made markers, piled up on the outward trip, gave heart to the whole party during their attempted return from the Pole.

Thursday Feb. 23, 1912. The data was so meager that it seemed a great responsibility to march out and we were none of us happy about it. But just as we decided to have lunch, Bowers' wonderful sharp eyes detected an old double lunch cairn [large snow cairn built on the outward trip], the theodolite telescope confirmed it, and our spirits rose accordingly. This afternoon we marched on and picked up another cairn; then on and camped only 2½ miles from the depot. We cannot see it, but, given fine weather we cannot miss it. We are therefore extraordinarily relieved. Covered 8.2 miles in 7 hours showing we can do 10 to 12 miles on this surface. Things are again looking up, as we are on the regular line of cairns, with no gaps right home, I hope.[1]

On a later expedition to the Antarctic a similar system of lining up artificial marks was used by Rear Admiral Richard E. Byrd. In place of snow cairns Byrd's expedition used orange-colored flags tied to stakes; and they marked their trail with a line of these spaced at quarter-mile intervals to the east and west of their depots of food and fuel. Of the flags thus set out, every fourth one was numbered, beginning with number one and mounting away from the depot on either side. Flags to the eastward had a capital E. A flag stick marked W2 would be eight flags or two miles west of the depot. Byrd's ground party, on its 200 mile trip southward, used this system of marking the trail and depots.

A party of several travelers in open landmark-less country can become landmarks themselves, or rather direction marks, by proceeding in what has become known as Indian file. No such party follows its leader blindly, nor should any party do so, for all must remember that any leader is subject to the same physical and mental influences as can make his followers deviate from the straight line. In extended Indian file the last man of a line can readily see the veering of the leader.

In the Alps, where this method is often used, it is seldom found that even the most experienced guide leading a roped party in a human chain can keep a straight line. It is the last man who guides him—who checks the natural transgressions of the moving column. Such a check of course is not always infallible, and itself must be checked periodically by compass; but it does put the compass where it belongs—as an instrument for intermittent and not continuous consultation. It works almost as well in a snowstorm as in good conditions. When you are walking, the compass oscillates, so the whole party has to halt while it is read, whereas the method just described does not hinder the speed of the party.

[1] Robert Falcon Scott, *The Journals of Captain R. F. Scott* (ed. Leonard Huxley), Vol. I of *Scott's Last Expedition*, London, © 1913.

R. H. Kahn had a personal experience of the technique of a party walking in Indian file. He related, in a scientific journal, how he joined a group of mountain guides who used this system in bad weather when they could not see very far ahead. The group was traveling on the ice fields of the Pasterz Glacier on the Gross Glockner, that fine mountain in western Austria. An old trick among the mountain guides of this district for snowstorm or misty travel was the human rope-linked chain. The first guide took what he calculated was the march direction, and tried to keep to it. The last guide took sight over the slowly moving column of people, to control any deviations from the straight. All the guides knew that the front man could not perform this task alone, as indeed he knew himself. Kahn himself could easily see that the leader constantly showed a tendency to veer to the right in a circular path. Constantly the last guide called out corrections to the front man. Aware though the leader himself was, of his tendency to swerve to the right, he could only partly correct himself and he still required—indeed relied on—the man in the rear to watch that he kept in a straight line.

In the arctic or antarctic the dog team and sledge, one of the most extensively used methods of travel, itself forms a line sufficiently long to be aimed and checked by the traveler. From leading dog to trailing sledge is fifty feet, a yardstick which can be kept aimed at a distant landmark, or oriented at a constant angle with the local grain of the wind-molded snowdrifts. Only in the thickest mist or blizzard is visibility down to below fifty feet; and under such circumstances the polar traveler usually stops and digs in until the weather lifts. But on the fells or mountains a party of three or more overtaken by mist or bad light may seldom carry their food or shelter with them. They must push on, their file extended to the limit of visibility and their visibility aided by white cloths or handkerchiefs pinned at the back of the head or on the back. In the dark or fog shouts are preferable to visual signs, and a good penetrating whistle is more audible than shouts. Every member of every climbing party should carry a whistle.

This chapter is concerned with the methods of keeping a

straight line, rather than with finding a straight line to keep: but it is important, of course, intermittently to check the party's general orientation, not only with the compass (as I have already indicated) but with the wind direction as given by clouds (and the higher the clouds the better), by the sun and shadows, by the moon and stars. All these fundamental navigational methods are of course discussed in later chapters. But apart from these fundamental methods there is an additional means of straight-line navigating that is worthy of discussion here—the method of the intentional error, the method of aiming (when the conditions of the journey permit) somewhat askew of the final target.

I can recall from my flying days a successful use of this simple trick. I employed it on my world flight with Wiley Post in 1931, when we were in an area in which there were no distinguishable features to relate to the map. The area was eastern Siberia; and we left Irkutsk for a "leg" of some 1,100 miles with the intention of refueling at a small airfield on the bank of the Amur River. The last several hundred miles of this leg were over northern

Amur River

Manchuria—over high grass country with no town, no roads—indeed precious few distinctive features of any sort. We knew that we were unlikely to land much before dusk and that the airfield was not lighted. We could not afford to waste any time looking for it. I purposely set a course to hit the Amur River ten miles to the left of our destination. When we reached the river I told Wiley Post to turn right. We rounded a bend and there lay the airport. We made our landing with just enough light. Wiley Post could not understand why I was so definite about turning to the right until I later explained it to him. There had been no check points for the last part of our route; and our maps were very questionable. If we had set a course directly to the field and had missed it when we reached the Amur River, we could have used up all our daylight by turning in the wrong direction.

Of course this method can be adopted by the pathfinder only when certain circumstances attach to the nature of his goal. It is necessary for the objective to be on some kind of definite line, such as a river, a range of mountains or a coastline. It does not need, of course, to be a straight line. The great thing, however, is that if your goal *is* on such a line you need no positive landmark until you reach the line.

This shows the value of the calculated intentional error—a simple method which can bring the traveler to the base line of his desired goal in no doubt whatever (unless he has been guilty of a really gross miscalculation) as to which way to turn. Any normal unconscious deviation is swallowed up in this intentional margin: by purposely aiming for a point either to the right or to the left of his objective, the navigator eliminates this uncertainty and is sure of his homefall.

Chapter 6

Use of the Ears

SOME YEARS AGO that famous traveler and explorer, F. Spencer Chapman, was kayaking along the east coast of Greenland with an Eskimo hunting party. The coast was free from ice, and in the heavy swell the waves were audibly beating against the shore; so that when a dense fog suddenly came up and reduced visibility to a few yards the party had no difficulty in keeping within sound of the shore. They were some distance from home, and Chapman seriously worried about how they were going to strike the narrow entrance to their home fjord. But, as he writes: "The Eskimos seemed quite unperturbed . . . . indeed they beguiled the time by singing verse after verse of their traditional songs and occasionally they threw their harpoons from sheer *joie de vivre.*"

It was not until after an hour of steady paddling had passed, that the leading hunter suddenly swung inshore and hit the narrow entrance with complete accuracy. It took some time for Chapman to satisfy himself about the method by which he had navigated with such precision: it was not until he had made some subsequent observations for himself that he could believe the trick. It was a simple one. "All along this coast," he wrote, "there were snow buntings nesting, and each male bird . . . used to proclaim the ownership of his territory by singing his sweet little song from a conspicuous boulder. Now each cock snow bunting had a slightly different song, and the Eskimos had learned to recognize each individual songster so that as soon as they picked out the notes of the bird who was nesting on the headland of their home fjord, they knew it was time to turn inshore." [1]

It may not occur to many people—and sometimes does not occur to experienced travelers—that they can use their ability to hear and interpret sounds in direction finding. Nearly all the time we hear sounds; but often they scarcely register in our conscious minds—or do not register at all. Only if we distinguish noises and consciously localize them can we use them for orientation on land or at sea. The opportunities for using this auxiliary method of navigation are surprisingly common, once we realize them.

The use of all our senses can be developed with practice, and perhaps none more unexpectedly and usefully than that of hearing. Every familiar noise of everyday life, whether it be a sound of man, or some human activity, or of some domesticated creature, or a sound of nature, can guide the traveler. He can listen to the sound of chopping, sawmills, church bells, whistles, to the rumble of trains and other industrial and highway noises, to the lowing of cattle, the crowing or cackling of poultry, the bleating of sheep, to waterfalls and rapids or the sea's surf. All these sounds can be used as landmarks, can be associated with the places to which they belong in the traveler's mental map, or they can become targets leading the traveler along a forward path indicated by no other sign.

Our human ears, like those of almost every animal, are designed to appreciate the quality and quantity of sound and its *direction*. Most animals which have forward-looking eyes (as opposed to eyes in the sides of their head), and thus "binocular" vision, also have ears formed to collect sounds coming from the front. Man can concentrate both sight and hearing together towards the source of a sound. Most humans have some difference in sensitivity between their two ears: right-handed people are usually more sensitive in the right ear; left-handed people hear better with the left. Provided that it is not overshadowed by true deafness in one ear, this difference in acuteness of hearing be-

[1] F. Spencer Chapman, "On Not Getting Lost," *The Boys' Country Book*, ed. John Moore, London, © 1955.

tween two normal ears is about one ninth, and is similar to the difference between the power of the right hand over the left in right-handed people. However, any difference in sensitivity between two ears is unlikely to affect the power of direction finding by sound; for this is almost certainly not usually based on the amount of sound detected by each ear, but on the difference in wave phase. It must be recognized that under the best circumstances it is rarely possible for a human to localize the direction of a sound more accurately than ten degrees in the horizontal plane: in the vertical plane localization is even less accurate.

No human ear has been found capable of hearing a sound with a frequency much less than twenty or much more than 20,000 vibrations a second. The upper limit is particularly variable in man. If we choose a note with a frequency of 1100 cycles per second, we have a sound which can be heard by every normal man and which has a wave length of about a foot. If a man turns his head so that the line through his ears makes an angle of 45° with the line joining him to the source of such a sound, the sound will reach one ear about 0.0004 seconds before the other, and the sound waves will be out of phase by about 2/5 of a complete wave length (cycle).

While sound location by wave phase seems to be the main method among humans and many other animals, it is certain that some other animals, particularly those which can rotate their external ears, can also appreciate and localize sounds by intensity. This may even apply to human sound location when the note to be located is a high one, such as that of the song of many kinds of birds.

The human trying to locate the direction or source of a sound probably unconsciously adopts the correct position for "scanning" the impulses, moving his head so that his ears rotate in the same plane as the source of the sound. Often an observed listener straining to detect a source will stop with his ear line at 45° to the sound line. If the sound comes from above ground level the listener tilts his ear line; that is, leans his head from one side to the other.

All these things the sensitive listener will do unconsciously, but sound location can often be improved if the listener goes through the scanning movements consciously—deliberately seeks for the angle where the sound waves are most out of phase, or for the face-on aspect where the volume of sound received by each ear is approximately equal. The phase detection process is much more an unconscious one than the volume detection process; indeed physiologists and neurologists to this day are not quite sure how it works—how the brain interprets the different stimuli and deduces the direction of the origin of the stimuli from them.

There are further processes in interpreting sounds which can be entrusted only to the conscious mind. Among these are allowance for the velocity and direction of the wind and assessment of the quality of the noise. Moreover, sound travels not only through the air—of course as a disturbance of the air—but through the ground and through water. The American Indian, keen to detect the sounds of galloping horses, puts his ear to the ground. The Fiji Islander, swimming under water and fearful of sharks, can identify the sound of a shark some distance away—and can even distinguish it from the sounds made by other fish.

More difficult than finding the direction of a sound source is finding its distance. This needs much conscious effort and training, and long experience; but every countryman who is familiar with the intensity of common noises such as the chopping of wood or the crowing of roosters can with experience get a fair estimate of distance by sound volume.

We now know that echo location was "invented" in the course of evolution independently by at least two orders of animals, the bats and some birds, long before man learned it himself by means of mechanical devices. But man can also use direct and simple echo location, at least when he is at a reasonable distance from the object whose distance he wishes to sound. When fog or darkness obscures vision in hilly country, the echo of a loud call can show the traveler his distance from a mountain side, if he remembers that in air sound takes nearly five seconds to travel a mile. Distance echo sounding is very useful to seamen, for sound often carries a long way over water; and many a vessel, close to a high rock-bound coast in fog or at night, has judged its distance offshore from the reflected sound of a pistol shot, siren blast or shout. Indeed, in the inland waterways of Norway, British Columbia, Labrador and Alaska, in dirty weather ships' whistles are quite regularly used with stop watches by captains and pilots. Each second between blast and echo means a distance of about 560 feet from the reflecting surface.

So clearly may sound sometimes carry over water that the seaman can hear the roar of heavy surf long before he can see the shore. But the distances at which he can hear sounds over water are markedly affected by the strength and direction of the wind. When interpreting shore sounds he must always consider this factor and do his best to allow for it. There are innumerable shore sounds. Each roosting or nesting place of sea birds produces one. It is pretty safe to assume that in most parts of the world the sound of sea birds at night indicates the direction of land. Few sea birds feed at night, and those that do, do so quietly. By day, it is true, sea birds of several kinds may be very noisy when a pack or flock discovers a rewarding feeding ground, but normally all sea birds are quiet except at their shore stations, their colonies. Generally speaking the voice of the sea bird—or indeed any bird—is the voice of the land. The land, of course, has many other voices which can be heard at sea. The shore-coasting navigator in fog or at night can distinguish the sound of trains, marine fog signals, factory whistles—and other signs of industrial activity. The sea navigator who, in fog, hears a ship's whistle or siren knows he has to make allowance for a moving vessel: he who hears bells at regular intervals, however, knows that the sounds are coming either from a ship at anchor, from a bell buoy or from some other kind of stationary marker. Always he listens for the sounds of the waves; and he remembers that, if and when he loses such sounds, it may not be because he has moved farther to sea, for the disappearance of breakers may indicate the presence of an inlet or a harbor.

Blind people are in no doubt about the value and possibilities of hearing their way about the world. The more fortunate majority—the seeing ones—usually never consider such things. But they can be most valuable, as helpful as they are unusual.

Chapter 7

Using Your Sense of Smell

MANY EARLY EXPLORERS were led to land beyond the horizon—by the nose. One wrote of the scent of rosemary off the coast of Spain more than ten leagues out at sea. Louis de Bougainville, when he was off the east coast of Australia in 1768, recounted that "a long time before sunrise a delicious odor announced the vicinity of the land which formed a great gulf open to the southeast."

There were several explorers before de Bougainville who were led on their way by the perfumes of nature, by the breezes carrying the scent of sweet spring flowers, of new-mown hay, of freshly turned earth. A journal of Sir Francis Drake's expedition in the Pacific in 1577 records that: "From hence wee directed our course towards the south-southwest . . . at which time wee had a very sweet smell from the land . . . and wee had sight of the land about 3 of the clocke in the afternoone of the same day."

Nature's smells may not only please but can guide, for various parts of the world have their own particular odors. Many miles to sea from the Falkland Islands the smell of burning peat may be picked up; off the Cape Verde Islands the scent of the orange groves may greet the voyager; to many voyagers in the tropical seas the sweetish rancid odor of the drying coconut may be recognized out of sight of the land from which it comes. Sea bird colonies on small islands produce the penetrating guano smell, with much ammonia—a smell which often reaches the traveler's nose before the island has reached his eye. Bush fires, forest fires, factories and oil refineries, all kinds of smelly industries indicate land not far off. Beaches and tidal lands have their own characteristic smells; and the sweet smell of new turned farmland—especially after heavy rain—can float on the breezes many miles to sea.

Often odors are at their strongest when visibility is low, as in fog, mist or rain, or at night. The Polynesians on their long voyages frequently carried pigs with them; pigs have a highly developed sense of smell. On smelling land far out of sight the pigs would become excited; the Polynesians watched them closely. Sea breeze odors tell not only of the nearness of land, but of its direction. New smells are quickly detectable to the sensitive seaman. He becomes accustomed to the ordinary spectrum of smells which belong to his own ship. This spectrum does not shift as does the smell pattern of a town or a village. Any new smell is much more readily distinguished at sea than on land.

Back in 1924, when I was third officer of an oil tanker twenty days at sea from a Californian port, I was on watch. I well remember how the monotonous smells of the ship were suddenly relieved by the fragrance of new-mown hay coming from land eighty miles away. Just at that moment, and at that great distance, I needed no other indication of the fact that we were nearing New Zealand—a fact which of course our modern navigational devices had already announced.

This also brings to mind an incident which happened earlier on the same trip. Our captain, who rather prided himself on his astuteness, announced that he could smell the distinct odor of tropical flowers from an island. There was a hurried examination of the charts: but nobody could find an island that could possibly have given rise to the smell. I regret to say that a fellow officer and I kept quiet about the fact that we had been blowing incense up the speaking tube from the engine room: we did not dare disillusion him.

On or over land the scents are much more numerous and confused, generally speaking, than they are at sea. Nevertheless there are many—both natural and pertaining to human civilization—which are diagnostic, readily detectable and useful to the traveler. In desert regions smells are relatively simple. Normally the only odors met with are near oases and human habitations.

Travelers have often been able to follow the direction to a water hole or oasis for several miles by smell alone, especially when the wind is in the right direction. In a recent paper read to the Institute of Navigation, Brigadier R. A. Bagnold referred to the use of smell in desert areas:

> In desert regions where the weather conditions in the evening and the early morning are generally very favorable and where the wind direction is fairly predictable it is sometimes possible to home on an occupied rendezvous by smell alone. In a lifeless country smells are so rare that one's nose gets almost doglike. For instance it is possible to home to a doubtfully located water hole hidden in broken country the size of a small English county after a D. R.[1] approach run of several miles. The author once found such a water hole entirely by the smell of one camel, which was picked up eight miles away.[2]

In the polar regions, which are in a true sense deserts, explorers have found much the same. Indeed, their own smells and the smells of their own animals in depots are their principal olfactory guides. Good guides, too, they can sometimes be, for it is almost a rule among dog team sledgers in the polar regions to try to locate their food depots by steering a little down wind so as to allow their sledge dogs (with their very acute sense of smell) to take the final line and find and close the depot.

Of course not only do dogs have a prodigiously better sense of smell than humans, but they live with their heads much nearer the ground; and scent is nearly always strongest near the ground, based (as it of course is) on tiny particles emitted by objects and floating in the air. Primitive man knew well how to track his quarry by scent, and he was never too proud to put his nose to the ground now and then like a dog.

But for modern man to hunt his game by scent, the game would probably have to be dead—and very well hung. It is not that modern man, compared with the primitive, lacks the capacity to

[1] D. R., which means Dead Reckoning, is a navigation term for a track or position arrived at by estimation.
[2] From "Navigating Ashore," *Journal of the Institute of Navigation*, VI, © 1953.

track by scent. He is probably blessed with an equal inherent capacity to do so, and an equally good sense of smell. But primitive man was aware of his olfactory powers and cultivated them: modern man has lost interest in them.

Yet there are plenty of smells that even the least practised of us can hardly overlook. Only a fool could fail to work upwind in his search for the source of a fire's smoke. More subtle is the traveler who can tell the difference between different fire smokes, who can distinguish, for instance, between a pinewood fire and an aspenwood fire. Such a distinction can be a valuable one in the Rocky Mountains of the western United States. As often as not, the smell of burning pine means a forest fire, but as indicated in Chapter I, the smell of burning aspen means a homestead, for aspen is the particular favorite of the domestic hearth of the Rocky Mountain cabins.

Often, indeed, a region, large or small, has its signature of smell. Cities have many such signatures. The fish market smells differently from the flower market, and the stockyard from the fish market. Sometimes cities (or parts of them) can smell, if not to high heaven, at least a long way in that direction. I well recall that, many years ago, while flying from Washington to New York with very bad visibility en route (and before the days of radio aids) we were able to get a most accurate fix of our position—directly above the glue works outside Philadelphia.

Chapter 8

Reflections in the Sky

WITH SOME NOTES ON STANDING CLOUDS

THE TRAVELER by land or sea, in nearly every part of the world, will pursue long stretches of his journey under a cloudy sky. The extent and nature of the clouds themselves may indicate the presence of mountain ranges or mountainous islands—I shall have more to say about such "standing clouds" presently—but a general cloud cover and overcast sky such as can be encountered almost anywhere (though it is very rare over certain deserts) is not by any means neutral to the traveler choosing his route or defining his position. There are many kinds of cloud sign that he can make use of, for clouds can, literally, reflect certain elements in the earth's surface below them. Cloud mirrors can, to the experienced natural navigator, indicate all sorts of things that are out of range of his line of sight.

On land off an ice-covered sea the traveler can, for example, detect the presence of open water, simply because it reflects less light than land or ice. The open sea's telltale sign is thus a darkness on the underside of the clouds. Usually it reveals little more than the presence of water: it is an unreliable indicator of the water's extent; even a small lead or pool in an otherwise complete expanse of sea ice can show a broad effect in the sky. Moreover, vapor often rises from open water in an ice field, especially when the temperature of the air is at or not far below freezing point. This vapor affects the light in such a way as generally to produce a dark cloud reflection. If the wind is blowing a comparatively small amount of open water can spread its telltale darkness over a wide area, and thus inform a navigator a considerable distance away. It produces what is known as a "water sky."

During an unsuccessful search in the arctic for the ill-fated expedition of Sir John Franklin, Lieutenant de Haven looked for an open sea to the northward and westward; he saw in that direction a water sky. Captain Penny later acted on this information, and confirmed the existence of open water in this area.

The Australian antarctic explorer, Sir Douglas Mawson, also gives an instance of the value of spotting this particular phenomenon in the absence of other means of navigation. "Soon after leaving the hills," he wrote "a direct course to the hut was made. There was no mark by which to steer, except a 'water sky' to the north, the hinterland being clouded over."

The converse of the water sky is "iceblink." An iceblink is a noticeable patch of brightness in an otherwise gray sky; and is a sign of an area of floe or shore ice surrounded by water, and big enough to produce a detectable reflection. Quite a small area of ice can produce a blink in the sky detectable from a long distance, and arctic explorers have always paid considerable attention to iceblink. From many examples, I can quote one written by Henryk Arctowski:

On January 19 [1898], Commandant de Gerlache pointed out the iceblink in the south. The sky was uniformly covered with a thick layer or stratus [cloud] and just at the horizon a white line appeared like a longitudinal slit, detaching itself by its brightness from the gray of the sky. It was discontinuous, a little undulated, not rising more than 10 to 25 feet above the horizon. At 8:00 P.M. Lecointe reported the first iceberg, which appeared like a dome rising sharply out of the sea at a distance of about 10 miles.

On land an overcast sky can signal many different things to the traveler. One of the simplest and most important of these things is the well-lit human city, town, airfield beacon, or even powerful lighthouse. The loom of these lights in the sky can often be seen when their source is below the observer's horizon.

In arctic or snow mountain country much of the anatomy of the land surface can be reflected in a high overcast sky—sometimes so distinctly that the sky can be said to provide a sky map. Great sheets of white, such as snow or ice fields, may contain a body of open water or exposed and naked rocks; the absence of reflection from these relatively nonreflecting expanses projects, upon the cloud screen if not their image, at least a dark indicator of their presence. Even new ice (blue or green) will show as grayish patches on the lower surface of the cloud layer, if it lies in quantity within a snow field. Patches of vegetation, or even those extraordinary plants which grow on snowbanks and are known as "pink snow," may be revealed in an overcast sky and sometimes even have a pinkish effect.

Conversely, the presence of ice patches and small snow fields in an otherwise vegetation-covered or bare rocky area will make a telltale steel-blue reflection on the under surface of a cloud. At the edge of a snow field, where there is a great difference between the heat reflection of the snow and the bare rock, a shimmering of the air can be produced which is detectable in strong sunlight above a ridge.

In deserts the shimmering which is caused by differences in heat reflection can produce a "desert blink" which is detectable in the clear cloudless sky which is practically permanent over some deserts. An area of white sand can produce a very marked desert blink because of its extra reflecting power. An oasis can produce a desert blink because of its lesser reflecting power.

In the desert the camel rider's eye is about ten feet from the ground. Oases often lie in hollows, and in some parts of the Sahara may be surrounded by ridges of hills up to a thousand feet in height, so they are often impossible to see from a distance. But the contrast in the radiation of the sun's heat between that of the green-palmed oasis and the surrounding desert sand produces a special kind of haze in the air above the oasis. Such a haze is known to the experienced travelers in the Sahara as "shabur." Shabur can appear over hollows and basins bottomed by pure sand and lacking in water and vegetation. The heat radiation from the surface all around the hollow is visible, while that from the bottom of the depression is in dead ground. At the level which the eye can see there is then a ring of air at a different temperature from the air in the middle. The consequent difference in the refraction of the atmosphere is immediately detectable.

In many parts of the world where the atmosphere is humid, clouds tend to form continuously on mountaintops; and many highlands, coastal ranges and high islands thus tend to have standing clouds or cloud crests around their summits. Often these clouds extend far above the peaks. As the clouds are continually forming at a particular point, they appear fixed in relation to the ordinary moving clouds passing by or above them. They can indicate, for long distances, the presence of peaks which are themselves below the horizon.

The standing cloud telltale of high land has been used not only by all primitive peoples but by the early European navigators. De Bougainville and Dampier attached very great importance to it, as their logbooks testify. La Pérouse, one of the early French explorers in the Pacific, lacked many of the modern navigational devices, but as his records show closely watched for the fixed clouds on the horizon that suggested an island or land mass.

Standing clouds often have a much woollier appearance than that of the normal trade-wind clouds, and readily betray the presence of an island by their shape as well as their immobility in the open ocean. Moreover, in the tropics, islands tend to produce not only standing clouds but distinctive reflections upon those clouds. Some islands—and particularly the coral islands—are far from high and mountainous. Flat and low though they are, they can still produce standing clouds simply because the white sands of a coral atoll reflect more heat than the surface of the surrounding water; the sharp kick in the temperature gradient above these islands may be enough to create the conditions in which a cloud can condense. Usually such a cloud is not directly overhead, but a little to the lee side of the island, because of the effect of the prevailing wind; and on the underside of this hovering cloud the lagoon of the atoll—nearly always bright turquoise in contrast to the deeper blue of the surrounding sea—is reflected. Such colored reflections can sometimes be observed miles before low-lying atolls appear above the horizon. Indeed, lagoons or other shallow waters can sometimes cause a reflection in a completely cloudless sky which is surprisingly conspicuous.

In the *Sailing Directions* of Matthew Fontaine Maury, the renowned American oceanographer writes of clouds hovering not only over coral islands, but over shoals: "They are often seen to overhang the lowest islet of the tropics and even to stand above the coral patches and hidden reefs, a 'cloud by day' to serve as a beacon to the lonely mariner out there at sea and to warn him of shoals and dangers which no lead nor seaman's eye has ever seen or sounded out."

Lightning from one particular direction in the early hours of the morning before sunrise is usually a sign of land to the tropical sea traveler—particularly when a large land mass or mountainous island carries a standing cloud.

So far I have generalized about standing cloud and cloud reflections. Let us now take a special example; for the study of clouds can help the natural navigator even further if he has a knowledge of local conditions.

When winter comes to the valley of the St. Lawrence River in eastern Canada, the waters of the river and its tributaries are warmer than the air, and a strip of mist columns is often formed which is intensified by the spray of the waterfalls. Near Quebec, for instance, stationary clouds are sometimes seen hovering over the cataracts—over the Chaudière and the Montmorency Falls. Later in the winter small, well-defined cumulus clouds can often be seen standing above the falls, at an elevation of three or four hundred feet. Higher up over the surrounding mountains, clouds form on the mountaintops and may descend some distance down their sides, or remain suspended and "standing" at some height above their summits. Clouds of the first kind are often seen before or after heavy rain, of the last kind usually in fine weather.

When fine warm weather succeeds heavy rains, and the surface of the earth has been exposed for several hours to the heat of the sun, clouds often form over the islands in the estuary of the St. Lawrence River. In good stable weather they appear towards noon. They hover over the small islands which are surrounded by a large area of colder sea. Not far away we can see the opposite of this—clear spaces in the heavens over lakes where a small region of cold water is encircled by land. This pattern of cloud of course derives from the fact that the sun heats the land more quickly than the water. Often the clouds of the St. Lawrence valley may be seen resting over the highlands all day, while the sky over the water is clear; and at nightfall the sky over the land becomes clear as it cools, and the clouds shift to lie over the river.

The average commonsensical traveler does not need specialized knowledge to understand these phenomena. He certainly does not need to be a trained meteorologist to detect the meaning of a stationary isolated cloud, if he studies the local conditions. But many pathfinders who tend to limit their observations to the things on the ground miss their opportunities.

Chapter 9

Directions from the Wind

THE WINDS of the world differ (of course) from each other in direction, velocity, temperature and humidity. But the differences are far from being haphazard or disorderly. Each district (practically without exception) has its own pattern of winds, usually with a particular wind from a particular direction that dominates at some seasons, and often at all seasons. I could not, of course, attempt to give details of the local prevailing or dominating winds in all parts of the world. It is not important to do so, for all that is necessary for the natural navigator is to find out what they are, learn how to recognize them and navigate with them as guide. Every human resident, almost without exception, of a country district knows his dominant wind or winds and can tell the traveler whether it is hot, cold, violent or gentle and the length of the day or the season for which it can be expected to blow. The dominant wind of any area is nearly always the same as the prevailing wind (i.e., that wind which blows longest from a given direction) and is the wind which leaves the biggest impression and directional effect on trees, snow, sand or other objects on the surface of the earth, either by blowing longer than the other winds (in which case it is also the prevailing wind) or by blowing more violently.

Generally it is true to say that at medium latitudes, that is, in most regions of temperate climate, the prevailing wind usually blows from the west in both the northern and southern hemisphere. In lower, more tropical latitudes, the prevailing winds—at least during the greater part of the year—lie between northeast and southeast and at the equator are often from the east. These

easterlies are called the Trade Winds; and it is not usually realized that these trade winds blow over the continents as well as
over the oceans.

To give an example, the prevailing and dominant wind in the
northern South Pacific is from the southeast. It is of medium
force and usually blows only during the winter months. It is the
most constant wind in velocity, and also blows for the longest
period of the year: throughout the year the other winds are more
variable in direction and force, and have no marked or lasting
effect on the surface of the land.

The compassless natural navigator can use certain simple and
pretty obvious principles in identifying the direction from which
winds come—even if he lacks local knowledge. Thus in the northern hemisphere a northerly wind will be generally colder than a
southerly wind, and in the southern hemisphere a southerly wind
colder than a northerly wind. In the southern hemisphere, moreover, a southerly wind is often accompanied by an extreme clarity
of atmosphere which very sharply outlines distant objects. Winds
blowing from deserts are unmistakable because they are dry.
Those blowing from oceans are moisture-laden—some are rain-
bearing. Those blowing from snow-capped mountains often bring
a marked drop in temperature. Some winds carry the signature
of their origin in the particles of dust, sand or smoke that they
bear. Wind can carry fine dust more than halfway across the
world: some great volcanic eruptions have tinted the sunsets
thousands of miles away for months after. I myself once wit-
nessed an example of the ability of the wind to carry smoke for
long distances. I was in Fiji at a time when there were extensive
bush fires in Australia. Their smoke was carried 1500 miles to the
islands. Any resident in Fiji at the time of the smoke winds
could tell the direction of the west simply enough.

Dust in the wind can be carried not only for vast distances, but
to great heights. Once I was in an aircraft flying across the
United States at a time of strong winds over the dustbowl region
of Kansas and Oklahoma. In broad daylight and at a height of
over 10,000 feet we were forced to fly entirely by instruments:
the dust obscured all vision.

In nearly all regions the prevailing wind has its own personality of velocity and temperature and humidity, which enables the wind navigator to identify it. He can also identify other winds which may prevail at different times and seasons in the same way. Nearly every coastal region, for instance, suffers both land and sea breezes, simply because the surface of the sea takes longer to heat up than does the land—but retains its heat much longer. After sunset in a coastal region the surface of the earth becomes colder, while the air above the sea remains warm. This warm air rises; and the cold air from the shore flows out to take its place and produces what is known as a land (i.e., off-land) breeze. The sea breeze—in the opposite direction—usually blows during the afternoon, while the warmed air over the land is rising and the air from the sea (at that time colder) streams in over the land.

In the open ocean the winds are by no means constant, but the prevailing wind often has not only its characteristic temperature, humidity and force, but its characteristic accompaniment of clouds. While the wind continues to keep its personality, the navigator can be pretty sure that it is not changing seriously in direction and can guide himself by it. All he has to watch for is a change. Below the equator, for instance, a vessel ploughing along under the stable and easily recognizable conditions of the southeast trades may sometimes experience a sudden decrease in temperature and humidity. Even without a compass its navigator would probably be correct in assuming that the wind had gone around towards the south.

The typical trade-wind clouds of the tropics are small isolated woolly tufts. They generally appear in a uniform layer below 8,000 feet, characteristically outlined against the blue sky. If these trade clouds disappear, and the sky becomes overcast with heavy billowing clouds, the navigator can conclude that in all probability the wind has gone around through the south to the southwest or even to the west.

For the ocean traveler, in the tropics and in temperate climates during the summer, changes of wind after sunset or during the night often mean the presence of nearby land. Often, too, these breezes bring land scent during the night or early morning.

In the polar regions the wind temperature gives the most reliable indication of open water, for this temperature is higher—naturally enough—when it comes from water than from ice or snow. A sudden drop in air temperature without a change in wind direction can conversely give conclusive evidence of the presence of a big iceberg in an upwind direction.

On land the traveler can use a constant wind both for orientation and for keeping a straight line. He keeps the wind directed to the same part of his body and all the time watches its strength, temperature and moisture content so as to note any changes immediately. Many travelers wet and raise their fingers to detect the direction of a very light breeze: they would be better advised to wet a cheek, a much more sensitive region of the body. Of course a slight breeze can be a rather unreliable guide, since it is more likely to vary than a strong one, but it may be of great value in cases where it carries a recognizable odor.

In dense bush it is not often possible to feel the wind, but it is easy to see the sky and to note the direction of movement of the clouds. High clouds are likely to be more constant in movement than low ones and to belong more certainly to the prevailing wind. Further, when the tops of the tall trees are visible, it is useful to observe which way the highest branches bend with the wind. If snow is falling the direction of its drift will also show the wind's direction.

All over the world local winds have such marked personalities that they have been named by the resident humans. The famous Mistral blows from the northwest across the eastern part of the south of France and the delta of the Rhone. It is a chilling wind that comes down from the mountains to take the place of the hot air that rises from the flat lands around the Camargue, so constantly bathed by the Mediterranean sun. The Mistral is accompanied by a bright sky and horizon. Violent, cold and dry, it blows often for periods of from five to nine days, and it is especially strong during the autumn and winter months. Another wind, the Autan, is also very strong, hot and dry, and blows from the south and southwest.

These two typical winds are encountered in a large part of France, but other winds of constant characteristics have become well-known to the inhabitants. According to Manciot, the Pontias is a northeaster which blows from the Col de Devez to the plains of the Rhone valley, and stops when the snow has disappeared from the mountains. The Pontias is a morning wind; and in the afternoon may be replaced by another coming from the southwest, the Vesine, which blows up the river Aigues, a tributary of the Rhone.

Incidentally, it has always seemed strange to me that winds are named after the direction from which they blow; for nearly all other natural movement, including the movement of the sea, is identified by the direction *to* which it is proceeding. The direction-from system of naming is a very ancient custom and was used before the introduction of the magnet, when (see page 44) the mariners in the Mediterranean divided the horizon into divisions according to the various wind directions. If we trace this Mediterranean dummy compass through the years, we can find all sorts of variations in the names given to the winds and in the number of divisions of the horizon—depending on the historical period and the nationality of the seamen. But throughout the years it is clear that the seamen and travelers were conscious of the character of the wind and of the locality *from* which it blew. One wind coming from the northern snow-capped mountains was named Tramontane. The dominant northwesterly wind of some parts of the Mediterranean was called Magister, or Maestro. Sirocco was, and indeed still is, the name of the hot dust-laden wind blowing off the North African deserts. Greco was the northwest wind which came from Greece.

Even when the prevailing wind is not blowing at the time, the traveler versed in the use of natural signs can identify its direction by observing animals and plants. Spiders cannot lay their webs against the wind (although they may take advantage of eddies or gusts to lay them across it) but the general orientation of the webs can contribute to the picture. A warning is necessary: a web which has been broken and very recently remade may show the direction of a recent wind which may not be the prevailing wind.

Most animals, especially birds and insects, naturally build their nests in protected positions. Most creatures who live by and with nature are very sensitive to the prevailing wind and use it to their advantage: you can use them to yours.

In the tropics the western side of rock or tree is that which is sheltered from the trade winds, and that where the shelters of the animals are most likely to be found. In higher northern and southern latitudes the eastern side is generally the most sheltered; and it is on the east, southeast or south (where it is usually drier and warmer than on the north or west) that the mice will burrow under dead trunks, the woodpeckers excavate their nests and the open-nesting birds will build. Out in the open, too, birds will tend to frequent and meet each other at places sheltered from the prevailing wind, even repairing to such places by habit when the wind is blowing from another direction. During the breeding season, for instance, many wildfowl will choose the edge of a lake or stream and congregate under the bank sheltered from the prevailing wind.

In South Africa protection from the wind is best found on the southeast of trees and rocks. Dr. S. H. Skaife of Hout Bay, Cape Province, has written very detailed accounts of the common carpenter bee of that region; and he informs me that this insect always has its burrow in that part of a dead trunk or branch which faces southeast. The rain-bearing winds of South Africa come from the northwest; this carpenter bee cannot tolerate dampness as it brings a fungus disease which is very harmful to it.

We see, then, that the wind can be your guide; and indeed it has guided many explorers of uncharted areas in the world—who have used winds at times when they had no other means of telling their direction. From the experiences of his most famous antarctic expedition, Sir Douglas Mawson found that:

In dense drift it was not a simple matter to steer a correct course for the Hut and it was essential not to deviate, as the rocky foreshores near which it stood extended only for a mile east and west, on either side abutting on vertical ice cliffs. With a compelling force like a hurricane at our backs, it was not a nice thing to contemplate finding ourselves on the brink of a precipice. The wind however, was steady, and we knew at what angle to steer to keep a rough course." [1]

[1] Sir Douglas Mawson, *The Home of the Blizzard,* London, © 1915.

Chapter 10

Some Special Effects of Sun and Wind

THE PREVAILING SLANT of the sun's rays and the prevailing direction of the wind may leave their signatures on the country in special ways. The experienced traveler can readily spot these signatures in certain kinds of country, even when the sky is completely overcast and the wind may be blowing in a direction quite different from its prevailing direction—or not blowing at all.

Let us take an example from mountain country in the northern hemisphere. In such country the southern slopes of the hills receive the most direct rays of, and therefore the greatest amount of radiation from, the sun. On the south slopes therefore are found greater extremes of temperature than on the northern slopes. In particular, the effect of alternate cooling at night and heating by day is much greater on the southerly slopes. Erosion by frost is therefore more rapid.

From this springs a general rule of mountain anatomy, namely that in the northern hemisphere the northern inclines are smoother, less eroded and offer fewer obstacles to the climber than the southern slopes. In the southern hemisphere of course the situation is reversed.

The sun leaves its signature very readily on fields of snow or ice. If such fields slope, the slopes which face the arc of the sun's daytime track will naturally melt more quickly than those tilted away from the sun. Rocks or trees in snow fields will leave "melt-shadows" where they have protected parts of the snow field from the rays of the sun. Such shadows give a rapid and positive indication of direction in all parts of the world.

In assessing direction by relative melting and by melt-shadows, it is necessary to take into account the direction of the prevailing wind as well as that of the prevailing sun. The modifying effect of the wind can be very substantial. Winds can melt snow quickly and, if of a high temperature, can sometimes have an even greater effect on the melt-rate than the direct rays of the radiating sun. Thus, while in general the snow line on mountains will be lower on the side protected from the sun, quite substantial exceptions to this rule may be expected. In the southern hemisphere, for instance, the general tendency is for the snow line to be lower on the south side of a mountain range than on the north; but in the Otago district of New Zealand, I have noticed, the region of low snow line has been swung through a large arc by the prevailing westerly wind; in fact the snow line is lower on the southeast and northern sides of the hills than on the western sides.

The directional melting effect of wind and sun can be observed on the glaciers of the temperate latitudes in a most interesting way. When small dark stones, leaves or other debris lie upon the snow, they absorb more heat than the surrounding white surface. Consequently, melting holes begin and small basins are formed in which water may lie. The depths of these basins are limited to what the slanting sun's rays can reach. Usually they are less than one foot in depth, though in some places they have been recorded up to three feet deep. They are useful in direction-finding because the swing of the sun's arc through the day traces a consistent semicircular edge on one side. In the Northern Hemisphere the southern edge of the melt hole is straight or almost straight and is aligned east-west; while the northern edge is the true semicircle with its arc open to the true south. In the Swiss Alps these melt holes in the snow are known as "noon holes" (*Mittagslöcher*) or "meridian holes" (*Meridianlöcher*).

The semicircular shape of noon holes is naturally best marked in low latitudes. In high latitudes during the summer they are of less value. North of the Arctic Circle the summer sun may never set in summer, and the melting occurs almost equally on all sides; and so the melt holes become practically round and have no directional value. But in the temperate and high tropical parts of the world they provide a constant and useful travelers' guide.

It is not even always necessary for small black bodies to be present to start them. In snow already pitted by wind, the shadow effect of the edge of the original wind pit may be enough to start differential melting and bring the pit to its telltale semicircular shape. In many snow areas of the world "pitted snow" or very small holes caused in the process of the melting of snow will show this same semicircular effect, the rounded edge being on the side farthest from the sun and the flat side nearer to the sun.

Just as small pieces of rock produce telltale directional noon holes, so do large pieces of rock on snow produce telltales: but these telltales are of rather a different kind. Few glaciers which flow through steep-sided valleys are free from rocks and earth eroded from the valleys' sides. Cliffs break in the ordinary process of erosion, and through the course of the years and months shed an intermittent cascade of rock onto the glacier below. Such rocks on a glacier form the beginnings of a lateral moraine; and when two glaciers meet their lateral moraines run together to form a central moraine on the joined glacier. Thus rocks may be carried along by moving glaciers in their middles or at their edges. When heated by the sun, large rocks protect the ice under them from melting, thus affecting it in exactly the opposite way from small dark stones.

The sun's action slowly melts the ice around and underneath the stone slab. Gradually it comes to stand on a pedestal of ice. A big platelike flat slab becomes a one-legged table; and the bigger it is, the greater is its protective action by shadowing the central core of the ice below it, and the higher does the pedestal become. In most temperate latitudes pedestals seldom become more than two or three feet in height whatever the size of the slab which they support; but in the high snow areas of the tropics where the sun's rays are steeper, the pedestal may be thicker and its height may reach seven, ten or, quite exceptionally, thirteen feet.

These glacier tables or ice tables (*Gletschertische*) as they are called in the Swiss Alps, are directional because of their tilt. In the northern hemisphere they normally tilt down towards the south simply because the greatest amount of melting takes place on the southern side. Normally the tilt increases as the melting goes on: the slab tilts more and more towards the south until, when the glacier table reaches a certain size, the slab slips off its

Glacier table. (*After Manciot*)

pedestal back onto the glacier face. The old pedestal then melts away (though often its remains can be seen) while a new one begins to be melted underneath the slab in its new position. Indeed, when melting is intensive, a new table can be formed under it during the same summer; and north of it the remains of its predecessor—and even occasionally its predecessor's predecessor —can be observed in line. These lines and the fundamental tilt of the slabs show a very reliable north-south direction to the mountaineer in the Swiss Alps. Large tables can be found on the glacier ice (not the winter snow) of the Unteraar, the Lower Grindelwald and Aletsch Glaciers.

In the arctic, glacier tables are rare and almost valueless for direction because of the low circular path of the summer sun. The sun's rays, falling seldom far from the horizontal, generally melt the ice all around a stone and quite far under it; and simply cause it to sink.

The signature of the prevailing wind may be detected in some kinds of country as readily as those of the prevailing sun. The wind carries erosive agents—water, snow, sand—which set their marks in unmistakable ways on the face of the traveler's terrain. The famous antarctic explorer, Douglas Mawson, knew well how often the prevailing wind and snowdrift set its mark upon the rocks and upon hard blue ice. Such ice may become channeled and pelted by the action of drift snow; and both snow and ice may become so polished by the prevailing wind that they grow very slippery. In one particular instance in the antarctic, Mawson noted a differential rock-weathering very similar to that which would have been caused by the sun in a more temperate latitude. The rocks facing the north appeared to be quite different from those facing the south: the southern faces were smooth and rounded by the wind; but their surface was somewhat broken by the chipping and splitting action of frost: the sheltered northern faces were rougher and more broken up.

I must stress that in most latitudes the effects of sun, wind and rain must be interpreted in conjunction with each other. Exposure to the sun may have an effect opposite to or modifying that of the prevailing wind or rain: results are much more pronounced when sun and wind work together. To show how sun and wind can write a joint signature across a natural landscape, I have chosen a particular area, the details of which can be appreciated by any interested observer.

In the Palouse region of the southeastern part of the state of Washington, and extending into northern Idaho, erosion and drift through the centuries have brought about a dunelike topography by working the soil into a succession of hills. In the winter, the wind blows almost continuously from the southwest, and tends to lay bare the windward slopes of the hilltops, and to pile deep snowdrifts on their leeward slopes immediately below their crests. Over the long years this has made the inclines facing southwest more gradual than those to the leeward, which are inclined to be steep.

In this region then, the location of the thickest snow cover is due principally to the great force of the southwest wind. The difference in the steepness of the slopes is very considerable.

Those facing the southwest are gradual—averaging less than eighteen degrees from the horizontal—whereas the northeast slopes incline about fifty degrees from the horizontal. This state of affairs persists throughout nearly the whole of the Palouse region so constantly that in the summertime any traveler can easily determine his direction anywhere in the area simply by watching the sides of the hills.

Chapter 11

Direction from Trees and Other Plants

WE SELDOM PAUSE to observe the shape of a tree, and therefore we do not often realize that the different forms of trees can teach us much about the directional influences of the sun and the wind in various localities. To understand how these two elemental forces affect trees, it is necessary to become "shape conscious" and familiarize ourselves with the basic outlines of the various trees. Each kind of tree has its own characteristic form, and it is therefore much easier to differentiate among the species if you think of them in terms of their silhouettes. Start with the shape, and with this impressed on your mind, it will be easier to study the details of leaves and flowers.

It is important for the pathfinder to learn to identify the common species of trees in his locality. In most parts of the world one can obtain popular books describing the trees of the region; a walk with someone who is familiar with the local trees will also be helpful. Moreover, once you have learned which trees are native to your area, you will be able to recognize any introduced species, particularly the ornamentals, which often indicate the proximity of towns and farms.

Nature designed the basic shapes of trees principally in order to satisfy their differing light requirements. The reason for the differences in the forms of various species, comparing the fir trees with the elm, for example, is that each has a greater or lesser need for sunlight, under the various climatic conditions to which they are adapted.

In the cold northern latitudes, many trees are dependent on lateral, diffused or indirect light. They adopt the pyramid shape;

of these the most common example is the fir. This tree cannot get overhead light, and there is therefore no advantage in its having a rounded crown such as the elm tree has in lower latitudes. Trees in the high latitudes are more openly branched and leaved than those of low latitudes, so that the light can penetrate even to the branches on the north. The leaves are generally rounded so that they are able to get direct light through the branches and diffused light from all sides.

NORWAY   WHITE   LOMBARDY   SYCAMORE
SPRUCE   OAK   POPLAR   MAPLE

Some trees of temperate climates, such as the cypresses, also have a pyramid form. They adopt this shape to avoid the excessive heat of the high sun at midday and to obtain the full benefit of front light in the morning and the afternoon.

A spectacular example of a large-leaved, tropical, palmlike tree which has a narrow, vertical form in order to avoid the midday heat and light, is the Traveler's Tree (*Ravenala madagascariensis*). This tree is thought by some people to have been so named because it is aligned in a north-south direction. This is not so: there would be no advantage in such an alignment in the equatorial region, where the sun is practically overhead at midday. Its name was suggested by the abundant store of fresh water found in the trunk at the base of the leaves.

Often, however, valuable indications of direction are given by the modifications of the basic shapes of trees through the effects of wind, sun, or these two elements combined. Even the most casual observer has seen wind-swept trees growing in exposed places of strong winds and has realized that they clearly show the dominant wind direction. But this knowledge is of little practical value unless it is interpreted in terms of north, south, east and west.

The dominant wind in an area is the one which has the most

Wind-blown tree (totara) at Auckland, New Zealand

effect on vegetation, either because of its strength or because of
the length of time it blows during the course of the year. It is
quite simple for the pathfinder to learn the direction of the dominant wind which causes the leaning of the trees in his own locality and to apply this knowledge in finding his way.

Trees do not necessarily have to lean away from the dominant
wind to show its direction. There are other, less obvious and
little realized effects. Wind can retard development, for example,
by damaging or desiccating the young shoots on the windward
side, while the sheltered side of the tree will flourish and produce
more branches and more abundant foliage.

Poplar tree at Heemstede, Holland. The growth on the right-hand side of the tree, which is the northwest side, has been retarded by the dominant northwest wind

The coconut palm normally leans towards the wind even in areas exposed to strong winds. During the many years I have spent in the South Pacific, I have observed hundreds of these trees, not only on my own coconut plantation island, but also on all the others I have visited. All of these palms lean into the prevailing trade wind, which in this area is the southeast. In common with other trees, the coconut palm has a much greater leaf growth on

the sheltered side and its head presents a flattened appearance to
windward.

Elm trees near Zandvoort, Holland. The right-hand side faces
southeast and shows the enhanced growth on the side sheltered
from the wind

When observing trees for directional purposes, it is essential to
choose a tree growing in an exposed position and one which is not
interfered with or sheltered by other trees or buildings. Do not
base your conclusion on only one tree, but examine several in
similar situations. Be specially careful that the trees you observe
have not been pruned by man or damaged by natural causes.

While the direction of the wind has the effect of retarding growth on that side of a tree, the effect of sunlight, on the other hand, is usually to enhance the development of branches and leaves, and its beneficial effects can be seen plainly. In places where the winds are variable, the full effect of greatest sunlight can be very striking in the distinct difference it causes between the northern and southern sides of the tree. In most parts of the Northern Hemisphere the arc of the sun from rising to setting is entirely on the south side of the tree, and the mid-point of this arc is true south. This is the direction of the most abundant foliage in certain species.

Among the trees which develop more foliage on the side which receives most sunlight are the common black and white poplars, the oak, plane tree, beech, Corsican pine, horse chestnut, Norway maple, British maple, ailanthus, box elder and North American black locust tree. Because of their greater branch and foliage development on the side where the light is strongest, in areas where the wind does not modify the effect, these trees often show a slight inclination of the trunk in that direction. Although elms are less affected by the direction of greatest sunlight than other trees of temperate climates, they sometimes show this same inclination of the trunk.

In Surrey, England, where strong winds are not particularly usual, I have observed that the oak and beech trees in exposed positions are more heavily branched and have greater foliage on the south side. In Virginia, the oaks and long-leaf pines show a decidedly heavier growth on the south side. The illustrations on pages 109 to 112 were drawn from photographs of trees which I examined. These trees are typical of most of the other species when growing in positions exposed to full sunlight in the temperate regions of the Northern Hemisphere.

In these regions the southern branches of many trees are more horizontal, while the northern ones reach up more vertically in their endeavor to obtain more light. This provides an excellent means of determining north and south.

This upward struggle of the northern branches to receive the greatest amount of top light is very pronounced in the horse

Longleaf pine tree, Virginia Beach, Virginia. The right side of
the tree faces south and shows the greater branch and foliage
growth on that side which faces the full daily arc of the sun.
This is an area where the winds have practically no effect on
direction of growth

chestnuts of the eastern United States and of Europe, and also in
the European lindens. In the elms, however, it is hardly noticeable. In Connecticut I have found it easy to get my direction
from the horse chestnuts merely by glancing out of a train window. In winter, when the trees are leafless, the side of greatest
branch growth is more easily seen. In summer a closer inspection
of the foliage from either side is sometimes necessary.

Unlike the trees mentioned above, there are some, such as the common spruce, the firs and the pyramid poplars, which usually remain straight and are uniformly branched on all sides in spite of uneven illumination. The cedars also remain straight unless they are very tall, when they have a tendency to bend towards the strongest light.

Cypresses and farm building in Provence in France. Note the large cypress tree with its bulge of greater growth on the southeast side, sheltered from the Mistral. Also of interest is the symmetrical shape of the small cypress sheltered by the large tree. The leafless trees in the foreground, on each side of the building, show the retarding effect of the dominant wind on the northwest side. The door of the farm building, on the sheltered southeast side, is typical of the Provence region. All of these features combine to give very positive evidence of direction to the traveler

So far we have considered only the separate effects of the wind and the direction of greatest sunlight on the growth and shape of trees. It is also necessary for the pathfinder to observe the combined effects of wind and light. In some cases these two influences will combine to intensify the effect; in other cases, one reduces the other. The sun has the stronger influence on some kinds of trees, the wind on others.

Early in 1955, my wife and I made a leisurely trip by car from the south of France through Belgium and Holland for the express purpose of observing and photographing the directional characteristics of trees. Similar observations were made in England and in the eastern United States. Following winding roads from the Mediterranean coast to Holland, we had no difficulty at any time in determining north, south, east and west by observing the trees through the car windows.

Through Provence in the south of France that chilling wind, the Mistral, blows from the northwest. The farmers in this region call the wind the "mud-eater" (*"mange fange"*) because its dry, cold gusts have the effect of drying up the ground. The farmhouses of Provence (locally known as *"mas"*) are built with their backs to the northwest, the direction of the Mistral, and have a minimum of windows on that side. The houses are usually sheltered from the wind by a row of cypresses which also shield the gardens. The position of these windbreaks would make it very easy for anyone to tell his directions, for they are naturally aligned northeast-southwest. The Mistral has a striking effect on the growth of individual trees, although it blows only for four or five days at a time, intermittently, during the winter. Every cypress in an exposed or unprotected position shows its bulge of greater growth on that part of the tree which is sheltered from the wind. Although trees in Central Europe actually receive the full benefit of the sun from morning to evening on the southern side, the wind's effects on their growth is much more pronounced than that of the sun. However, the decidedly greater growth of branches and leaves on the southeast is to some extent caused by southern sun, though not enough to make it a true southerly growth.

Proceeding on our journey, north of Avignon we left the cypresses behind but observed the same marked effect on the common poplars. Although we were out of the area of the violent Mistral, the trees throughout central and northern France, Belgium and Holland clearly showed that the direction of the dominant wind was still northwest. In this region almost all isolated trees, of various species, even if not leaning away from the wind, show evidence of retarded growth on the side where the wind blows strongly. The silhouettes of clumps of trees present a smoothly rounded edge pointing into the prevailing

Greater branch and foliage growth on the sheltered south-east side is common to all the cypress trees in the region where the Mistral blows

northwest wind. The sheltered sides of these groups of trees have a more ragged configuration. This striking evidence of direction can be seen many miles away.

Summing up, we have to give full consideration to the separate effects of wind and sun on trees, and at times to their combined influence. The information gained in this manner can be applied in finding our way.

Beeches and a birch near Heemstede, Holland. The rounded edge of this clump of beech trees points to the northwest and is caused by the retarding effect on growth exerted by the dominant northwest wind. Note also the enhanced growth on the southeast side of the birch tree which overtops the beeches

In any place where the wind blows predominantly from one direction, the flower plumes of reeds will be found to form a thin wedge only on that side of the stem away from the wind. I have seen this not only throughout Europe but also in many other places in the world, including the vicinity of my home in the Fiji Islands, where the southeast trade is the dominant wind.

It is often stated in boys' books that moss will be found on the north side of trees in the northern hemisphere. This is a rather dangerous generalization if other factors are not taken into account. Moss and lichens do not necessarily thrive where they receive the most shade but—and this is more important—where the moisture is retained the longest. Humidity is an even greater factor than shade. It is a question of knowing from where the rain-bearing winds in your locality blow, and the direction of the

Flower plumes of reeds grow away from the direction of the dominant wind

greatest shade. Combining these two factors, you should be able to determine where moisture will be retained longest and where moss will grow. In North America, as a general rule, there is less evaporation on the north and northeast sides of trees and rocks. On the other hand, in the Seine and Burgundy regions in France, mosses and lichens are usually found on the northwest side of trees and rocks and in the Jura, in Switzerland, on the southwest side. Each locality has its differences in climate, and you should determine for yourself which side retains moisture the longest in your particular area. Only in this way can mosses and lichens be a valuable guide to direction.

This information will be all the more worthwhile when evidence is obtained from growths on trees or rocks exposed to all weathers. It may also be of interest to know that some mosses take on a darker brown hue when growing in greater sunlight and are more green or grayish-green when found in more shaded spots.

Other plants growing on trunks or branches of trees can be useful to you in determining direction if you continually observe the habits of each individual species under local conditions. These plants are known as epiphytes. Each species has its particular preference for light, shade or moisture.

The Indians of North America used all possible indications in order to orient themselves in the forests. Père Joseph François Lafitau, speaking of the Iroquois tribe, with whom he spent five years, wrote in 1724:

The savages pay great heed to their 'star' compass [the Pole Star] in the woods and in the vast prairies of the continent of America, as well as on the rivers whose courses are well known to them. But when the sun or the stars are not visible they have a natural compass in the trees of the forest from which they know the north by almost infallible signs.

The first is that of their tips, which always lean towards the South, to which they are attracted by the sun. The second is that of their bark, which is more dull and dark on the north side. If they wish to be sure they only have to give the tree a few cuts with an axe; the various tree rings which are formed in the trunk of the tree are thicker on the side which faces North and thin on the South side.

Lafitau's statement that the tips of trees point south is not wholly accurate; in fact the tips of certain trees in North America, such as pines and hemlocks, lean to the southeast.

The tree-ring method known to the Indians was also described by Leonardo da Vinci in Italy more than four hundred years ago. Throughout North America and Europe more recent observations have confirmed da Vinci's statement that as shown by annual tree rings, the heart of a tree is nearer the bark on the south side, and that the bark of old trees is usually thicker on the north and northeast sides.

Section of tree trunk

In a test made many years ago by the New York State Forest Commission on 700 black spruce trees in the Adirondack Mountains, 94 per cent showed a greater growth of the trunk section toward the north and east, while only 6 per cent had thicker growth on the south and west.

Plants and trees can give us much help in finding our direction because of their liking for certain environments. Some species flourish in full sunlight, others in shade; some prefer moist conditions while others need arid zones. Many types, such as those with small leaves which spin with the wind, have a tolerance for wind, while other plants, including many with large leaves, need sheltered positions.

Thus we find that in many cold and temperate parts of the Northern Hemisphere the leaf-shedding trees grow on the warmer, south-facing slopes, while the evergreen pines and conifers are found on the northern slopes.

In the Rocky Mountains, limber pines will nearly always be found on the south-facing slopes, while Engelmann spruce trees are on the inclines facing north. Seeing either of these species, you can be very certain which slope you are on.

In the eastern Grass Veld of South Africa the north-facing slopes are exposed to intense sun and hot winds. This results in a vegetation which can stand the dryness, such as thorn trees, milky sap plants, and aloes. On the protected south-facing slopes, however, there are grasslands. These inclines also get the benefit of the rain-bearing winds blowing from between southwest and southeast. In the higher ridges of the Drakensberg and Stormberg

Mountains in South Africa this causes patches of forest, usually on the sides facing these winds.

For another example, on the Banks Peninsula in New Zealand, and in the Southern Alps there, the trees and shrubs are invariably found on the southern slopes of the spurs, which face the rain-bearing winds and are also the side protected from the sun. The northern inclines are generally bare.

In the hilly parts of central and southern Europe vineyards are usually situated on the southern slopes because the vines require the greatest possible amount of light and warmth. In European farms and gardens, peaches, nectarines, mulberries, grapes and other sun-loving plants are grown against the southern side of garden walls.

Many plants throughout the world indicate direction because of their need for light or their permanent alignment to avoid the excessive midday light and heat.

For example, there are many species of wild lettuce which are common throughout Europe, Africa and temperate Asia. They have violet or yellow flowers. All of them have vertical leaves and align their edges north and south so that they can get the benefit of the morning and afternoon sun and avoid the full midday heat. The leaves of these species are similar on both sides. Those of most other plants, however, differ on the upper and lower sides, with many more breathing spores or stomata on the lower side, which is protected from the sun.

The yellow-flowered prickly wild lettuce (*Lactuca serriola*) was introduced into the United States in about 1863 and is now found very generally throughout the country. It has similar directional characteristics. Some of the narrow-leafed domestic lettuces also align their leaves in a north-south direction when allowed to seed. The Cos and Deertongue varieties are particularly noted for this.

In the United States, too, the pilot weed or resin weed (*Silphium lacinatum*) directs its leaves in a constant north-south direction when it is not growing in the shade. It grows to a height of from three to six feet and is commonly distributed from Ohio to the Rocky Mountains and from Minnesota to Texas. Often

PILOT WEED

Two views of this plant show its compass-like habit of
adjusting the leaves in a north-south direction. The one
on the left is seen from the east and the other from the
south

called "the compass plant of the prairies," its directional qualities
were well known to the old pioneers. Longfellow wrote of it in
Evangeline:

Look at this vigorous plant that lifts its head from the meadow,
See how its leaves are turned to the north, as true as the magnet;
This is the compass flower, that the finger of God has planted
Here in the houseless wild, to direct the traveler's journey
Over the sealike, pathless, limitless waste of the desert.

This weed has been introduced into Europe and is often found
there as a cultivated plant.

A closely related weed often called prairie burdock (*Silphium
terebinthinaceum*), shows the same peculiarity. Only the younger

NORTH

The North Pole plant of South Africa (*Pachypodium namaquanum*). The tops are all bent permanently to the north to obtain the full advantage of the midday sun. (*After Marloth*)

plants of this species, however, manifest this north-south orienta-
tion. This weed is widely distributed throughout the southern
United States and is often found growing with the prickly pear
(*Opuntia*) in the Southwestern deserts.

In South Africa, a plant which gives direction to the lost traveler by its curious, uncanny growth is the so-called "North Pole"
(*"Noord Pool"*) or *"half mens"* (*Pachypodium namaquanum*).
It is an amazing sight to see hundreds of these plants with their
heads all turned towards the north. A traveler should have no
trouble in finding his way in such a locality. The name *"half
mens,"* meaning "half a person" in Afrikaans, is given to these
plants because from a distance they resemble silhouettes of slender people buried up to their hips in the ground. The crown of
this plant, particularly of the taller specimens, always points to
the north, and the rosette of leaves on the crown forms an angle
of 30 degrees with the horizontal. The "North Pole" plant is
found in the mountains on both sides of the lower Orange River
in Namaqualand. Plants of this species which are eighteen
inches high may be as much as twenty-five years old. Their curiously shaped stems are leafless for ten or eleven months of the
year, and sometimes in periods of drought they may have no
leaves for several years, and look like petrified sentinels on the
rocky slopes. When the rains begin, a rosette of grayish-green,
feltlike leaves covers the head of each plant. The flowers, which
appear in July or August, are large and showy, pale yellow in the
lower part of the tube and deep maroon at the mouth.

This plant is not to be confused with a different South African
species, *Euphorbia fasciculata,* which shares the name *"Noord
Pool"* and is reputed to bend the apex of its stem towards the
north.

In North and Central America the giant barrel cactus, *Foro
cactus,* is similarly influenced by the direction of the midday sun
and has a permanent lean to the south. In desert areas this plant
is a most valuable guide, besides providing a source of water.

In northern temperate climates there is a marked tendency for
the flowers of plants to face south or east. This can be important

not only to anyone trying to orient himself, but also to the person planning his garden for the most effective display.

In middle northern latitudes such plants include the viola, pansy, daffodil, some lilies and the Shasta daisy. This orientation of the flowers is more pronounced when they are not crowded or shaded but are able to get the full influence of the sun.

Many other plants, especially when shaded, turn their flowers towards the greatest source of illumination. Among these are tulips, phlox, Sweet William, coral bells and canterbury bells.

Some flowers are true sun followers from sunrise to sunset, while others are influenced only by the early sun, after a night of darkness, and give up their chase of the sun by midday. The daisy-like leopard's bane (*Doronicum*) which flowers in the spring throughout Europe and North America, is a true sun-follower. From sunrise to sunset the flowers turn towards the sun, but they are about forty minutes late (roughly 10 degrees).

Contrary to popular opinion, the common garden sunflower (*Helianthus annuus*) does not always point to the sun. It appears to do so in fairly high latitudes, where the sun is always at a low angle and the light is not so intense as in lower latitudes. In the vicinity of New York, however, one close observer found that 95 per cent of the flower heads of this plant always face east.

Study of the ecology of plants shows that there are many factors which determine why particular plants and trees grow in certain places and not in others. Among these factors are the chemical content of the soil, the temperature, the amount of moisture and drainage, the duration of daylight, the amount of light or shade, and exposure to or protection from winds.

A little known and remarkable fact is that the chemical content of some plants indicates the ore content of the soil in which they are growing. This knowledge can be very useful to those searching for minerals. The Finnish scientist Kalervo Rankama terms this "geobotanical prospecting." The usual procedure is to burn the plant and analyze the ashes. Finnish geochemists actually found a rich copper-nickel deposit by examining the ashes of birch leaves.

In the United States, Mrs. Helen Cannon, a scientist employed by the U. S. Geological Survey, located several important uranium ore deposits by analyzing the ashes of deep-rooted trees in desert areas. Previously these deposits had been missed by prospecting with Geiger counters and spot drilling.

Prospecting for zinc ore has been very successfully carried out this way. There is, for instance, the classical zinc pansy, *Viola calaminaria et zinci*, which shows a decided affinity for zinc and accordingly is found on waste ore dumps of zinc mines in many places in Central Europe. This zinc pansy may contain up to several per cent of zinc oxide. Another zinc indicator of the *Thlaspi* genus, commonly called pennycress, which grows in Germany and Sweden on ground rich in this element, is said to have up to 16 per cent zinc in the ashes.

The lead plant (*Amorpha canescens*), a shrub two to four feet high, with blue flowers, is found in Missouri in ground containing silver and lead.

Although this method of prospecting has received special attention in recent years because of the present increased interest in rare minerals, it has been known in principle for many years. In 1897, in northern Australia, it was reported that a small plant, about six inches in height, with large flowers (*Polycarpaea spirostylis*), contained a large percentage of copper and was an actual indicator of copper deposits.

In Norway is found the attractive alpine plant *Lychnis alpina*, less than a foot in height, with pink flowers, which grows in soils rich in copper. In the copper ore deposits of the Röros area of Norway, hardly any other plants than these can survive.

There are even plants which indicate gold. Two of these, commonly called "horsetails" or scouring rushes (*Equisetum arvense* and *Equisetum palustre*), may contain up to four and a half ounces of gold per ton of plant material.

Four species of milk vetches (genus *Astragalus*) are considered the best plants for indicating uranium. They are *Astragalus thompsonae, Astragalus confertiflorus, Astragalus Preussi* var. *arctus* and *Astragalus Pattersoni*.

Two other good indicators of uranium are the prince's plume (*Stanleya pinnata*) and woody aster (*Aster venustus*).

Chapter 12

Anthill Signposts

ALL INSECTS, being cold-blooded, are sensitive to changes in temperature; and few insects are more so than those highly specialized social creatures, the ants and the (quite unrelated) termites or white ants. Both of these orders of insects build hills to house their communities; and many of these hills are to a greater or less extent oriented to the sun. The ants of cold regions, or regions which are cold in winter, build their nests to get the greatest warmth. Other tropical ants build their nests in the coolest places. Sometimes this results in buildings which have a shape and alignment consistently oriented in a compass direction. What they build, in fact, are signposts for the natural navigator.

In the parts of the Northern Hemisphere which have cold winters, in both the new and the old worlds, several kinds of ants build their mounds on hill slopes facing southeast, the direction in which the winter sun rises. So cold are the nights that the ants are almost paralyzed by the low temperature: they need the earliest rays of the morning sun to get the longest possible working day. That is why they build their mounds aligned in a southeasterly direction and show a general preference for living on southern or eastern slopes (depending on which kind of slope gets the most heat). When they build their hills close to trees or tree stumps the hills are generally found on the warmer side, which is (in the Northern Hemisphere) the south or southeast side.

Perhaps the most striking example of a signpost ant is the yellow ant of Central Europe. *Lasius flavus* is particularly common in the pasture lands of the Swiss Alps and in the Jura Mountains

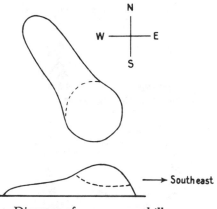

Diagram of compass anthills

and it is on their southeastern slopes that the ants of this species generally build their nests. When their mounds are built in open ground, they are oriented most accurately to the southeast, so much so that the native humans of the area often use them to pick up bearings when they are lost in a fog or away from home. The Swiss even have a local name for these directional anthills—"*teumons.*"

These compass anthills are steep on their southeastern edge to get the greatest amount of warmth; and it is in this part that the ants live, and here that the ants continue to build as they add new earth to their anthill. The result is that the hill slopes gradually to its northwestern end; the northwestern part, indeed, is often quite abandoned, and represents the home of previous generations.

Established yellow ant mounds usually develop distinct characteristics other than their compass alignment. On their southeastern side the ground is often loose and sandy, with scattered vegetation, with thyme and a fine gray-green grass predominating. On the northwestern sides the soil becomes compacted into a consistent humus—which tends to become covered with low-growing but dense vegetation of bulb type plants, which eventually carpet this part of the mound completely. A big hill of the

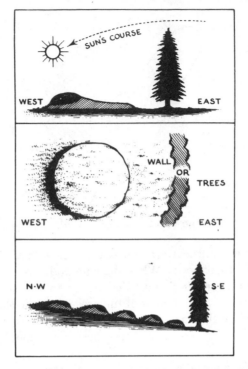

Three exceptions to typical anthill growth. (*After Linder*)

yellow ant is six to seven feet long, two and a half feet wide and about fifteen inches high. On open ground it takes its most typical oval shape: when the mounds are surrounded by, or built against, a rock wall, or encircled with trees, they are often round; for in such circumstances the ants get their greatest warmth from sun rays striking from above, and there is no longer much advantage in extending the mound towards the direction of the rising sun. Nevertheless, under these conditions the mounds can still be used for direction finding; for the ants still tend to inhabit the southeastern side of the nests.

Exceptionally, though, the ants may inhabit the northwest end of their nests—when the mound is close up to a tree or rock which shields it completely from the southeast.

North-south termite mounds of northern Australia, seen from the east
(*above*) and from the north (*below*)

Another European ant, the black ant, *Lasius niger,* builds nests of pine needles. These nests do not have the oval shape of those of the yellow ants, but their inhabitants consistently tend to live on the eastern side of the hills, which show the greatest activity to the watchful traveler.

In the western part of the United States we can find two further examples of the consistent orientation of anthills. The western harvester ant, *Pogonomyrmex occidentalis,* which is also known as the mound-building prairie ant, builds the only entrance to its mound at the bottom of its southeastern side. The nests of the silver ant, *Formica argentata,* are similarly oriented in the fields of the lower mountain areas of the state of Colorado.

In desert areas where ants seek cool as opposed to warm conditions, certain ants, like *Messor arenarius* of the Sahara, build the walls of their hills in a crater-like form, with the high side facing the local strong winds—and give safe signposts to the natural navigator—at least if he already knows the direction of the prevailing wind, as (we hope this book will have persuaded him by now) he should.

Termites or *White Ants.* Termites are social insects which belong to an order of insects quite different from the ants. The order has a more exclusively tropical distribution than that of the ants, so it is not surprising that most of the "compass" termites construct and orient their nests to avoid the excessive heat of the midday sun.

Some of the most interesting termite mounds can be found over the vast hot desert areas of northern Australia. They all belong to the well-known termite *Lamitermes meridionalis.* They are most conspicuous structures which have been christened "magnetic anthills." Some of them reach a height of twelve feet; few established hills are less than three feet high. All of them are oriented almost exactly true north and south. On their eastern and western sides they are steeply flattened and their average length is about four or five times their height. They rise to a sharp and serrated top ridge.

Magnetic anthills (if we may forget that termites are not ants and use the popular expression) owe their straight north-south shape to a technical necessity. These hills are built of mud and the termites can only build them under very wet conditions: yet in order to become secure they must dry most rapidly. If they are built north-south the morning sun can dry the eastern side, the afternoon sun the western side, and no part is left in shadow for very long during the day.

A further advantage in the directional shape of this kind of mound is that the termites can move quite quickly from one side of the hill to the other. This they need to do in order to obtain the most comfortable temperature during the day; for they can withstand neither the heat of midday nor the direct heat of the morning or the afternoon sun. In the winter they move in the opposite way, to the east galleries for the morning warmth, to the west side in the afternoon.

These magnetic anthills are one of the most important travelers' guides through the thousands of square miles of northern Australia in which they are found. They have certainly made it difficult for anybody to lose his way in this area. During the last war I was Director of Air Transport for the Allied Air Forces in Australia and New Guinea, and several times I flew over Queensland and over Australia's northern territories. I often saw the military ranks of the magnetic anthills. From the air their number is most spectacular and the consistency of their orientation almost uncanny. Close to the airport townships of Darwin and Katherine I inspected these termite hills on the ground. In this flat monotonous country with no mountains on the horizon, they made living signposts that no traveler could forget and few could fail to use.

Just as in northern Australia, farmers and travelers on the edge of the Kalahari desert in southwest Africa have a termite signpost to guide them. The common termite here, as Dr. S. H. Skaife of Cape Province informs me, builds its mound some ten to fifteen feet high and orients it with the tip bent towards the north.

Map showing directional characteristics in Australia. This map shows that over a vast area of the Australian continent it is a simple matter to find one's direction by means of such natural features as the direction of the sand dunes, the prevailing winds, and, in the north, the striking north-south termite mounds which abound in a large area of northern Australia. (*After Madigan*)

Chapter 13

Finding Your Way in the Desert

THOSE WHO MUST FIND their way in deserts know that in all the deserts of the world there are indigenous nomadic people to whom the desert is a familiar home, and for whom the solution of the many difficult problems of travel is second nature. The desert explorer must, through his powers of observation, attain the proficiency of the true desert people. For them navigation is a necessity for survival. From an early age they know it is a matter of life and death.

Naturally enough, the desert nomads have a very well-developed visual memory for topography. In their minds every journey's landmarks are engraved and recalled in succession as they go their way. Their conversation together is of many things, but most particularly of landmarks and travel conditions. Every meeting of nomads in the desert produces talk of the state of going, the condition of water holes, the amount of feed available at pastures. They are particularly observant of traces of each other's caravans, and can tell with incredible accuracy just how many camels and horses have passed one way and how long ago they passed. In the vast sand-free pebbled areas which form most of the Sahara, even when the caravan tracks and the camel tracks (called *medjhed*) have become obliterated, generations of nomads have marked the way from water hole to water hole with rock cairns. These pyramids of stone, called *amer*, or *redjem*, are usually perched on some skyline point so that they can be seen from afar.

I confine this chapter to those methods of navigation which are peculiar to desert areas or any places in the world containing sand. The desert traveler must remember that these are the special techniques to be used in conjunction with many of the other general techniques described in this book, which of course apply just as much to desert areas as they do to other regions.

Even if we ignore the cold deserts of the arctic and antarctic, we find that about a sixth of the land area of the world is desert. No great continent is without a desert or semidesert arid area. In North Africa lies the Sahara, the largest and best known desert in the world—three million square miles of level plains, jagged mountains, rock plateaus and sand dunes. Only 10 per cent of it is sand: by far the greater part is gravel from which the sand has long ago been blown, to pile up in the depressions where most of the dunes are found. A track in the Sahara's desert gravel lasts for many years. South Africa's Kalahari is another great desert: and from the deserts of Arabia arid zones stretch almost continuously into Syria and through Persia into India's Baluchistan and up into Russia's Turkestan. In central and eastern Asia lie the Ordos desert and the great Gobi, a saucer-like plateau north of China which includes large parts of Inner and Outer Mongolia. Ringed by mountains, its basin stretches as an almost endless, almost level, plain with scattered rocks and buttes. South America has its great desert; Australia its vast central desert; and North America its great basin: the desert area of the southwestern United States has flat plains with scanty cactus vegetation and abruptly rising mountain islands which remind one of parts of the Gobi and the Sahara.

The two special keys to desert navigation are given by the behavior of sand and the behavior of animals.

In the desert regions of the earth man has established only the tiniest of communities. Except in the oases, the earth has never been subjected to cultivation; and across the desert's broad sweep the winds have left their marks for man to read. Each desert has its prevailing wind, just as has each ocean; and these winds can make permanent impressions on the landscape which dominate the scenery when it is calm or when the winds are temporarily varying. A temporary wind blowing across a desert in a direction other than that of the dominant wind may leave its marks, but usually these are but ripple marks, and insignificant in comparison with the effects of the dominant wind.

The dominant winds of the desert are really very constant in direction; and since the greatest part of most deserts is plateau land, these winds are not interfered with by local topography as they are in mountainous land. The first thing the desert traveler has to learn is the direction of the prevailing wind and the principal ways in which it arranges the shifting sand.

Desert sand mostly consists of hard mineral grains small enough to be moved by the wind but not small enough to be carried up into the air for long periods and distances and dispersed as dust. Sand is blown, but not at random, for by its very nature it piles up into definite features. Sand dunes have a history and an anatomy: they are not just disorderly masses of sand. They can be classified into three main types, which we shall examine presently.

Sand, when driven by wind, settles in sheltered places, gradually filling in depressions and protected spots. When a rock or some other obstruction rises in the desert, the blown sand accumulates on the leeward side of it, where it ultimately consolidates into a streamlined shape. The crest and the long axis of this sand drift will lie in the direction of the prevailing wind. On the windward side of an obstacle like a rock or shrub, a steep sandbank will heap up. On the sheltered side the bank will slope away more gently as a streamlined dune, or perhaps I should say a near-dune.

The three main kinds of dunes in the desert are the longitudinal dune, the seif dune and the barkhan.[1] Of these the commonest is the longitudinal dune. Typically it is a continuous bank of sand of even height which lies parallel with the dominant wind. In the sandy parts of hot deserts longitudinal dunes are very extensive. In the Atlas regions of the Sahara the Great Western and the Great Eastern Erg are composed of a vast system of these longitudinal sandhills running northwest to southeast or north-northwest to south-southeast. In the central Sahara the alignment of the dune system turns southward, and in the Sudanese (east-

[1] Or "barchan."

ern) Sahara, towards the southwest and even towards west-southwest. In the Libyan desert—the northeastern part of the Sahara—the dune axis is north-northwest. Here, as everywhere, it is in the general direction of the prevailing wind.

Such is also the case in Inner Mongolia, where the dunes in the Ordos desert are oriented northwest to southeast parallel with the wind. Some of the dunes are bare, for this desert has an exceptional quantity of loose sand, but others have been consolidated with vegetation and appear as small hills covered with tufts of grass or low brush.

In Australia the inland desert dunes run generally northwest, with a more westerly trend at both the north and south margins of the western desert, and once more this reflects the direction of the winds which blow almost permanently in that region. The dunes are low (on the average about forty feet high, with a maximum of about a hundred feet), straight and naturally parallel, with a rather regular distance of a quarter of a mile between ridges that may be truly hundreds of miles long.

Unlike the longitudinal dune, whose one side is almost a mirror image of the other, the individual seif dune has a form very like that of a sand drift behind a rock. Its length (or axis) lies in the direction of the prevailing wind, but its long crest, unlike that of the longitudinal dune, is sharply ridged, much more steeply on one side than on the other. Indeed, one end often appears as a rounded convex slope while the other falls as a concave slope or even a precipice, so abruptly that it may give the appearance of a collapsed front. This front is at right angles to the dominant wind. And it may change temporarily when a strong wind veers out of its prevailing direction. Seif dunes are seldom found alone, but much more often as a range forming a continuous ridge connecting a succession of summits from sixty to six hundred feet apart. Usually several seif dune lines run parallel with each other at intervals varying (depending on the area, but rather uniform within the area) anywhere from four hundred yards to five miles.

A barkhan is a crescent dune shaped like a horseshoe. The slopes down to the hollow are steeper than the outside slopes and the hollow faces down wind. In the sandy desert of Peru the barkhan dune is known as *medaños;* and there it is the sand dune's most typical form. Where other deserts might have longitudinal dunes, this desert has a ragged interrupted line of these rather small crescentic mounds In the horseshoe's hollow the

Barkhan or crescent dunes in snow (*above*) and sand (*below*)

steep slopes are sheltered from the wind; and there the sand lies at the steepest angle of rest, about 33 degrees from the horizontal. At any greater angle the sand would slide, for gravity would overcome surface friction. The end of the barkhan dune which faces the wind slopes least, only about 5 or 6 degrees from the horizontal. The angle of the sides is usually from 10 to 13 degrees.

This desert dune topography is not entirely confined to the world's present deserts, for many great areas in temperate zones date from an arid past, though subsequently conquered by vegetation and cultivation. What we could almost call the "fossil shapes" of their desert dune topography remain, as does even the alignment of the dunes with the prevailing wind—showing, incidentally, that the type of country has changed more than the wind. Old dune formations in Germany, Poland, Hungary and on the moors of Gascony lie east-west, for instance; and the dunes of Sweden are aligned with a foehn wind which comes down the Scandinavian Alps, a dominant westerly, deflected south.

Animals as Desert Guides. The question of survival in deserts might, by a purist, be thought not strictly relevant to a discussion of desert navigation. However, a common-sense view recognizes that the two subjects are mixed closely together. The armed forces of many countries, of course, have made detailed studies of desert survival; and there is already a mass of literature dealing with the solution of the problems of exposure and living off the land. One of the most important survival methods which involves navigation is that which enables the traveler to find water. Water holes may not necessarily be on the intended route of the desert traveler; but a knowledge of their direction can always help him to find his position. Among the best indicators of desert water are animals. Anybody who can spare enough of a desert day to sit quietly and out of sight near a water hole, will learn a great deal about the behavior of water-seeking birds and other animals.

There are 289 species of pigeons and doves in the world; and there is no desert (apart from the ice deserts of the north and south) which does not have one or more species native to it. Birds of this order are easily recognizable by their shape and style; and nearly every species has a habit of perching in trees or shrubs near desert water holes, especially towards the evening. Usually the desert pigeons drink once or twice a day. Occasionally they drink at daybreak: always do they drink in the early evening: never do they drink during the heat of the day. It is, then, in the evening that it is important to watch the direction of their flight. An experienced watcher of desert pigeons can even tell whether his birds are on their way to or on their way from their evening drink, for their flight from water is characteristically heavy, and is accompanied by a louder flapping of their wings.

A remarkable story of desert pigeons is told by H. A. Lindsay in his *Bushman's Handbook*.

In the desert of the Australian Northern Territory a whole party of surveyors were bushed without water. David Lindsay took the strongest camel and went off to look for water. He failed to find it. But on his way back to camp that evening he saw a solitary rock pigeon flutter across a gorge ahead of him. He followed its flight line up a hill; and, in a spot where nobody would normally think of finding water, came across a rock hole containing thousands of gallons.

If it had not been for one little bird the entire party might have perished.

Each of the world's deserts has its own particular, sometimes even peculiar, birds—besides pigeons and doves. The Australian desert has its speckled finches, locally known as diamond sparrows, which congregate in thick flocks never far from a water hole. Among the best indicators of water in the Gobi deserts are wagtails, and larks and other small sand-colored birds. The Australian desert has cockatoos and other deserts have parrots. Nearly all deserts have quail. When geese migrate through desert country (as they often do) their presence may be considered as an indication of water—particularly when they are flying low, for then they follow rivers or chains of ponds or isolated lakes.

King Solomon is said to have discovered the retreat of Balkis, Queen of Sheba, among the mountains between the Hejaz and the Yemen, by means of a plover which he despatched in search of water during his progress through Arabia.

Birds are not the only indicators of water, by any means. Gazelles and other desert antelopes herd towards the water holes, particularly in the evening. Bees and hornets go on watering flights and are excellent guides to water. The tracks of mammals and humans on the desert sand do not of course by themselves invariably lead to water; but when different animal tracks converge they will probably do so.

Not all animals, of course, invariably show the presence or direction of water at evening drinking time. A number of species can go without water for several days. If you see an emu or the large red kangaroo or the gray kangaroo in the Australian desert, for instance, you—and the animals—may easily be from twenty to fifty miles from a drinking place.

Chapter 14

Finding Your Way in the Polar Regions

THE WORLD'S AREAS of permanent, or near-permanent, snow and ice are by no means confined to the polar regions. The suggestions in this chapter apply, especially in winter, also to Alaska and Greenland, to the whole northern part of Canada and the Soviet Union, to northern Scandinavia and Finland.

The North Pole area itself is only a large floating mass of ice without any actual land, while the South Pole region is really a very large continent. In the last years the antarctic has attracted a great deal of attention not only on account of the disputes about sovereignties of that country but also because of the possibilities of the presence of rare minerals. This large land mass is in my opinion the adventurous area of the next fifty years. It is also the last of the earth's unknown regions, except for the oceans.

Already I have discussed many methods of pathfinding which apply to snow-covered lands. Among them are the study of reflections in the sky (page 87), the construction of back-tracking landmarks (pages 73-74), the direction of the prevailing wind (page 93), the observation of wind-polished rocks and of the movements of high clouds, the directions of sun and shadows, and steering by sighting on companions, whether they be fellow humans or dogs.

Special to the problems of pathfinding in snow regions is the study of wind-made snow forms. All the accounts of the great polar explorers—Scott, Amundsen, Nansen, Shackleton, Mawson and Byrd—show that they paid very great attention to snow forms in finding their way on their famous journeys. Many of us read and reread their epic stories full of suspense and self-sacrifice. Just now polar travel is reviving. Explorers are using techniques out of reach of those great pioneers, though no doubt they dreamed of them. I expect the explorers of the present generation will find just as much thrill and drama under extreme conditions as the men of a generation past, and will be poised (as they were) just as excitingly between success and failure.

I am certain they still watch and use the sastrugi, the snow mounds, the wind ripples on the snow and the distribution of sea ice to help them in their navigation in the same way as their predecessors did.

The polar regions have much in common with the hot sand deserts. They are themselves cold deserts, for one thing; and for another very cold snow behaves physically in many ways which are similar to the behavior of sand. Snow crystals are smaller than most of the usual sand particles. But the wind can arrange them in much the same way. In the snow deserts, then, the wind forms snow dunes or snowdrifts, just as in the hot deserts it forms sand dunes and sanddrifts. What is more, these snow dunes have very much the same shape and properties as sand dunes, though generally speaking they are smaller and less stable. Like the sand dunes, snow dunes reflect the direction of the dominant or prevailing wind, and thus are a very considerable aid to the navigator who is traveling on an antarctic or an arctic day when the sun is clouded over, or in the long antarctic or arctic night when he cannot see the stars.

One of the commonest snow dunes is the counterpart of the longitudinal sand dune. Over extensive snow-covered areas the prevailing wind drives the drifting snow and packs it hard into ridges, from a few inches to three or four feet in height, which run parallel with the wind's direction. These are known as "sastrugi": the word is derived from the Russian word "*zastrugi*" meaning snow waves. Smaller than the longitudinal sand dunes, sastrugi are almost always placed much closer together; but they are built in the same way.

So many polar explorers have found sastrugi valuable in navigating when other means of orientation were obscured by weather, that accounts of sastrugi have become almost commonplace in the logs of their expeditions. I can quote, for instance (as I often do in this book), from the famous book *The Home of the Blizzard* by the eminent Australian antarctic explorer, Sir Douglas Mawson:

> Close to the Magnetic Pole as we were, the compass was of little use, and to steer a straight course was a difficult task. The only check upon the correctness of the bearing was the direction in which trended the old hard winter sastrugi, channeled out along a line running almost north and south. The newly fallen snow obliterated these, and frequent halts had to be called in order to investigate the buried surface.[1]

Admiral Richard E. Byrd also added his tribute to the directional value of sastrugi in his book *Little America*. This tells of his explorations in and around the famous United States base on the antarctic continent, reestablished in a new location (as I write) for the International Geophysical Year. Admiral Byrd refers to them:

> . . . rough sastrugi which we had to cross diagonally and which made the compass bound about badly and steering, therefore, difficult. As is always the case (in this region) these sastrugi trend in an ESE to WNW direction. . . . It has been a stimulating afternoon after the almost unchanging travel for the past three weeks over the sastrugi surface of the Barrier.[2]

In just the same way Sir Ernest Shackleton recorded the frequent use of sastrugi in his great book *The Heart of the Antarctic*. In his famous polar dash he was often denied a sun sight for days at a time; but all the time, when low clouds obscured the sun and even prominent surrounding landmarks, he was able to steer by aiming his sledges at a constant angle to the prevailing direction of the sastrugi.

[1] Sir Douglas Mawson, *The Home of the Blizzard*, London, © 1915.
[2] Richard E. Byrd, *Little America: Aerial Exploration in the Antarctic: The Flight to the South Pole*, New York, © 1930.

Just as sastrugi are the counterparts of the longitudinal dunes of the sand desert, so does snow occasionally form, or rather drift, into mounds which have a crescentic shape similar to the barkhans of the sand deserts. Snow barkhans are not only smaller than sand barkhans, but their sides are much less steep. In just the same way as those of sand barkhans, the hollow part of a snow barkhan or snow mound points down wind.

Winds make ripple marks upon the snow in much the same way as they do upon sand. These ripples are very small and never more than a few inches high. They are not valuable as an indication of the prevailing winds, because they can be formed very quickly by any substantial local wind. These temporary snow ripples are set at right angles to the wind, just as are water waves; they are quite different from and much less useful than the sastrugi and the snow barkhans, which take the direction of the dominant wind and are much more permanent.

I make no apology for quoting Sir Douglas Mawson once more, as his observations and accounts are always full of the most clever combination of natural navigational methods. Throughout his book we can read of many occasions upon which he used one indication to check another. Here is an example:

At 11 a.m. on Sunday, November 24, we moved off to the southeast in a wind of fifty miles an hour. The light was bad, and steering had to be done by sastrugi and wind. However, momentary glimpses of the sun served to check the course. The lunch camp was five miles from the depot, and a good mound with a top of black bunting was left there. At almost every halt, thus far on our journey, the snow cut for pitching the tent had been gathered up into a mound which, in addition to forming a landmark, could often be used as a back-mark for checking the course. Our depot thus had a mound four miles on the southern and five miles on the northern side of it. It was not marked as well as I had hoped, but under the circumstances we could not do better. Moreover, at intervals during the day, some very distinctive snow ramps had appeared in the valley, some five miles to the northeast, and their position was fixed relative to the course.[3]

[3] Sir Douglas Mawson, *The Home of the Blizzard*, London © 1915.

Sea ice in navigation. On the seas of the polar regions true pack ice, or pancake ice is continually formed when the temperature of the surface water is somewhat below zero. Such open sea ice rarely if ever appears in any but rounded flat pieces made up of small fragments and occasional large floes.

Icebergs are formed in quite a different method: they are pieces which have broken off glaciers which flow into the sea. Rough and irregular in appearance, they show varying wave erosion marks at different angles—different because as their ice melts or breaks off, their center of gravity periodically shifts and the whole berg assumes a new position. An iceberg which shows no wave erosion lines cannot have drifted far; but neither icebergs nor large true floes are of much use in navigation, since their position is due to current drift and is relatively unaffected by opposing winds. Considerable local knowledge of dominant currents and dominant winds is necessary before such ice formations can be used to establish position. But from one particular kind of ice formation—"bay ice," more useful conclusions can often be drawn.

Low, smooth, flat pieces of ice, which look as though they might be part of a jigsaw puzzle, will (if they are fairly close together) not be far from the frozen cove from which the pieces have been broken off by tidal and other effects. Bay ice with fresh edges is seldom far from home: bay ice which is largely dispersed and whose pieces are rounded or edged with a raised rim of crushed fragments, has probably been carried for a long distance by wind or current. Fresh bay ice is the telltale of the nearness of a bay; old bay ice of the general direction of a prevailing wind or current.

While not strictly navigational, one note on sea ice is worth the attention of the polar navigator. Even though true ice floes are formed by the freezing of sea water and contain the sea percentage of salt at the moment of formation, this salt leaches out quite quickly, so that the traveler seeking fresh water has to do no more than cut ice from the upper part of the older, larger floes. When he melts the ice he will find the water quite fresh.

Chapter 15

Directions from Hills and Rivers

THE TRAVELER in mountain and valley country has only to study the map to realize that most mountain ranges are arranged in an orderly way and that the rivers which rise in them and flow from them show orderly trends. Not only are the mountain chains themselves prominent landmarks, but the streams which flow down them usually have a directional trend. Only in flat plains do streams and rivers meander to a very great extent, and it is a traveler's rule (as old as travel) that the lost wayfarer has only to follow a river to pick up his bearings or reach some form of civilization.

Take for example the Coastal Range in the north of New South Wales in Australia, which continues almost throughout the length of Queensland. This chain of hills creates a vast watershed on each side of the range. The rain on the coastal side forms into rivers running eastwards to the sea while on the western slopes the rivers run inland in a westerly direction. As this coastal range is followed farther into northern Queensland, the rivers on the west side empty into the Gulf of Carpentaria while those on the eastern slopes flow into the Coral Sea.

All over the world, mountain ridges and valleys tend to be grouped in more-or-less parallel series. For instance, from New Hampshire into Maine and the Maritime Provinces of Canada, is found a consistent group of low ridges, locally called "horsebacks." They run in a northeasterly-southeasterly direction, nearly parallel with the Appalachian Chain.

These horsebacks occur with reasonable regularity, like ripples on a water surface. Few of them rise for more than fifty feet above the surrounding country and most of them average between fifteen and thirty feet. On their southerly side the slopes are gradual, on their northerly side steeper.

Such trends in land forms are common features of the surface of the earth and can easily be detected on a small scale contour map. Every traveler is advised to consult such to map to get a general idea of the trends in the surface anatomy of his region, for this affects not only mountains and rivers, but lakes and ponds. In the horseback area of eastern North America, for instance, many lakes and ponds are embraced by the horsebacks, where natural drainage has somehow become plugged with accumulations of silt. These ponds have a bank several feet above the water, behind which the ground slopes away into a swampy area—swampy probably from seepage through the banks—and the dry land bank bordering many of these ponds is hardly wider than the average-sized roadway and may often extend several miles. When it does so it is in a consistent direction—in this case northeasterly.

The river follower should make a point of observing all the other features I have described from which he may naturally navigate, for the ancient method of pursuing a river may occasionally lead to a serious mistake. There is a famous story from Iceland of a farmer in the north of the large island, who traveled up one of the rivers which flows north from the central desert, to round up his sheep. Late in the year great mists often descend upon the barrens of central Iceland; and this shepherd, becoming lost, actually crossed the water-parting without knowing that he had done so. Obeying the ordinary rules of river following, he made for the nearest stream and pursued it on its way to the sea. Many days later, nearly dead from exposure and exhaustion, he staggered to the door of a farm in the *south* of Iceland. He had followed the wrong river, and only his physical condition and tenacity had brought him to the end of the journey over a hundred miles longer than the path to his own home.

The traveler, then, had best be pretty sure that his river method

will work, when he embarks upon it without auxiliary navigational aids. But in nine cases out of ten rivers will lead, if not
home, at least to somebody else's home. It is often extremely
difficult to follow a river by walking along its precise bank. Tributaries are frequently most difficult to cross at their mouths. It
may be easier for the lost wanderer to follow ridges which are
periodically in sight of the river, provided the conditions are not
too overcast. In flattish and desert country, where there is little
rainfall or only seasonal rainfall, river beds often dry up; and if
the gradient is a gentle one it is often quite difficult to tell which
way the river flows when it carries water. But nearly always the
river's last flow will have carried shrub debris or at least a certain
amount of floating vegetation. The position in which this is held
on the dried bed will indicate very clearly which way the river
runs.

To tell direction from rivers is relatively easy over vast areas of
the Soviet Union. In the greater part of that country the rivers
flow northwards through the great plains to the sea. People without even seeing a river always call the eastern bank the high
bank, and the western one the low bank.

The erosion of the eastern banks, causing high bluffs, is undoubtedly due to the piling up of waters by the continuous westerly winds. Another possible contributing factor is the deflecting
force (known as coriolis) caused by the rotation of the earth.

In my opinion, it is quite possible that the reason for the extensive fertile plains in the Soviet Union and Canada is that the
northward flowing rivers have, over hundreds and thousands of
years, gradually but continually moved to the east due to the
erosion caused by the heaping up of waters by the westerly winds
and in small measure by deflection of the moving waters in an
easterly direction because of the rotation of the earth.

In mountain country it is sometimes easier to pursue ridges
than to pursue rivers. If the country is very steep this can be
dangerous, for ridges may end in sudden precipices, whereas the
worst interruption to the path of a river is a waterfall or rapids,
whose banks can usually be easily negotiated. Ridge following

pays good dividends in gently rolling country, particularly in densely wooded country. The animals which live in forested hills often pick their routes to feeding grounds along these ridges, and tread natural pathways which can be followed with advantage, especially by the traveler who has studied the general pattern of the local topography beforehand.

Chapter 16

Estimation of Distance

It is very important to be able to judge distances when you are making an overland trip, particularly when the journey involves many detours. Not only should you keep an accurate account, mental or otherwise, of the direction of each detour, but you should also try to remember the distance traveled on each route. Distances can be counted in number of paces, which, for the individual, can be translated into miles depending on the type of country and the average length of the pace. Alternatively, distance can be calculated from the time in relation to the speed of walking in miles per hour.

For the average person walking over fairly flat country, a thirty inch pace will result in a speed of three miles an hour. If greater accuracy is desired, you can test yourself to find your average length of pace in normal walking.

On occasions when it is necessary to record accurately the distance covered on a particular route, paces may be counted. Instead of counting each pace, try counting only the right-foot paces, and multiply by two when you reach a hundred. To make recording easier, start out with some small pebbles or seeds in one of your pockets, and transfer one pebble from one pocket to the other at each hundred paces. For a thirty-inch pace, one thousand right foot steps will equal one mile, requiring ten pebbles or seeds to the mile.

Distances very often are found to have been underestimated when judged before starting out and overestimated when judged while your trip is in progress and you have become fatigued.

When judging distance ahead of you by eye, certain conditions will cause overestimation of distances, while others will result in an underestimation.

Objects look much nearer than they actually are when:

> Looking up or down hill.
> There is a bright light on the object.
> Looking across water, snow or flat sand.
> The air is clear.

Objects look much farther away than they actually are when:

> The light is poor.
> The color of the object blends with the background.
> The object is at the end of a long avenue.
> You are looking over undulating ground.

In judging distances, the following table will be found very useful:

At 50 yards	The mouth and eyes of a person can be clearly distinguished.
100 yards	The eyes appear as dots.
200 yards	The general details of clothing can be distinguished.
300 yards	Faces can be seen.
500 yards	Colors of clothing can be distinguished.
800 yards	A man looks like a post.
1 mile (1760 yards)	The trunks of large trees can be seen.
2½ miles	Chimneys and windows can be distinguished.
6 miles	Windmills, large houses and towers can be recognized.
9 miles	An average church steeple can be seen.

A simple means of judging distances which can be used either on land or at sea is the finger method. It is based on the principle that the distance between the eyes is about one-tenth of the distance from the eye to the end of the extended finger. When the width of a distant object is known and you wish to determine how far away it is, proceed as follows:

With the right arm extended in front of you, hold the forefinger upright and align it with one eye on the end of the distant object. Without moving the finger, observe with the other eye and note how many feet along the length of the object it appears to have moved. The range of the object will be ten times this distance. When the height of a distant object such as a mountain, a building or a vessel is known, hold the head sideways and follow the same procedure.

If you wish to get greater accuracy, measure the distance between the center of the eye-pieces of your binoculars when adjusted to your eyes, and multiply this distance by ten; in this way the exact distance at which to hold the finger may be determined readily.

The finger method was used by the British Army during the First World War and was found to be of very practical value. It has since been used at sea in place of a range finder, for keeping ships in station.

Visibility with the curvature of the earth

It is useful to know how to judge distance at sea, whether it be the distance of a ship or of land. Because of the curvature of the earth, the greater the height of the observer's eye, the greater his range of vision; that is, the farther away will be his visible horizon.

For an accurate determination of the distance of the horizon at sea, take the square root of the height in feet of the observer's eye, and multiply it by 1.15. The result will be the distance in miles from the observer to the horizon. For instance, if the height of the eye is 9 feet above sea level, by multiplying 3 (the square root of 9) by 1.15, we find that the horizon is about 3½ miles away. Hence any low floating object just on the horizon will also be about 3½ miles away.

When the object whose distance is to be judged is between you and the horizon, you can estimate the proportionate distance between yourself and the object and the horizon, and thus get a close estimate of the object's distance, calling on your familiarity with perspective.

When a ship is partly below the horizon and partly visible above the horizon, if you can form an idea of what type of vessel it is, you can estimate the height above the water line of the part of the ship just level with the horizon. You then add the square root of its height above the water line, to the square root of your height above the water line and multiply by 1.15, which will give you the distance to the ship, even though you cannot see its full outline.

For example, suppose you see the crosstrees on the foremast of what appears to be a large steamship. Although the hull is out of sight, you assume that in a ship of this particular size the crosstrees will be at a height of about 64 feet from the water line. The square root of the height of the object equals 8. Adding 3, the square root of the height of the observer, we have 11, which, multiplied by 1.15, gives us the answer: about 12 2/3 miles.

If the height of some prominent object, such as a mountain or headland, is known, the same method may be used. Many trees are of known average height: for example, the coconut palms of low islands, the tops of which may be taken with little error as being about eighty feet above the water line. Thus, if the tops of the palms appear in line with the horizon and the height of the observer's eye is still 9 feet, the palms are about 13 ¾ miles from the observer.

If you don't want to bother with multiplying by 1.15, as in the preceding examples, it won't make very much difference for your purposes if you omit this step. Your result will still be out by 13 per cent, at most.

Chapter 17

Finding Your Way in Towns

As you approach the outskirts of a town there are many indications which announce to you its close proximity. Converging roads, railway lines, telegraph wires and heavy power lines all point the way to a city. As the greater number of people are coming into a town in the morning and are leaving in the afternoon the direction of heavy traffic in or out at these times will show the way to the heart of the city. A number of aircraft climbing or losing altitude is an indication of an airport and, usually therefore, a town. At night another guide is the red obstruction lights on high buildings in the vicinity of an airport.

Most people will naturally point their television aerials facing a station for better reception. If you are aware of the location of the station or stations chiefly serving an area, the direction in which the aerials are pointing will be worth noting. Often such stations are located near the center of a city. This can be useful to aviators. The value of this indication will depend on your knowledge of the situation in your region.

To a newcomer, a strange town presents many of the same problems in direction finding as those set by pathfinding in dense woods. They are both unknown areas and there is the same need for accurate orientation. Although the consequences of being lost in a city are not likely to be as serious as those of losing your way in the woods, they can sometimes be equally as exasperating, especially as it is the habit of most people, when asked, to give confusing directions to a visitor in a town. The average person takes so much for granted because of his familiarity with the place that he will give an absolute jumble of vague directions and follow them up with that most annoying phrase "you can't miss it." Even with the aid of systematically numbered and named houses and streets you can still get lost if you do not quickly orient yourself at the start. The first impression is the most important one.

Begin your visit by learning the general layout of the streets in terms of north, south, east and west. Establish these directions from a known point which may be your hotel or house. Draw a simple map marking in this "home base" and all prominent landmarks. As you travel, keep an imaginary thread connecting you with your home base so that you know exactly at all times the direction of the place from which you started. Mentally record each turn you make; for example, "left home base and walked two blocks down, turned to the left for one block, then right. . . ." This constant relation of your present position to your starting point will prevent you from being incorrectly oriented. This method was used by primitive peoples who were able to point to the place from which they came at any given time along their route. Combine this method of relating everything to a central point with the more modern one of establishing north, south, east and west and so have the advantage of both.

If there is some high point, a building or a hill which is visible from all parts of the city, you can relate your directions to this as long as it is not too far from your focal point.

There may be circumstances under which you find it difficult to record your turns mentally; in such a case use the street on which your house is situated as a base line and relate all your directions to this. Even if you are not able to go directly to your house you can locate this line and proceed along it to your base.

Everything depends on your early experiences in a new place when associations which become basic are being established. If at the outset you wrongly orient yourself then it is practically impossible to adjust. Most of us have experienced that confused, bewildered and unpleasant feeling of uncertainty which accompanies an illusion of orientation in a strange city. Everything seems reversed and you begin to lose all confidence in your ability to find your way.

In 1929 I accompanied Roscoe Turner on his attempt to break

the air record between Los Angeles and New York. It was my first flight to Long Island; and after a long and trying nineteen hours' flying, we landed at Roosevelt Field in very bad weather. It was in the middle of the night. I was overtired, and when I oriented myself on leaving the airfield I established the wrong directions. I kept feeling that I knew my directions perfectly and kept finding that I was absolutely wrong. What is more, on subsequent visits I carried my capacity for illusion with me. Everything seemed reversed. I made mistakes so consistently that I began to lose all confidence in my ability to find my way. For years after that, when I was in the region of Roosevelt Field, I always felt that north should be south and that west should be east; and even though I knew perfectly well that these directions were wrong, I somehow could not rid myself of them and had to translate them correctly in my mind with an act of conscious will each time I visited the area.

I have since found that my experience is not unique. Indeed, it has been shared by most people with whom I have discussed the phenomenon. A first mistake in orientation at the beginning of a visit to a strange town seems to be curiously ineradicable. It can be prevented only if the natural navigator makes sure that he has the right directions when he first establishes his base in a city.

At first glance it may appear that some cities have spread out without any particular pattern but closer study may reveal some form of alignment. As a newcomer to a city you should endeavor to find out whether this pattern is regular or irregular. In the newer towns which have been planned, and not just evolved from small villages, the tendency is to lay them out symmetrically; and as long as the terrain permits the streets will be at right angles. A true north-south alignment is the easiest pattern to follow. Salt Lake City is a good example because in this city the main streets run north, south, east and west. The compass point orientation exists even though a river flows through its center. Once you have established which direction lies north and make it a habit to record your turns, you should travel with confidence in a place like this. Other cities in the United States such as Chicago,

Denver and Kansas City are also aligned to the compass points. It is also easy to find your way in Melbourne, Australia, which has been laid out in regular blocks with the streets at right angles to each other.

A river, lake or hill may have an important influence on the way a city is planned. When a river flows through a town, it is probable that the streets conform to the configuration of the shore. A town which is fronted by a lake may be aligned to it. Similarly, when a community is situated between hills the streets will be patterned accordingly.

There are many examples in the United States of this alignment to a physical condition. Cleveland, Ohio, is oriented parallel with Lake Erie and at right angles to the lake shore. If you realize in such a case that the general orientation follows and runs directly parallel with the lake front, it should not be too hard to keep track of your direction. Manhattan, in the city of New York, is aligned running parallel and at right angles with the Hudson River and the East River. Fifth Avenue is practically parallel with these rivers and is nineteen degrees east of north.

In cities built on hills, such as Wellington, New Zealand, the alignment will be irregular because the roads are planned with consideration for the slopes, so that they will not be too steep for vehicles.

In some cities, streets parallel with each other are distinctively numbered or named. One example is Brisbane in Australia, where the streets running in one direction have women's names while those at right angles have men's. In other cities, the main streets may flow out from a central point such as a square or a circle. In this case memorize the pattern of streets around and from it, and keep your directions related to this point. This method of orientation is particularly necessary in the older cities such as London or Paris which have expanded without a clear plan or pattern.

After you have firmly established in your mind the general pattern of the streets of a town, consider then the other means of telling direction. The orientation of buildings to sunlight can be very significant. When an architect designs a building, he takes into consideration which area will benefit most from sunlight and faces the house in that direction accordingly. In the temperate and cold climates of the Northern Hemisphere you will find that buildings are generally oriented facing south, which is the direction of the greatest sunlight. In the temperate and cold climates of the Southern Hemisphere the orientation will be opposite, that is facing north.

In cold climates, where possible, the living rooms face south to get the greatest warmth and light, and kitchens will usually be found on the north side. The long and narrow Friesian farmhouses in Schleswig-Holstein in Germany, face the south to get the greatest warmth from the sun, with the longer sides running east and west. A careful inspection of this district has shown that 77 per cent of the houses are aligned in this way. This orientation has the advantage not only of the greatest warmth from the southern sun but the narrow ends of the houses face the strong cold westerly winds. In other areas in which cold violent winds are prevalent, windows and doors are situated on the side away from the chilling wind. Such an orientation is found in Provence in France.

In the hotter parts of the world the orientation rules of houses may be quite different. Often it is desirable to avoid the sun rather than court it, and to court the wind rather than avoid it. As you descend to the Mediterranean from the hills of the Massif Central of France, you can notice a pretty rapid transition from sun-facing houses to patio-style houses on the coast—houses in which the main living rooms look onto a central court which can be completely shaded from the hot summer sun. Houses of this style are the norm in nearly the whole of Spain, and were an early invention of the first great Western civilization, for the Sumerians built in this way more than five thousand years ago in sunny hot Mesopotamia.

In other parts of the world with hot climates, houses are generally oriented to get the greatest cooling from the prevailing wind. In the islands of the South Pacific, wherever possible, the long axis of the houses is aligned at right angles to the southeast trade wind to get the cooling air through all the rooms.

An additional means of telling north from south is found in Holland in the absence of window shutters on the north side of houses. The thrifty Dutch generally place their shutters only on the south side of their houses because the sun shines only on that side. These shutters, which are hinged back when not in use, are very often gaily decorated and can be a useful sign of direction in this country.

In Christian countries churches have nearly always an east to west orientation. This dates from ancient days, when they were designed with the altar to the rising sun. The tradition has been followed as consistently as possible throughout the evolution of the magnificent church architecture of western Europe. In Spain, Germany, England, France and Italy, and in many parts of Holland and Scandinavia the churches and cathedrals, both mediaeval and modern, show this east-west alignment. The chancel, which contains the altar and forms the most easterly portion of the church, is nearly always the oldest part of the church and is often lower than its greatest part—the nave. Around the eastern end of the chancel there is often an apse, which is in turn lower than the chancel and forms (usually) a projecting semicircular part at the church's easternmost end. Between chancel and nave are often found great wings, one north, one south, which give the church or cathedral the shape of a cross, and the towers or spires may be built over this central transept or (more often) over the western end of the nave.

In the populated centers there are still effects of nature which can tell you your direction. These natural signposts, apart from their value to a stranger, also can be informative and interesting to a resident of a town. They will help him practice his observation, increase his awareness and prepare him for the time when he visits a strange city. Both the newcomer to a town and the one who lives there can apply the knowledge gained from this book to interpret some of nature's causes and effects which are peculiar to built-up areas. One of these is the fungus, moss or lichen growth on any building, which can be a consistent feature for direction. First of all, find out where the rain-bearing winds come from in your locality, combine this information with a knowledge of the arc of the sun and you will then know the direction which retains the moisture the longest. Once you have established this for a particular town, you will have a perpetual aid for direction finding by noting which sides of buildings have this growth.

The direction of the greatest sunlight will have a bleaching effect on paint work, particularly on darker colors. By studying which sides of structures show this effect you will have another clear sign of direction. Further to this, interpret the effects of a combination of sun, wind and rain which causes peeling of paint or other deterioration on houses, buildings or fences. This effect also can be seen in the corrosion of ironwork in buildings and bridges. Even though you may be unable to determine which of these forces has the biggest influence you will be able to see a consistency in the direction of the greatest weathering. For example, you may have established that this weathered appearance is on the southeast side of one building: as you travel through the locality you will notice that the same side on most of the buildings is similarly affected. You have, therefore, a constant and automatic directional aid just by observing which side shows this effect.

I have stressed repeatedly throughout this book that to be guided by nature, you must add up all the natural signs. The rule is the same in finding your way in towns, where many of the individual aids and methods to which I have devoted chapters can be used in conjunction with each other. The use of the sun and shadows for telling direction when you are traveling in built-up areas is, as ever, a most reliable guide. The moon and the stars can be used at night in the way I have outlined in these two chapters. The movement of high clouds, the direction of the seasonal and dominant winds for the districts, are all aids which can be used also in finding your way in towns.

Chapter 18

Orienting as a Sport

NAVIGATION IS an art, so it is not in the least surprising that it has been developed into a sport. The sport of orienting [1] is a new one. It originated in Sweden not many years ago and it is now estimated that about 350,000 people (a very high percentage of the Swedish population) now engage in this form of pathfinding. Even more significant is the fact that every year in Sweden about forty thousand boys and girls qualify for orienting proficiency pins. The pastime has certainly become a very popular one.

Essentially, orienting consists of cross-country races on a course that is arranged from point to point. Each point must be reached entirely by map and compass. Many forms of competition have been devised, so that people of all ages and of varying physical condition can take part. In a simple cross-country orienting contest—the most popular form of competition—all the competitors start out with map and compass from one common point at time intervals of about a minute. Upon their maps is marked the compass direction and location of the first control point or "control station." Each participant takes what he estimates to be the shortest possible route to get there. The control point—which may be a hill, a dead tree or some other unmistakable landmark—carries a sign which gives the compass direction and the distance to the next. Competitions are nearly always scored on time, so

---

[1] I think it is a pity that the Scandinavian enthusiasts have introduced this sport in English-speaking countries under the name "orienteering." I believe that the adoption of this name has hurt their cause. An exact translation of the Swedish word is not "orienteering," but "orienting." This word is already an English word and is widely understood. The coined word does not sound natural.

that each is a race to the finish, but it is a race that tests skill as much as speed.

A less rigorous form of orienting is point orienting, in which the competitors follow on foot a course clearly marked on the terrain, and locate on their maps the exact position of the control points that they come across on their journey. Their log is subsequently judged and awarded appropriate marks. Some orienting competitions are conducted in summer by bicycle or by car, in winter on skis or skates. It is even possible to hold an orienting competition indoors with maps and photographs of the terrain and its landmarks; the contestants have to indicate the compass direction to a number of points on the map. In all these forms of competition skill in the use of map and compass is at a premium.

Another of the less exacting forms of orienting is miniature orienting. This is a game devised to teach children to walk by compass and is excellent training. In a school yard or park the pupils have to find, by compass direction alone, a succession of control points. Each point is marked by a card which is concealed from the direction in which it is likely to be approached—for instance, by being attached to the back of a tree.

Orienting, pioneered in Sweden, has now become popular in the other Scandinavian countries as well as in Belgium, Holland, Switzerland and France. Lately it has been introduced with some success into the United States, Great Britain, and Australia and New Zealand.

There is no doubt that the spread of orienting through the world owes much to the fact that it can be easily adapted to Boy Scout programs. It is a sport wonderfully suited to the temperament of youth. A boy or girl who takes up this keen, active and competitive game will develop in later years into a skillful country rambler. Many a hunter, fisherman, hiker, rock climber, explorer of the future, will go far afield on guideless trips with perfect efficiency and safety because of his experience in orienting.

There is no doubt that orienting owes much of its success to the fact that it can evoke the pioneering spirit over country that is well explored and well mapped. The Swedish exponents, Bjorn

Kjellstrom and Stig Hedenstrom, who have introduced the sport into many other countries, say that through orienting they can experience the thrill of discovery—that a vista of new adventure is opened up to them.

My only criticism of this excellent sport as at present conducted, concerns its obsession with the use of map and compass. As a professional navigator, I would be the last to condemn any sport designed to improve familiarity and efficiency with these two fundamental instruments; but in my opinion, orienting enthusiasts would derive far more pleasure from their pastime if they were also guided by natural signs. If natural navigation were introduced into orienting competitions—as it could be without any great difficulty—it would not only increase the interest and sheer fun of the sport, but would give the competitors even more accuracy and speed in finding their way, and would also prepare them for the time when they may find themselves without a map and compass.

To take an example, the natural signposts provided by the sun and shadows could be easily used on orienting courses. Nobody can read a compass when he is running; but he can easily look for shadows. In a competition in which time counts, the experienced sun-watcher should easily outstrip the compass-needle-watcher. He needs of course to know the rate of movement of the sun at his latitude and season. The tables at the back of this book can be read as easily as a compass and the relevant information memorized without difficulty at the start of an orienting race.

How much more meaningful and adventurous would orienting be if each contestant were to set out to find his way from start to finish using natural navigation, primarily—checked only secondarily by compass and map. The whole sport of orienting arouses the senses of wonder and discovery. How much more dramatically would these senses be aroused if the explorers put a premium on their ability to derive conclusions from nature.

Like many other professional navigators, I must have been playing the game of orienting all my life without knowing it, for it is just that precision which is cultivated in the sport which has appealed to me in my professional job. I know no greater feeling of satisfaction than that which comes with a landfall over a long distance of sea (by ship or by air—it does not matter which), when the point of destination shows up at the exact spot to which the course has been set. An accurate homing at the end of a land journey is perhaps a little less dramatic, but the fascination of the problem is just the same and the satisfaction just as profound.

In the armed services, at the present time, the use of map and compass is taught only to specialized groups. I am certain that the simple use of these instruments should form a part of everybody's military training, and should be conducted on lines similar to those followed in the Scandinavian sport of orienting. But I would go further. I cannot imagine any branch of the armed services in which the usefulness of a man could not be sharpened and his efficiency improved by simple training in the elementary principles of *natural*—as opposed to instrumental—navigation.

Chapter 19

Directions from Waves and Swells

MOST NAVIGATORS of today would be lost at sea if they were deprived of the use of compass, sextant, chronometer or radio. So accustomed are we to navigating with these instruments that we watch the waves rising and falling with their monotonous regularity, without appreciating that they have a definite order and pattern. The natural navigator can study the anatomy of sea swells and use them to find his way.

In nearly every part of the world's oceans, some sort of swell is chronic. In mid-ocean even a glassy sea has a detectable up and down movement. Only under quite exceptional conditions is this movement so small as to be invisible. This chronic sea swell is the lasting telltale of the direction of the prevailing wind, for the prevailing wind arouses it and maintains it. It takes a prolonged and exceptional wind from a direction which is not the prevailing one to divert and reorient a swell. Normally, the momentum imparted to the swells by the prevailing winds persists throughout all the vagaries of weather. Winds may suddenly change, but the directions of the swells will not. It is important of course to distinguish between swells and waves. When the wind changes, the motion and direction of the surface waves will soon follow these changes; but the fundamental chronic swell will persist for far longer. Soon after the wind has established itself in a direction other than the prevailing direction, we can begin to detect the peculiar effect of wave motion working at an angle to the long fundamental chronic swell.

The natural navigator can in many circumstances, though not all, get useful information from wave motion, and in practically all circumstances from swell motion. For instance, waves can sometimes be indicators of the direction of unseen land. When there is fairly high ground near the shore of this unseen land, and a wind is blowing off the land, the benefit of the protection of the land barrier will be felt by mariners even if they are well out of sight of it. For in the wind shadow on the lee side of the land, there is a reduction in the size of the waves and (if the wind blows off the land in its prevailing direction) also of the swells. The voyager, sailing or drifting, who discovers that the sea has subsided although the wind is still blowing with the same strength, can be fairly sure of the direction of the land from which this protection comes.

Of all early pioneers, the Polynesians squeezed most meaning from the ever-changing appearance of the sea. Living as they did, and still do, in the island-dotted Pacific Ocean, they developed a most particular and critical interest in the effects of islands upon the shape, direction and motion of the waves and swells. It was much better for them to watch these things than to try to take soundings; for most of the coral islands of the Pacific Ocean are isolated in waters of very great depth. To Polynesian eyes, wave formations became as useful as landmarks to the landsman.

The Polynesians were not the only native navigators of the Pacific who understood wave marks and swell marks. Even more skillful were the Micronesians—a mixed Polynesian and Mongoloid race which lives in the Caroline and Marshall Island groups. These archipelagos are in the western Pacific, north of the equator, and consist of hundreds of small, low-lying coral atolls, isolated in large expanses of water, often visible only for short distances, and seldom visible from each other.

Throughout these archipelagos the Micronesians navigated in the same way as did the Polynesians. But they also had something that the Polynesians proper never seem to have invented— charts of the anatomy and topography of local surface waters. These unique charts were, in a sense, models, for they were made out of the ribs of coconut palms tied together with coconut fiber. Within a framework were meticulously arranged bent ribs tied into a sort of net that most accurately represented the curvature

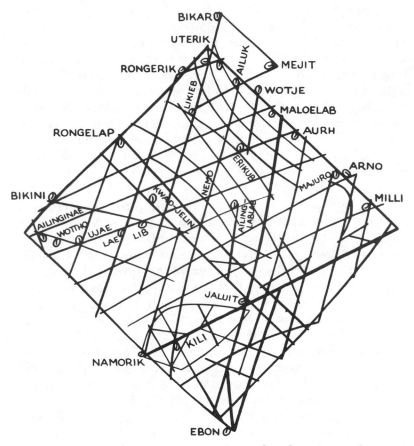

Marshall Islands stick chart made from ribs of coconut palms, with shells representing islands

and meeting points of the dominant swells around the islands. The islands themselves were represented on the framework by small shells. The charts were not made to distance scale, so much as to time scale, for the Micronesians and Polynesians thought of their journeys only in canoe- or catamaran-days from one place to another. On some of these Micronesian charts small islands were shown disproportionately large, because of their sheer importance to the maker and users of the chart. Indeed, the Micronesian charts were really aids to memory. There were three chief kinds: simple instruction charts used for training; general charts of large areas; charts of local areas.

The Micronesian charts were (as far as we can judge) very personal and individualistic, for each master navigator made his own and incorporated in it those ideas which were of particular interest and help to him. It is for this reason that charts of the same areas differ considerably, as we can see by examining the handful in the museums of the world. Unfortunately, there are, as far as I know, only forty-three surviving examples. In a Micronesian chart of a particular archipelago, the directional characteristics of all the swells throughout the group are carefully marked. Further, sticks on the charts indicate the distance from land at which coconut palms can be seen. Other lines showed the position and distance from the island of the meeting of the waters of the oncoming swell and the tide ebbing from the island's lagoon. In many cases, this meeting place is actually out of sight of the land.

As a dominant swell approaches an island, its pattern of parallel ridges begins to be modified. This modification may start at a point out of sight of the island and consists of what is at first a gentle curving of the swell front, as if to embrace the island. As the swell system nears the island, this curvature becomes more and more pronounced until it almost fits the obstruction. At this point that part of the swell directly in front of the island starts to break up into smaller waves which gradually build up and finally collapse as breakers on the reefs. This wave motion from the direction of the prevailing swell is easy to see.

This is not all the story; for we can find on the opposite side of the island a counter-swell. Certainly this is much less noticeable than the prevailing swell on the prevailing windward side of the island. But anybody who knows enough to look for it, can find it. I have seen this counter-swell particularly well from the air, and have easily recognized its curves, which also embrace the island, though never so closely as the curves of the main swell. The counter-swell and the main swell meet, of course, on a line which runs through a point a little on the lee side of the island, and lies at right angles to the direction of the prevailing swell. The slight eddies and disturbances can be often traced along this line for a considerable distance; and it was this line of meeting of two opposing swells that the Micronesians looked for. When they were steering for an island and by some chance had missed it, they would reach the swell line and simply sail down it to the island. Moreover, they could even find and use this swell line at night, for in the tropical seas eddies and turbulence bring up luminescent organisms to the surface and make the swell line into a subtle, but nonetheless authentic kind of flare path.

Not only did the Micronesians seek and use these junction lines of swell and counter-swell, but they also used the crossings of the swells of one island with those of another. They were always sailing from island to island, making mental notes in their heads, or physical notes on their model charts of the expected curvature of this swell, or interruptions to that swell, of the eddies and meeting points of those swells: and of course they also watched the sun and the stars, and studied the flight of birds, and navigated in many other ways that I have already mentioned in this book. Seasoned navigators of my acquaintance have invariably expressed amazement—and in some cases disbelief—when I have described to them the early Micronesian method of navigation and have shown how these peoples could successfully make wonderful inter-island journeys. Necessity, of course, is the mother of invention; but it is undoubtedly astonishing that, a thousand years ago or more, native navigators could observe and make charts of such subtle things as the peculiar ground swell on the prevailing windward side of some islands—which is caused by a reflection of the main swell thrown back by the shore which runs over the top of the oncoming swell and against it. The Micronesians and Polynesians could even distinguish this swell a long way out at sea.

Chapter 20

The Color of the Sea

It is popularly supposed that the color of the sea is derived largely from the reflection of the sky above. It is true that the state of the weather may make a slight difference to the apparent color of the sea, which tends to be brighter in sunlight and duller under overcast, but every experienced sea voyager knows that the fundamental color of the waters he travels on depends upon their composition. There are two tendencies, each of which is influenced by more than one factor.

The color of the sea tends to be green when the quantity of particles or organisms in it is high and when the quantity of salt in it is low. The color tends to be blue when the quantity of particles or organisms is low and the quantity of salt is high. The intensity of the coloration—green or blue—depends slightly upon the amount of sunlight, but more particularly on the depth of the waters—the deeper the darker.

Following these rules, we find that equatorial waters tend to be blue, temperate and arctic waters green. In hot climates—and particularly in enclosed seas in such climates, like the Red Sea and the Mediterranean—so much evaporation takes place that the sea contains a percentage of salt considerably above the average. This makes it blue, as also does the fact that tropical seas generally contain *fewer* organisms than those of more northerly or southerly latitudes.

Conversely, towards the poles the seas suffer less evaporation and are diluted by melting ice. Their salt content is therefore below average: moreover, right up to the ice edge the cooler seas swarm with organisms. They are consequently very green in color.

All the same, green water is occasionally found in the tropics. There is a special reason for this. When we mix the primary colors yellow and blue we produce the color green. This happens when blue tropical seas overlie yellow sand. The green water of the tropics, then, is most often an indication of shallow water. It is not always so, however; for when the bottom sand is not its usual yellow but (as is fairly common in some coral areas) white, the shallow water will be very blue—but a characteristic light blue.

Green water can be also found in tropical regions near the mouths of large rivers such as the Amazon and the River Plate in South America. Both these rivers bring down tremendous quantities of silt which they deposit some distance out to sea. The sediment content near their mouths renders the water a muddy green—not blue. But far beyond the region in which these rivers drop their mud their fresh waters dilute the sea and lower its salinity. This also renders the waters green, and the effect of the water of the River Plate can be noticed a thousand miles out to sea.

Anybody who studies a simple current chart of the oceans of the world will see that the waters are not arranged in simple bands of temperature corresponding to latitude. On the contrary, most parts of all oceans are in a constant state of circulation, both at the suface and at great depths. There are a few areas, of course, in which the circulation is not great; but these are rare. One of the most famous of them is the Sargasso Sea in the tropical North Atlantic Ocean. Here the waters are very saline and almost lacking in living organisms and solid particles—so much so that the Sargasso Sea is bluer and clearer than any other water known, salt or fresh, with the possible exception of the famous blue deep fresh water lake high up in the mountains of Oregon, Crater Lake.

Owing to the constant circulation of the oceans cold green arctic water penetrates in places almost to the tropics, and warm blue tropical water almost to the arctic regions. In their passage through the oceans these currents are very well defined, and the boundary lines between the ocean streams can be readily detected by the navigator from the sudden change in color and in temperature. The contrast between the so-called Gulf Stream and the Labrador Current is so well defined that the line between them extends for hundreds of miles, is readily visible from the deck of a ship, and, being relatively constant in its position, offers a ready and valuable means of determining position.

The Gulf Stream was so named from the erroneous idea that it originated in the Gulf of Mexico; but we now know that it passes from the Strait of Yucatan to the Strait of Florida, and that very little of it enters the Gulf of Mexico. Originating in the tropical Atlantic, this great ocean current has a very high salt content and not enough oxygen to stimulate the growth of many living organisms. It is very warm and very blue and can be readily distinguished from the adjacent waters through or alongside which it passes.

The Labrador Current, on the other hand, flows down from the region of Greenland and the Canadian Arctic along the coast of Labrador, carrying with it many icebergs from the great glaciers of the high arctic regions. It flows along the eastern seaboard of North America between the land and the northeastward flowing Gulf Stream. It is very cold and contains relatively little salt and a vast quantity of marine life. It is therefore very green. At its convergence with the Gulf Stream the contrast in color is spectacular and the contrast in temperature even more so, for in places the temperature may suddenly rise or drop 30°F. as the voyager crosses the convergence.

From this example—and there are many others perhaps less spectacular that could be drawn from nearly every sea in the world—we can understand how important changing sea color and sea temperature was to the early "primitive" and European navigators. In the logbooks of the latter we can find frequent references to such things as "the green hue of soundings." It is an axiom that all ocean travelers, especially those in small craft, should have a knowledge of ocean currents and enough experience to identify them. All such navigators pay close attention to changes of air temperature and quickly confirm whether such changes also apply to the surface of the sea. When a small change of temperature is noticed in the open sea and there is no local weather change to account for it, it may be readily assumed that it is due to some shore effect or to some current from a polar or equatorial direction.

Less than two hundred years ago the determination of longitude by chronometer was far from commonplace and many voyagers and geographers like Benjamin Franklin and John Williams took pains to encourage a system of what they christened "thermometrical navigation." They made charts giving accurate positions of the warm and cold currents in the Atlantic Ocean and encouraged voyagers to take frequent sea temperatures. Surprisingly accurate results were obtained. With the improvement of the chronometer, and its more general use in navigation, thermometrical navigation fell into disuse. But it is still a useful tool for the natural navigator, who can quickly learn to detect even quite a small change in temperature simply by dipping his hand in the water—just as the Polynesians did throughout the Pacific perhaps a thousand years ago.

But I must return to the subject of color navigation. We have already seen that in the tropics green water may be a good indication of the presence of sandy shores (provided the sand is yellow) or of the mouths of rivers. There are other color indications of the presence of land, and of the depths of reefs and passages. Anywhere within the tropics, where coral reefs break the water or great coral heads live under its surface, the experienced mariner has only to watch the color of the sea to know where he can pass safely, for the depth of the underwater coral heads has its telltale in the color change of the water. Water over coral usually looks yellowish when only a few inches to a couple of feet deep. Beyond this, the deeper the darker. Within the Fiji Islands there are vast areas of water as yet uncharted. Following the old Polynesians (who knew all about this color change with depth, and who sailed their catamarans with great accuracy and boldness in and around the reefs) I have myself navigated my motor cruiser day after day at full speed, knowing

—entirely by the color of the coral water ahead—just what un-charted reef we could safely pass over.

I would add one rider to this only. I would never care to boast of having done this in bad weather or when the sun was very low. In such conditions the color guide becomes unreliable and the method of navigation positively unsafe.

Not all color changes in the sea are indicators of current con-vergences or the proximity of land. In many parts of the oceans of the world certain kinds of minute organisms may swarm and produce an orange or red appearance. This does not necessarily show nearby land; but a brown or muddy appearance in the water almost certainly does, for it will be caused by silt, and silt comes only from a river or estuary (or, most exceptionally, a volcanic eruption).

Patches of luminescence in the water usually indicate a reef or a shore line, but do not invariably do so; for some organisms may show in patches in the surface waters of the open ocean and shine at night with their own light. Nevertheless a so-called "phosphor-escent" sea should make the natural navigator careful of a reef. The word phosphorescence is not quite right, incidentally, for the luminescence of marine organisms has nothing to do with phos-phorus. Gallego, the early Spanish voyager in the Pacific, showed himself a wise man when he wrote in his journal of 1566: "when the night overtook us we were without knowledge of any port, having much thick weather with wind and rain. Guided by the phosphorescence of the sea, we skirted the reefs; and when I saw that the reefs did not make the sea phosphorescent, I weathered the point and entered a good harbor at the fourth hour of the night."

Chapter 21

The Habits of Sea Birds

THE GRACEFUL SEABIRDS have been masters of the sea many thousands of times longer than man. According to the latest enumeration, there are about 8600 known species of birds in the world. Only about 200 of these have become fully specialized inhabitants of the seas and open oceans. Ever since man became a mariner these successful and beautiful birds have guided him at sea. Their lines of flight have led him to land, for sea birds are unerring navigators. The presence of one sort or another has told the navigator that he has moved from one zone of waters to another; for each part of the ocean has its own particular characteristics of temperature, depth, salinity and movement and supports its own special communities of marine life. It is this marine life that supports the sea birds and each zonal community has its own characteristic set of winged navigators, diving, skimming and flying over the waves.

No voyager at sea should travel without a bird book, such as W. B. Alexander's *Birds of the Ocean* which covers the sea birds of all the world. And no seaman could help but understand the sea better if he read such authoritative works as Dr. Robert Cushman Murphy's *Oceanic Birds of South America* or (if he is interested in the North Atlantic) James Fisher's and R. M. Lockley's *Sea Birds;* or the former's monograph, *The Fulmar,* or the latter's monographs *Shearwaters* and *Puffins.*

I should like to begin with a quotation from Dr. Murphy's classic work:

. . . if the quality of the water may tell us something about the birds, the birds should also tell us much about the water. The Snow Petrel requires water which is cool; Tropic Birds prefer water which is clear, dense, saline and moderately warm; the Brown Booby clings to water inhabited by flying fish which in turn, are limited to water of definite temperature and gaseous content.[1]

From the authorities I have mentioned, and from the works of many other learned ornithologists who have been equally fascinated by the wonderful birds of the sea, I have attempted to distill some of their knowledge which, with some of my own, may be of value to the natural navigator.

A reader of Dr. Murphy's *Oceanic Birds of South America* comes to understand very rapidly and clearly that in the tropical zone of the oceans bird life is generally surprisingly scarce. This is in very striking contrast to conditions in the higher latitudes. On the whole it is the sea-bird community of the higher latitudes (both north and south) that tends to include species that range far from their breeding grounds into those parts of the open ocean most remote from land. The majority of tropical sea birds, on the other hand, do not often range far from their nesting places on island groups and continental coastlines. There are some tropical species, of course, about which we know very little, and some extremely abundant birds like sooty terns and noddies seem to disappear to sea where nobody can find them. Certainly, where conditions are suitable the numbers of the tropical sea birds are somewhat astronomical. In many of the more undisturbed archipelagos in the tropical oceans, especially in the Pacific and Indian Oceans, the sea birds breed truly in millions. Of course nowadays, and particularly on the larger islands, the presence of man and certain inimical animals that he has introduced has succeeded materially in reducing the sea bird population. But there are still many small islands whose sky is darkened by the nesting birds.

Despite this, it must be reiterated that the voyager may travel for days across tropical oceans and see no birds at all. One ex-

---

[1] Robert Cushman Murphy, *Oceanic Birds of South America*, New York, © 1936.

perienced observer recorded, on a long cruise in the tropical Pacific, an average of only one bird for every 125 miles of open sea. The observer many miles from land in tropical seas may expect no aid to finding his position from the sea birds. He must take advantage of all the other aids to location available to him. It is when he is nearing his landfall that the tropical sea birds become useful to him—the more so if he can make a careful note of their number and rely on his own powers of simple identification.

To give an example: on a voyage between San Francisco and Tahiti it was noted that for the first two days North American coastal birds were seen. After this for five or six days only an occasional petrel was observed. When the observer neared the equator, scattered woolly clouds became thicker and grayer, the swell increased and rainstorms came. Suddenly, numerous birds appeared. Among these were storm petrels and red-tailed or white-tailed tropic birds. Then as islands were approached large numbers of terns were seen. As the ship sailed farther along the birds dropped away again as suddenly as they had appeared.

Most frequently is this sudden appearance and disappearance of sea birds notable to the voyager and natural navigator. Birds appear and disappear as one passes out of or into the doldrums or from the part of the sea dominated by one ocean current to that dominated by another. As we have seen in an earlier chapter, neighboring waters can differ astonishingly in their characteristics, and birds' distributions can have edges just as sharp as the edges of the currents. One current may be rich in its ability to support bird life, while the next is poor. At the convergences of ocean currents not only may bird distribution suddenly change, but there may also be a great concentration of bird life at the actual meeting place, for here water frequently upwells from the depths and brings food to the surface. There is nearly always a big concentration of bird life along the line (page 171) where the Gulf Stream meets the Labrador Current.

The two accompanying charts, based on the observations of many bird watchers, show the relative frequency of birds in the North and South Atlantic. The top chart shows the average num-

After Jespersen

From Murphy after Spiess

Frequency of birds in the Atlantic Ocean

ber of birds seen per day. It can be seen, for instance, that birds tend to become more plentiful as the voyager penetrates farther north into richer, shallower waters. A hundred birds can be seen a day in the waters around the Faeroe Islands in the North Atlantic, whereas in the middle of the Atlantic sometimes only one may be sighted per day. Thirty-four birds a day were noticed around the Cape Verde Islands and (to illustrate the matter further) on a line between Bermuda and the south of Spain one bird per day was seen in the middle of the Atlantic, increasing to four, seventeen and then fifteen approaching Gibraltar. The lower diagram for the South Atlantic shows much the same state of affairs: an increasing number of birds with latitude. Generally speaking, the farther the voyager goes south of the equator, the richer become the waters through which he sails and the greater the number of sea birds.

As a further aid to the natural navigator, I have summarized the habits of a representative number of sea birds in the following pages, concentrating most on those which are of real value in determining the neighborhood and direction of land. From pages 204 to 213 plates and accompanying descriptions of forty-three species of sea birds will be found. The illustrations have been specially drawn by that great naturalist and observer of the *living* bird, Francis Lee Jaques, who has depicted each species with special accent upon the distinctive features by which it may be easily recognised. Further, since the importance of birds as indicators of land varies much according to the season, and particularly the breeding season, I have compiled a tabled summary which embraces seasonable notes. I must stress that these notes are purely for guidance and that it will be a rule that isolated observations or a small number of observations should not be followed. It is absolutely necessary to take into account the law of averages and all I have made are *reasonable* assumptions about the distance from land that a certain observed number of birds may indicate. No evidence from bird numbers at sea should be regarded as conclusive, unless it involves more than a handful of observations of several different species or unless it is coupled with indications from other natural signs. After all, the art of natural navigation often consists in receiving pieces of information from a number of sources, each of which by itself may well be unreliable, but the sum of which when taken together becomes a certain guide.

Notes on Specially Useful Sea-bird Guides. The information here summarized about the habits of these representative species is intended to augment the tabled summary, pages 214-217.

Penguins. There are fifteen species of penguins in the world, all confined to the Southern Hemisphere and to waters which are at least fairly cool. Half of the species breed on the sub-antarctic islands or around the shores of the antarctic continent itself. Nearly all the penguins breed in large social rookeries where they are very noisy and can be heard for considerable distances. During the breeding season vast numbers will be found swimming towards or from their rookeries close to the shore: however, in the antarctic and sub-antarctic large concentrations of swimming penguins are not necessarily an indication of the nearness of a breeding colony, for the birds often congregate where crustacean food is available hundreds of miles from base. Most familiar perhaps to the natural navigator are the more northerly species. Four of these are jackass penguins, characterized by a broad white eye stripe which widens on the side of the face and neck to join a white breast; the blackfooted or common jackass penguin is found along the coast of South Africa as far north as 15° south latitude. In South America the Magellan jackass penguin is found up to 24° south on the east coast and extends also onto the west, where also is found Humboldt's jackass penguin, which extends with the cool Humboldt Current as far north as latitude 6° south. There is also a small species of jackass penguin confined to the Galápagos archipelago on the equator off the west coast of South America—the only place where penguins reach the equator. There are also penguins which breed on the south coast of Australia and New Zealand, one of which penetrates as far north as latitude 22° south on the coast of Western Australia.

Albatrosses. The most highly adapted and specialized of all the oceanic sea birds are the albatrosses. Thirteen species are known in the world: the family belongs to the order of tube-nosed birds which also includes the petrels and shearwaters. The wandering albatross is the largest known living sea bird, with a wing span up to eleven and a half feet and a weight of about seventeen pounds. It has a wide range in the southern oceans between 30 and 60 degrees south. Some individuals come a little north of 30° south in the Humboldt Current on the west coast of South America, penetrating to about 23° south. Only four species regularly live north of this latitude. One of them, the waved albatross, nests only in the Galápagos Islands on the equator and is the only albatross with a tropical breeding distribution. There is no albatross in the North Atlantic Ocean, but three species nest in the North Pacific. Of these, by far the rarest is the white-bodied short-tailed albatross. So scarce was it that recently it was thought to have become entirely extinct. Fortunately this is not so; a colony of ten pairs nested on Torishima, an island belonging to Japan, in 1954. The Laysan albatross has a white head and underparts and dark brown wings and back: it nests in the north-westerly islands of the Hawaiian archipelago. The commonest albatross of the North Pacific is the sooty-brown black-footed albatross, which has a rather wide nesting distribution on the more northerly Pacific islands from Hawaii to the Marshall Islands, Volcano Islands and Bonin Islands. The North Pacific species of albatross usually breed from April to October. Even at that season small numbers of individuals seen may be a long way from land.

The modern seaman does not seem to believe in the old superstition so solemnly recounted in Coleridge's *Ancient Mariner.* He does not think it unlucky to catch an albatross. I was once an apprentice on a ship running from Australia to New Zealand, and it was quite a common practice for the crew to catch albatrosses to examine them. One method that I used myself was to trail a small open triangle of brass on the end of a line. Attracted by the shining metal, the albatrosses got their curved bills caught in the triangles. It was then quite easy to haul them aboard. Incidentally, an albatross when hauled aboard always becomes violently sick. Many writers have christened this "seasickness," but I believe myself that it must be a defense mechanism for, on its breeding cliffs, the albatross and its young both vomit at intruders in order to scare them away. Anybody who catches an albatross should study its sharp bill with a good deal of circumspection. It is hooked and very strong and can inflict a nasty wound.

Petrels. Besides the albatrosses, there are three other families in the great order of tube-nosed sea birds. There are nineteen members of the storm-petrel family, many of which are dark with white rumps. The storm petrels are small and have a flitting, mothlike flight, skimming the water closely for surface food. Many but not all of the storm petrels are ship followers and outside the breeding season can be sighted thousands of miles from base. As far as scientists know, they tend to breed in the season after that in which they are hatched, so that during the breeding seasons there are few or no nonbreeding adolescents far to sea. Thus storm-petrel numbers can be a useful indication of the nearness of land where there is an active breeding colony.

One of the most abundant storm petrels of the world is Wilson's petrel, for from its breeding headquarters on the antarctic continent and its surrounding islands, it penetrates in the off-season far north into the Pacific Ocean where it certainly crosses the equator on the west side, and into the Atlantic and Indian Oceans where it regularly crosses the equator. In the North Atlantic it scarcely ever reaches Britain; but on the west side it is well north of the Sargasso Sea by April and is often seen in numbers off the eastern seaboard of the United States feeding along the convergence of the Gulf Stream and the Labrador Current. Indeed, it is one of the best bird indicators of the Labrador Current. There is some evidence that the return journey to the south of the Wilson's petrels of the North Atlantic is made on the east side of that ocean from the Bay of Biscay along the West African coast. It is occasionally abundant, in June or after, off the coast of Portugal; and birds are still off the West African coast until December and early January. Wilson's petrel can be fairly easily confused with two other storm petrels, which breed in the North Atlantic—Leach's petrel, whose headquarters is mostly on the western side but of which there are over half a dozen colonies in Britain, the Faeroes and Iceland, and the storm petrel whose headquarters is in north and west Britain, but which breeds also in Iceland, the Faeroes, northwestern France, the Bay of Biscay, Madeira and on islands in the western part of the Mediterranean.

A large family of fifty species embraces the giant petrel or stinker, a great many birds that carry the general name of petrel, and the shearwaters. These birds have a more gliding, albatross-like flight than the little storm petrels; and while there are always large concentrations of them near their breeding grounds in the proper season, they usually have fairly long periods of adolescence and may be observed sometimes in fair numbers long distances from their breeding grounds at any time of the year. However, a knowledge of the natural history of many of them may be a great aid to the natural navigator.

The commonest petrel of North Atlantic waters, for instance, is the fulmar—a truly oceanic bird which may have a period of adolescence as long as seven years. There is scarcely any part of the northern North Atlantic in which fulmars have not been seen in every month. Nevertheless, a knowledge of this bird has proved often very useful. On one occasion during the Second World War, one of Britain's great "Queens" was making a voyage from Britain to North America. There was, of course, the usual security blackout about the vessel's route, but at least one member of the passenger list who had not been let into the secret was well aware that the great liner was in the Denmark Strait between Iceland and Greenland. The North Atlantic population of fulmars has two main color phases, one white-headed and white-breasted and the other darkish gray-blue. The dark fulmars nest only in the high arctic where the temperature of the sea surface in July is around freezing point. Although there are no breeding colonies of dark fulmars very near the Denmark Strait, it is an assembly place of many of these dark forms from the arctic; and from January to April the dark birds equal, and from May till August greatly outnumber, the light birds in that region—at least in the western part of it fairly close to the Greenland coast.

The fulmar is one of the few birds of the world that is truly bi-polar, for it is either of the same species as, or very closely related to an antarctic petrel which used to be known as the silver-gray petrel but now is generally called the antarctic fulmar. This breeds on the antarctic continent and on some of the sub-antarctic islands and operates into the Indian, Atlantic and Pacific Oceans, though normally only in the regions of cool water. However, aided by the cool Humboldt Current, it sometimes nearly reaches the equator on the Pacific Coast of South America and may even occasionally have crossed it. The race of the true fulmar that breeds in the North Pacific is in many ways intermediate between the antarctic fulmar and the Atlantic fulmar; and, ages ago, the North Pacific may have indeed been colonized by fulmars from the antarctic. Afterwards, they must have spread across the polar basin into the North Atlantic.

The known breeding colonies of the Pacific fulmar at present are in the Kuril Islands, in the Komandorski Islands east of Kamchatka, in certain of the Aleutian Islands, in the Semidi Islands off the Alaska Peninsula, on the Pribilof, St. Matthew and Hall Islands in the Bering Sea and on certain promontories near the easternmost end of Siberia. The Pacific fulmar is always to be found in the Bering Sea and operates through most of the year a long distance down the Pacific Coast of North America; however there are very few records indeed of fulmars as far south as the state of California between May and August.

The North Atlantic fulmar nests in some eastern islands of the Canadian arctic archipelago, Greenland, Iceland, the Faeroes, Britain, Jan Mayen, on one island in Norway, on Bear Island, in Spitsbergen, Franz Josef Land and Novaya Zemlya. There is so much ice around the western part of this range that fulmars are almost entirely absent from Davis Strait and Baffin Bay in November and December and withdraw yet farther—even from the Labrador coast and most of that of Newfoundland—in January and February. A steamer traveling eastwards from New York to London in the winter is seldom likely to pick up fulmars until it reaches the eastern part of the Grand Banks of Newfoundland. Generally speaking, the southward limit of fulmars at sea in the North Atlantic Ocean is about 49° or 50° on the east side: on the west the distribution dips down in particular strength to about 41° or 42° north on longitude 50° west, which is southeast of the Newfoundland Banks, a most favored feeding ground for fulmars. There are useful maps of the fulmar's distribution through the year in James Fisher's monograph, *The Fulmar* (*New Naturalist* series, 1952).

A typical petrel of the southern oceans is the Cape pigeon. Like the fulmar, it is a regular follower of ships and can be often seen far from land. Nevertheless, the observation of large numbers of these birds may generally be taken as an indication of nearby land, for even outside the breeding season they tend to congregate in feeding packs not far from shore, or from the edge of the antarctic ice. The Cape pigeon breeds on the more southerly of the sub-antarctic islands—South Georgia, the South Orkneys, the South Shetlands, the islands of Graham Land, and Kerguelen Island, possibly also on Bouvet and the Crozets. Away from its breeding grounds, it has a wide distribution in the southern oceans, extending north with cool currents as far as (for instance) northern Peru in the Humboldt Current, and the Marquesas. On the African Coast it reaches Angola and Mozambique; and it also reaches Australia, but it very rarely crosses the equator.

A typical petrel of lower latitudes in the southern oceans is the Kermadec petrel, one of the many species of petrels and shearwaters that have white underparts. This petrel nests on the island of Juan Fernandez in the South Pacific, also on the Kermadecs, Lord Howe Island, and the Austral and Tuamotu Islands; formerly it also nested on Norfolk Island. A closely related petrel nests on South Trinidad Island in the South Atlantic. The Kermadec petrel roams some distance across the equator, often to 15° north, reaching the coast of Mexico; isolated individuals of this species at sea should not be taken as indicators of land. A few have been recorded as far as 210 miles from their breeding grounds on Juan Fernandez, but large numbers do not begin to build up until the breeding land is approached.

One of the most interesting and important of the shearwater group of the petrel family breeds in such large numbers on the islands of Bass Straits, between Tasmania and the south coast of Australia, that smoking and salting the young birds for the

local market has become a large industry. An experienced observer saw what he estimated to be 150 million of these short-
tailed shearwaters at one time en route to their breeding grounds
on these islands. In its off-season from March to November, this
bird may be encountered far to sea especially when migrating
through the western Pacific north to eastern Siberia, and the
Bering Sea, where it can be very numerous within sight of the
Aleutian Islands. It appears in the Bering Sea most commonly
between April and October. Not many short-tailed shearwaters
cross to the eastern Pacific at latitudes lower than the Bering Sea,
but small numbers are occasionally seen off the coast of California, which are believed to be individuals that have linked up
with the flocks of the sooty shearwater, which normally migrates
along an easterly Pacific route from its winter home in the Bering
Sea and adjacent waters, to its breeding grounds in and around
New Zealand and South America.

Indeed, among the shearwaters, there are several examples of
birds which breed in the Southern Hemisphere and migrate to
spend their off-season in the northern summer. It must be
stressed that while on migration and while in their winter
quarters, their presence and direction of flight may give no indication whatever of the proximity of land. An important species
which falls into this category is the great shearwater, or Tristan
great shearwater of the Atlantic Ocean. Its only known breeding
place is in the archipelago of Tristan da Cunha in the South
Atlantic, one of the most isolated island groups in the world.
This great shearwater appears to spend our summer entirely
in the North Atlantic. In May the birds begin to arrive off the
east coast of the United States and when their population builds
up, groups of a hundred or more may be seen in favorite places,
such as at the convergence of the Gulf Stream and the Labrador
Current or off the Newfoundland Banks. The great shearwaters
swing eastwards across the North Atlantic and often arrive off
the western shores of Britain in June. They work their way home
down the eastern North Atlantic, departing from European waters
in November. In effect this species makes a slow roundabout
cruise of the North Atlantic during its off-season and at each

point in this roundabout there is an appropriate time when a peak abundance can be expected. For instance, on a line from Nantucket Island, Cape Cod and Nova Scotia to the mid-Atlantic in 51° north 30° west, the great shearwater peak is in about the last week of May. In the first week of June the species is abundant on the Grand Banks.

James Fisher has seen great shearwaters at Rockall, about 300 miles west of the mainland of Scotland, as early as May, but the peak visitation in west Britain is in about July and not until later is the species common off the Scilly Isles and to be met with occasionally in large flocks off the Cornish coast.

Another important shearwater is the Manx shearwater. This is a species more local than some of the great wanderers from the Southern Hemisphere; and within its curiously scattered world range it has several well-marked races. Such races nest in New Zealand and Hawaii, on the west coast of Mexico and on islands off it, in the Mediterranean and the North Atlantic. The Mediterranean and North Atlantic races are sufficiently different to be distinguished in the field. We now know from marking records that the North Atlantic race migrates from the British Isles across the equator to the eastern coast of South America. But when the Manx shearwater is not migrating, it usually stays within 200 miles of shore or at least over the shallow waters of the 100 fathom continental shelf. During the summer breeding season in the Northern Hemisphere, big "rafts" of Manx shearwaters sitting on the water or big packs in flight mean birds which are operating from some land base. As Manx shearwaters relieve each other on the nest at intervals of up to a week, their operational range from base can be quite considerable. Many of the birds that breed in Wales regularly feed in the Bay of Biscay. At the end of the season, the Mediterranean birds pass out of the Straits of Gibraltar and turn north, reaching as far as the entrance to the English Channel. The Manx shearwater is rare on the American side of the North Atlantic; it is not certain that it still nests in Bermuda; and the New England coast is certainly well out of its range. Yet, a bird taken from its burrow in Wales and flown to Boston, returned under its own power across the Atlantic in less than a fortnight.

I should mention the last and smallest family of the tube-nosed birds, the diving petrels, of which there are four species, confined to the cooler waters of the Southern Hemisphere and sub-antarctic. These extraordinary little birds are shrimp-feeders and can actually swim with their wings under water. At sea they may be sometimes present in quite large numbers a long distance from base in places where sea conditions provide copious food.

The Steganopodes. The Steganopodes are an order of sea birds comprising the tropic-bird family, the frigate-bird family, the cormorant family, the gannet family and the pelican family. Not all the members of these families are marine, though the order certainly must have evolved in the oceans of the world.

Tropic Birds. The curious tropic-bird family contains three members, all of which are indeed mainly tropical in their distribution. Tropic birds are useful guides to the natural navigator, for normally they are seldom observed in groups of three or more unless land is close.

During the summer around Bermuda the white-tailed tropic birds which nest there operate to a distance of sixty or seventy miles, flying out to the feeding grounds early in the morning, returning shortly before sunset. A group of three or more such birds seen flying at these times of day will surely indicate by the direction of their flight the direction of the land. The white-tailed tropic bird is found in all three tropical oceans: in the Atlantic it breeds not only on Bermuda, but at many islands in the Bahamas and West Indies, possibly in the Guianas, on Fernando Noronha just south of the equator, on Ascension, and on islands off the West African coast just on the equator. It has a wide breeding range in the central and western Pacific and in the Indian Ocean. Where tropic birds breed on inhabited islands they can sometimes be seen flying about without their tail feathers: these slender and beautiful plumes are often removed by the natives who highly prize them.

The white-tailed tropic bird is one of the few species seen

in the area of the Sargasso Sea, though it is not very common there except in its western part. A voyager traveling from this sea area towards the West Indies or Bermuda during the tropic bird's breeding season (May-August) can observe the increasing numbers build up as he goes.

The red-billed tropic bird is found in western Mexico, Central America, the southeastern West Indies, the Cape Verde Islands, St. Helena, Ascension, Fernando Noronha and Rocas Rock. These last four breeding places are on islands in the Atlantic just south of the equator. The species also breeds on the coast of Ecuador and in the Galápagos Islands; and at the southeastern end of the Red Sea and near its entrance to the Indian Ocean.

The red-tailed tropic bird is not an Atlantic species, but breeds in the Indian and Pacific Oceans over a wide area from Madagascar to the Galápagos Islands and from the oceanic islands off south Japan to the Hawaiian islands and the Kermadec Islands and northern Australia.

Frigate Birds. Of all the sea birds the fantastic frigate birds, with an enormous wing expanse in proportion to their weight, are the most skillful and maneuverable aviators. Their advanced design serves them well, for they are interceptor fighters in their role as marauders of the skies. Though frigate birds are true sea birds, they are essentially land based—and hence of value to the natural navigator. If they land on the water for any length of time their plumage actually becomes waterlogged. They eat almost entirely fish, but rarely catch fish themselves. Normally they sit and wait and intercept and rob a returning fish-laden booby or tern. As their victim comes in they take off, gain altitude and power-dive it until it disgorges its belly-load of fish—which the interceptor deftly catches in the air. I have stood on a small Pacific island around sunset and ducked my head from what sounded like a landing airplane: it was only a booby trying to land before a frigate bird could catch up with it.

The frigate birds are not always easy to distinguish from each other. There are five species in the world, all tropical, which range more or less throughout the coasts and islands that lie in the belt 1800 miles north and south of the equator. On the west coast of America they range between Southern California, and northern Peru and Sala y Gomez Island off the coast of Chile; and in the open Pacific as far north as Hawaii, as far south as New Caledonia, north almost to Japan, south to New Zealand, Tonga, and northern Australia. They are widespread in the tropical parts of the Indian Ocean.

It is altogether exceptional to record a frigate bird as far as three hundred miles from land; and the presence of any large number of them almost certainly means land within a hundred miles. Since they do not normally settle on the water they shun nights at sea, so that the direction of their flight at dusk will normally be towards land and is well worth observing. Incidentally, frigate birds have very keen vision; and a bird seen passing at a respectable height above the voyager is extremely likely to be homing directly by sight.

Apropos of frigate birds, I can cite a good example of the principle I have been trying to establish in this chapter—namely that there are exceptions to every rule and observations should be as varied as possible before a collection can be made from which conclusions can be drawn. I remember the case of a French doctor who, failing in his attempt to swim the English Channel, sought fame by drifting across the Atlantic on a raft. With him he took my former publication *The Raft Book,* which was designed to help people adrift at sea during the Second World War. In this book I repeatedly stressed that reliance should not be placed on any *one* sign.

Ignoring these warnings, this doctor put his trust in one single observation of a frigate bird to estimate his nearness to land. If indeed he correctly identified his bird as a frigate bird, his observation of it when many miles from land was most exceptional, in view of all the recorded observations of others over many years. Doctor Robert Cushman Murphy expressed the situation well in a recent letter to me:

. . . a storm driven waif once in a thousand years or perhaps in ten thousand years would probably account for the present situation of Frigate Birds of several species distributed widely over the warmer ocean waters. The fact of the distinctness of the present day species in several distinct oceanic areas is further proof that they are essentially relatively local in their habits.

He added further:

During the preparation of my book *Oceanic Birds of South America* I ran down many alleged records of Frigate Birds in remote oceanic areas, and I found that an error was involved in nearly all such instances.

Cormorants (or Shags). There are thirty species of cormorants or shags in the world, though not all of them are sea birds, and few indeed are birds of the open sea. So much is the average cormorant a coastal bird that in olden times it was called the sea crow or sea raven and was the shore-sighting bird carried by primitive European navigators. Captain Cook noted that cormorants were never seen more than twenty-five miles from the shore, and all the vast experience of bird watchers in recent times has done no more than confirm this figure. So if the natural navigator sees a cormorant, and better still, cormorants, he is pretty certain to be within twenty-five miles from land.

Cormorants and shags have a very wide range through all parts of the marine world (and some inland waters) except the islands of the central Pacific. On the whole they are more numerous and have a slightly greater variety of species in the Southern Hemisphere. One particular cormorant is the dominant bird in what is perhaps the greatest community of sea birds in the world, for the guanay or guanay cormorant is the most abundant species all along the bird islands of the guano coast of Chile and Peru.

Cormorants are seldom found on any islands remote from continents, though on the Galápagos Islands a peculiar isolated flightless form occurs; and some species have colonized the subantarctic islands in very great numbers.

Gannets and Boobies. Gannets and boobies are always good indicators of land, for they breed in large numbers on many oceanic islands, yet do not normally operate on ration runs far beyond the hundred fathom continental shelf. The family, of which there are nine members, are all great fishermen, and the birds may be seen leaving land on their way to their fishing grounds, especially in the early morning. Normally there is two-way traffic through much of the middle of the day, and in the evening a procession of incomers with their bellies full of the last load of fish for their young.

The visitor to a gannet or booby colony can often walk among the nests, for many species nest on flat ground or even in the branches of bushes. As he walks through, the adults and young often readily disgorge freshly caught or freshly fed fish, no doubt a form of intimidative display.

In these modern days such a habit might seem only in the remotest sense useful to the traveler: at least, this is what I thought myself until one day in the Pacific the whaleboat in which I was landing capsized off Baker Island. Our party was unable to return to our schooner for five days, and during this time I used my knowledge of the regurgitating habits of the boobies to provide us with meals of freshly caught and quite edible fish.

The six boobies are of tropical distribution, the three gannets of temperate distribution. Perhaps the most widespread booby is the brown booby, which breeds on the oceanic islands of the tropical Atlantic (not St. Helena), on several islands off the West African coast, on many in the West Indies, and widely in the Pacific from Mexico to Colombia, from Hawaii to the Kermadec Islands, from Formosa to Northern Australia. It breeds also on islands on the tropical belt in the Indian Ocean and in the Red Sea.

Usually the brown booby fishes within a range of about thirty miles from its nesting grounds. The farthest that a single brown booby has been recorded from land is a hundred and twenty miles, in the Caribbean Sea. Normally it would be pretty safe to assume an outside limit of seventy-five miles from base for several brown boobies seen at sea. At dawn such boobies are likely to be flying from land, at dusk towards it. A dozen or more together are almost certain to be within thirty miles from land.

The red-footed booby breeds on bushes, not on the ground, and is confined to islands which can provide woody vegetation.

Apparently it finds too much difficulty in taking off from the ground. Notwithstanding this limitation, it is rather more widely distributed than the brown booby in the tropical parts of the Indian Ocean and western and central Pacific. It has fewer colonies than the brown booby around the tropical Americas. In the central Atlantic, unlike the brown booby, it may breed on St. Helena.

Red-footed boobies are at their most plentiful within twenty-five miles from base; smaller numbers range to fifty miles and only individuals, and that rarely, beyond seventy-five miles.

The blue-faced or masked booby has a similar distribution to the other species, though the number of colonies known is not quite so great. Like the red-footed booby, it is absent from the islands off the coast of West Africa.

The three boobies that I have just described are the most widespread, and useful maps of the distribution of each of them are published by Fisher and Lockley in their *Sea Birds* (*New Naturalist Series*, 1954).

Like the boobies, the gannets seldom wander off the hundred-fathom continental shelf, which means that they are unusual more than a hundred miles to sea and decidedly rare over three hundred miles from the coast. When a gannet is breeding it relieves its mate at the nest at least once a day, and the operational range of adult North Atlantic gannets from their colonies is probably between sixty and ninety miles, a matter of five or six hours' flying and feeding time for this powerful bird. With its six foot wing span and seven and a half pounds weight the gannet is the largest sea bird of the North Atlantic.

Every colony of the North Atlantic gannet has been found and indeed the number of nests of these colonies is now counted every ten years by Fisher, Vevers, Lockley and their colleagues. At the last census in 1949, there was one colony off the coast of Brittany, two in the Channel Islands, one in Wales, three in Ireland, one in England, eight in Scotland, one in Norway, one in the Faeroes, five in Iceland; and on the western side of the Atlantic three in the Gulf of St. Lawrence and one on the coast of Newfoundland and two on islands off it. About 100,000 nests were occupied in all in that year. The breeding season of the gannet begins with the arrival of adults as early as January or February in Britain—in March or April in North America. Egg-laying starts in May and the young are away early in September. Young gannets are distinguishable from their white parents, going through various stages of dark plumage in their four years of immaturity. During this period they operate to sea farther than the adults and reach quite a distance down the west coast of Africa. Gannets penetrate the Mediterranean out of season, sometimes even as far as Palestine. Occasionally they reach the Gulf of Mexico on the American side. The winter distribution of the main pack of gannets on the North American eastern seaboard depends somewhat on the state of the Labrador Current. Suffice it to say that the adult gannet is in the nesting season always a good indicator of the direction of land, indeed of a particular rock (for the number of colonies is so limited that we can usually fix a flight line on a particular one). Out of season all gannets, young and old, are certain indicators of the continental shelf.

Very similar to the northern or North Atlantic gannet is the Cape gannet, which breeds on islands off the coast of South Africa from Hollams Bird Island to Algoa Bay, and which in the off-season migrates a considerable distance up the coast of West Africa, sometimes crossing the equator.

Closely allied also is the Australasian gannet. One race of this breeds on islands in the Bass Strait and around Tasmania, from July to January, and is distributed when young or in the off-season, in the neighboring seas and as far as Point Cloats in Western Australia and Brisbane in Queensland. The other race of the Australasian gannet is confined to New Zealand.

In the season of 1946-1947 a census of the dozen or so occupied colonies of the New Zealand gannet (two were off the South Island, all the rest off North Island) showed that the population of this race was between 18,000 and 24,000 pairs. The Australian race nests probably in five colonies only and may total about two thousand pairs.

Pelicans. Of the six pelicans in the world, only one, the brown pelican of America, can seriously be regarded as a sea bird. The other great birds, if they do not live inland, are birds of estuaries and lagoons and scarcely ever range out of sight of land. But the brown pelican breeds and roams on the Pacific coast of tropical America from Chile to California and on the Atlantic coast from Florida to the Amazon. Like the gannet, it secures its food by diving from a height, but unlike the gannet it seldoms travels to the limit of the continental shelf, except in parts of its range among the guano islands off Chile and Peru. Normally the brown pelican operates within twenty-five miles from shore and any string of pelicans flying can be regarded as at this distance or less.

In the big gull-wader order of birds six families—the sheathbills, the phalaropes, the skuas (or jaegers), the gulls, the terns and the auks are sea birds, or mostly so. The sheathbills comprise two curious pigeon-like species confined to the antarctic and the sub-antarctic and seldom ranging far from the sea-bird colonies on which they are modest predators and professional scavengers.

Phalaropes. One of the most extraordinary transitions in nature is found among the waders; for two slight and delicate birds, which breed on the arctic tundras in the summer (and behave very much like their relations the stints and sandpipers) become —in winter—birds of the open ocean. The gray phalarope, or red phalarope as it is called in America, breeds all round the arctic regions, in a belt somewhat more northerly than (but much overlapping with) that in which breeds its cousin the red-necked or northern phalarope.

The sea voyager sees the phalaropes in their gray winter plumage, a much more modest dress than that which they wear in the breeding season. The passage south of the gray (or red) phalarope takes place partly over land (at least in the North American continent and western Europe) but also over sea, particularly in the northern half of the North Atlantic. By no means sufficient information has yet come to hand for us to establish the precise wintering places of the bulk of the gray phalarope population. We know that some birds reach South Africa and even New Zealand; but it appears that the bulk of the winterers remain concentrated in three main sea areas. One of these is in the Humboldt Current to the west of the border between Chile and Peru. Another is certainly along the extreme western part of West Africa and around the Cape Verde Islands. A third is in the northwestern part of the Indian Ocean and towards the entrance of the Red Sea.

From its rather wider breeding distribution in the arctic and northern regions of both Old and New Worlds, the red-necked phalarope or northern phalarope also migrates south overland and over sea. Probably more individuals of this smaller species take the land route than of gray phalaropes. We can be certain that one of the wintering concentrations of the red-necked phalarope is (like the grays) in the northwestern part of the Indian Ocean and the southeast entrance to the Red Sea. Winterers are also seen on the waters of the Persian Gulf and rather widely in the seas of the East Indies, around the Philippines, Borneo, Celebes, the Moluccas and New Guinea. Very few, if any, gray phalaropes winter here.

Only a few red-necked phalaropes appear to migrate to South America and its adjacent seas, or to South and West Africa.

Skuas (*or Jaegers*). The skuas are four, all gull-like birds which have become marine birds of prey and which migrate enormous distances, often across the equator. Only when large numbers of one kind of skua are seen can the navigator infer the presence of nearby land. Small packs may operate hundreds of miles from land when there are other sea birds to parasitize—for the skuas earn much of their living by pursuing other birds and by compelling them to disgorge the contents of their stomachs.

Largest of the skuas is the bonxie or great skua. Like the fulmar it is one of the few bi-polar birds in the world. Its breeding headquarters is in the south. One race actually nests on the antarctic continent and other forms are found in all the sub-antarctic islands and as far north as Tristan da Cunha. The species breeds also in the Falkland Islands, in Chile and south Argentina, and in the South Island of New Zealand and its adjoining oceanic islands.

An extraordinary outpost breeds on the other side of the world in the North Atlantic Ocean, where it is confined to the northern part of the British Isles (particularly Shetland), the Faeroe Islands and southeast Iceland.

From these bases the great skuas appear to operate widely over the oceans. Individuals of various races have been observed in the Pacific as far as Japan on the west, and British Columbia on the east. Others penetrate into the Indian Ocean nearly as far as the equator; and great skuas have been seen in the central Atlantic which may have been either from the southern colonies or from the north—nobody has yet been able to find out whether the wandering range of the two widely separated breeding populations overlaps. Certainly in the North Atlantic the great skua ranges very widely, reaching the eastern seaboard of North America, most of the North Atlantic oceanic islands, Baffin Island, Greenland, Spitsbergen and the north coast of Russia; and individuals have penetrated at least halfway into the Mediterranean and some distance into the Baltic Sea.

The arctic skua or parasitic jaeger has an entirely northern breeding range, nesting near coasts and also hundreds of miles inland on suitable moors and tundras, widely around the Old and New Worlds north of latitude 60° N—and in some cases, as in Kamchatka, south almost to 50° N. From this breeding headquarters it migrates over land and sea tremendous distances, and has reached islands not far from the antarctic continent. Undoubtedly a good proportion of the arctic skuas winter in the tropical seas, but many certainly push on as far as South Africa, southeast Australia, the South Island of New Zealand and southern South America.

The pomarine or twist-tailed skua or jaeger has a rather more northerly breeding distribution than the arctic skua and a smaller population. There is no evidence that it penetrates as far south as the arctic skua, for it has not so far been observed in southern South America or near the antarctic continent. Certainly a great many winter just north of the equator in the seas west of the western bulge of Africa. Others also reach southeast Australia and New Zealand.

The smallest of the skuas is the long-tailed skua, which also breeds in the arctic north. Migrating over land and sea, it does not appear to winter into Asia beyond Japan or to visit Australasia; but it has been recorded in the tropical Atlantic, in West Africa and in South America. There is a considerable mystery, still, about the true wintering headquarters of the long-tailed skua.

Gulls. There are forty-two species of gulls in the world. I might have headed this paragraph "Sea Gulls," were it not for the fact that about half the gulls in the world (both individuals and species) see relatively little of the sea; and some never see it at all.

Gulls, in fact, are primarily shore birds. Of all the gulls in the world only two species—the kittiwakes—are truly oceanic. Perhaps we should call all the other gulls "shore gulls."

Most shore gulls are beach feeders or inland feeders and thrive on seaweed, mollusks, star fishes, sea urchins and crustaceans. Intertidal feeders, they are also great opportunist scavengers, and to a certain extent predators. They haunt the colonies of other sea birds to pick up anything they can get (and a living egg or young bird if possible). Great numbers of gulls of several species have become parasitic on the world's coastal fishing industry, haunting fish-curing wharfs and trawler docks to feed on scraps. Normally no shore gull is ever found at a greater distance from the shore than fifty miles, though some members of some species will occasionally work as far as the edge of the continental shelf when this is more than fifty miles from the coast. Most exceptions to this rule occur when gulls follow ships, especially trawlers. Certainly most trawlers of all the nations that work the North Atlantic and Arctic waters carry with them their own wake of expectant gulls (and in some areas also very many fulmars). Most gulls will leave an ordinary vessel before it gets out of sight of land, and return to their scavenging occupation on the shore; but they do not always leave a trawler or drifter, and it seems that quite regularly gulls will accompany the Fleetwood and Milford Haven trawlers right out through the north entrance to the Irish Sea and 250 to 300 miles to the Rockall Bank. James Fisher has even once seen a black-headed gull at Rockall—and the black-headed gull is the most inland of all the British gulls, and must have needed a strong stimulus to go so far out of sight of land.

The commonest gull of the Northern Hemisphere is the herring gull, though in parts of western Europe its close relation, the lesser black-backed gull, is almost as common. The herring gull has a very wide distribution on the coasts and to a certain extent also the inland rivers and lakes of the north temperate and sub-arctic regions of all the lands around the North Pole. It migrates to a certain extent in the autumn, though not as far as the lesser black-backed, ranging mostly coastwise in rather desultory exploration of new territory.

Many of the big light-headed gulls are dark-mantled and dark-winged. The southern black-backed, Dominican or kelp gull is the only large black-backed and wholly white-tailed gull in the Southern Hemisphere. It is darker on the mantle than any other gull, even the great black-backed of the Northern Hemisphere. It breeds in southern South America, South Africa and New Zealand, on Tristan da Cunha and Gough Island, and on practically all of the chain of sub-antarctic islands that embraces the antarctic continent.

About half the gulls of the world are dark-hooded or at least assume chocolate or black heads in the breeding season. A typical example is the handsome laughing gull of North America. This breeds in Central America, the Caribbean, and northwards on the west to Southern California, on the east to New England, and coasts south in the autumn to winter as far as Brazil and northern Peru.

A typical resident coastal gull of the Southern Hemisphere is the silver gull, which is found on the South African coast north to about 30° S. and is also common in New Caledonia, Australia, Tasmania, New Zealand and some of its satellite oceanic islands such as the Chatham and Auckland Islands.

As previously mentioned, the only gulls which are truly oceanic birds are kittiwakes. Of the two species, the red-legged kittiwake is extremely rare and as far as is known breeds only in three small island groups in the Bering Sea. But the common kittiwake has a wide breeding range in the North Pacific and North Atlantic Oceans and adjacent parts of the Arctic. Indeed, the kittiwake's breeding distribution extends to the northernmost high arctic lands: it is a very successful species. To the south it breeds in the Atlantic as far as the Gulf of St. Lawrence on the west and Brittany on the east. Its breeding range on the Pacific does not extend beyond western Alaska and the Kuril Islands.

Much has yet to be learned about the kittiwake's distribution at sea and its life cycle. It is certainly true that the kittiwake is absent or at least exceptionally rare in mid-Atlantic from mid-June to mid-August. In the winter kittiwakes wander freely in the North Atlantic, reaching latitudes much farther south than do the fulmars. Some even reach 24° N. occasionally. At all times of year kittiwakes are very common off both eastern and western Atlantic seaboards between 40° and 50° N.

Terns and Noddies—with a note on Skimmers. There are thirty-nine kinds of terns in the world and three kinds of the closely allied but peculiar skimmers. Terns are smaller and more swallow-like than the gulls and are not difficult to identify as a family. They usually breed in large colonies, sometimes—in the tropics—*very* large colonies. Terns of one kind or another are found almost from pole to pole; and one species in particular, the arctic tern, makes what are certainly the longest migratory journeys of any bird.

The most beautiful of all the sea birds, in my opinion, is the white tern, with its streamlined delicate appearance. It was in 1935 that I first saw these tropical terns—on Palmyra, an island eleven hundred miles south of the Hawaiian Islands. The lovely creatures were so tame that when I tried to photograph them they hovered around my head too close for a clear snapshot. The white tern builds no nest, yet nests on shrubs and trees. It just lays its egg on a round branch, fixing it with a sticky mixture of its own making.

The white tern seldom operates farther than forty miles to sea, and is therefore a useful indicator of land, for the voyager who sees several together can be pretty sure of his maximum distance from land.

The white tern breeds on the oceanic islands of the South Atlantic just south of the equator (Fernando Noronha, South Trinidad,

Ascension and St. Helena) in the Seychelles in the Indian Ocean and probably on some other archipelagos, and in many islands in the Pacific Ocean, from Laysan in the north to the Kermadecs in the south.

Perhaps the most typical of the tropical terns—certainly the most abundant—are the noddy and sooty terns. These wander more than the white tern, and their presence over the seas is by no means a sure indication of the nearness of land. The sooty tern is the more venturesome of the two and ranges farther off-shore. A lot remains to be discovered about the distribution at sea of these two species. Both species are almost confined, in and out of the breeding season, to the belt of the world between the Tropics of Cancer and Capricorn, though both breed a short dis-tance north of the Tropic of Cancer in the Dry Tortugas off Florida, the only tropical sea-bird colony in the United States of America. The breeding season of the sooty tern differs much from one place to another, and on Ascension Island is not annual, but at approximately ten month intervals.

The arctic tern is typical of a largish group of black-capped terns. It has been proved by ringing that an arctic tern hatched in west Greenland can double the Cape of Good Hope and reach Natal on the east coast of South Africa in the autumn of the same year, a distance by sea of over eleven thousand miles. The breed-ing distribution of the arctic tern extends to the highest arctic regions from the north temperate and sub-arctic regions all round the pole. From these high latitudes many individuals migrate all the way to the antarctic continent. The Atlantic element of this migrant population crosses from the American arctic to the west coast of Africa by flying the North Atlantic diagonally from north-west to southeast. It can be understood that on migration the arctic tern cannot be relied on as an indicator of the nearness of land.

In general, terns are rarely seen on the water because they are poor swimmers. They prefer to hover over schools of fish and crustacea, making quick swoops to the surface (or just below it) for their prey. Nobody has ever seen an arctic tern alight on the North Atlantic during its long migration across that ocean; but terns at sea will sometimes rest on any driftwood available, or on ships.

The curious skimmers, of which there are three species in the world, can scarcely be described as sea birds. They are usually denizens of tropical estuaries and enclosed lagoons, as well as rivers and other fresh waters. Occasionally they will feed in the shallows offshore, but never do so, as far as I am aware, out of sight of land. With their curiously elongated lower mandibles, the skimmers fly to and fro ploughing a furrow in the water. It is commonly believed that they feed in this way, but Dr. Robert Cushman Murphy points out that during this maneuver their bill is usually closed. He considers that the skimmer "ploughs the main" with its bright red bill in order to lure small fish to the surface, which it catches by doubling on its tracks.

Auks. Our last family of sea birds certainly originated in evolution in the northern part of the Pacific Ocean, possibly the Bering Sea, for in those waters the auks attain today their greatest diversity. Essentially auks are sea birds which have specialized in being able to fly both over and under the surface of the water. They manage to swim with their wings with great skill and at a speed which approaches, though it does not attain, that of a penguin.

On the whole, all the members of the auk family—puffins, guillemots and auklets—operate from their bases to the edge of the continental shelf, and are seldom found more than about seventy miles from shore unless the continental shelf extends farther. Very rarely are any species seen over deep waters or in mid-ocean.

The largest surviving members of the auk family are the puffins. The tufted puffin of the Pacific has a wide distribution from the Bering Sea to California, and is a familiar bird to most visitors to the western seaboard of the U.S.A. In the Pacific is also found the handsome horned puffin which has a close counterpart in the common puffin of the North Atlantic. Though puffins, like most other auks, seldom operate beyond the continental shelf, individuals quite often appear to cross the long deeps between the Scottish continental shelf and the isolated Rockall Bank; and there have been a few transatlantic recoveries of marked puffins. Thus the observation of a few puffins cannot safely be relied on to indicate the nearness or direction of land.

The Atlantic puffin moves a fair distance south in the winter, and at that time quite a number can reach not only the Canaries but the Azores, which involves them in at least a half Atlantic crossing, during which they probably swim as great a distance as they fly.

Abundant are the two members of the guillemot or murre genus. Both species are found in the North Pacific, the North Atlantic and parts of the Arctic Ocean in between, though the arctic murre is alone found in the higher latitudes as a breeder. I use the name "arctic murre" to avoid a good deal of confusion; because in the Atlantic this species is known as Brünnich's guillemot or Brünnich's murre, and in the Pacific as Pallas's murre. Similarly the more southern species, the common guillemot or common murre, is known in the Pacific as the California murre. Neither of these two murres often operates farther than the edge of the continental shelf. Of the two, the arctic murre in the winter is the more likely to penetrate towards the deep ocean. In places where the continental shelf extends an unusual distance, such as the southeasterly edge of the Grand Banks, both murres (but particularly the arctic murre) can be sometimes abundant: and occasionally, in the summer, rather large numbers of the arctic murre have been seen east of the southern tip of Greenland nearly 150 miles from land and over rather deep water. But normally both species coast in the off-season and pursue fish by diving to fair depths in the coastal waters above the shelf.

There is a fair confusion between the two sides of the Atlantic over the vernacular names of some of the auks. In America the word guillemot is used almost exclusively to describe the black guillemot (or, as it is called in the Pacific, the pigeon guillemot). This widespread arctic and sub-arctic species is a particularly resident and coastal bird, staying near its breeding places in the winter even in the arctic, where it can find a living in the "leads" in the floe ice. The natural navigator should learn this bird in both its distinctive summer and subtle winter plumage, for it is a very useful indicator of the proximity of land, feeding as it does in shallows, hardly ever migrating, and living a somewhat self-sufficient life in pairs and little flocks—never in big packs.

In contrast to the black guillemot, the little auk or dovekie—the smallest of the auk family in the North Atlantic—is perhaps the least coastal of the Atlantic auks. Breeding in the high arctic, it moves far south of the edge of the sea ice only in some winters, when it may suddenly invade more southerly seas in exceptional numbers. Interested as it is, more in ice-edge than land-edge, it can be seen (in winter particularly) quite frequently in mid-ocean and in fair numbers.

In the Pacific the dovekie has many counterparts which, like it, are plankton (mainly crustacean) feeders. The crested and paroquet auklets are not often seen in great numbers off the continental shelves, and when moving out of the breeding season tend to coast or island-hop. They are fairly reliable indicators of the proximity of coasts throughout the year.

Smallest of the auk family is the tiny least auklet. Like the crested and paroquet auklets, this breeds in and around the Bering Sea, the home of the auks. In winter it coasts out of the Bering Sea as far as the sea of Okhotsk and the islands northeast of Formosa; on the American side of the North Pacific as far as the State of Washington.

1. WANDERING ALBATROSS. 1a. *Swimming*. Adult albatross, principally white, with black and white markings on upper parts of wings and tail; sides of head usually have pink or orange patch; bill, pink or yellow.

Young albatross, mostly brown and black on top of wings, white underneath.

This, the largest of the albatrosses, has a maximum wing span of a little more than 11 feet. The wandering albatross is similar to royal and other predominantly white southern albatrosses.

2. SOOTY ALBATROSS. Adult, sooty-gray or brown, darkest on wings and head, black bill and flesh-colored feet. Younger birds similar except for white markings on neck.

It is representative of the dark southern albatrosses.

3. BLACK-FOOTED ALBATROSS. 3a. *End view*. Adult, sooty-brown, with white around reddish-brown bill. Feet black.

Young similar but with lighter upper parts.

From the descriptions of this albatross and ones depicted in figures 1 and 2, any of other ten species may be identified as belonging to albatross family.

4. KERMADEC PETREL. 4a. *End view*. Body, brown above, with either white or dark under surface. Head sometimes white; white patches on under side of wing tips. Bill, black. Feet, black or yellow.

The Kermadec Petrel is similar to the many other petrels and shearwaters that have white underparts.

5. SHORT-TAILED SHEARWATER. Head, tail feathers and upper parts of body, sooty-black; under surface, sooty-brown; bill, blackish-brown; feet, purplish-black. General appearance similar to sooty shearwater and to other dark petrels and shearwaters.

6. FULMAR. 6a. *On water;* 6b. *End view*. Head, neck and under surface, white, with dark spot in front of eye. Bill, gray, green or yellow. Upper part of tail, pearl gray. Main upper surface wing, slate-gray with whitish patch. Feet, gray or flesh-colored. High arctic color phase in Atlantic much darker, grayish blue replacing white. In Pacific this color phase has more *southerly* distribution than white phase.

Although somewhat similar in color to many gulls, the fulmar should not be confused with them. Its flight is quite distinctive, much more stiff-winged and dynamically soaring. It glides much greater distances than gulls, much more swiftly, and in gliding its wings are held stiffly almost straight out; those of gliding gulls are "angled."

PLATE III

7. NORTH ATLANTIC GANNET. 7a. *End view.* Body, mainly white; head and neck, yellow with patch of dark blue skin on throat; quill feathers blackish-brown; bill, white; feet, black.

Young, dark grayish-brown above with white spots, and white underneath.

8. AUSTRALASIAN GANNET. Adult similar in appearance to North Atlantic and Cape gannets, but with outer tail feathers white and central tail feathers grayish-brown. Head, yellow with slate blue patch of naked skin on throat. Bill, slate-colored; feet, grayish-black.

Young, white spotted grayish-brown above, and white underneath, with brown blotches on throat and sides.

9. RED-FOOTED BOOBY (*White phase*). 9a. (*Gray phase*). Adult, generally white with variable yellowish tint on head, neck, back and tail. Outer wing feathers, dark brown with tapering band of brown along rear edge of wing. Tail, longest of any of boobies. Bill, in males, blue with red at base. Legs and feet, both sexes, red. Young, generally brownish.

A variation of this bird, found in great numbers among those with white plumage, is predominantly gray with dark brown wing tips and white tail. This gray phase is shown in 9a.

This same bird may also be seen with brown coloring and white tail. It can be distinguished from the masked or blue-faced booby by its smaller size and bright red feet.

10. MASKED OR BLUE-FACED BOOBY. Adult plumage, white, except for dark brown wing tips, tail and rear half of wing. Skin of face, black; bill, horn color with bright orange at base in males and pink or light red in females; legs and feet, olive drab in males, and lead color in females. Young birds have head, neck and upper parts smoky-brown, somewhat mixed with white feathers.

Being larger than any of the other boobies, it may be distinguished from the red-footed booby, and although the feet may vary in color, they are never red. It may also be recognized by its black tail.

11. BROWN BOOBY. Head, neck and chest, chocolate brown; under parts of body and wing, white with paler brown under wing toward tip; top of wing pale brown; base of bill yellow, and bluish-white toward tip; legs and feet yellow.

Young birds, grayish-brown above, slightly lighter on belly and darker on breast. General effect, brownish-gray instead of white. Bills, darker than those of adults.

12. RED-TAILED TROPIC BIRD. 12a. *Turning in flight.* Adult, silky-white, sometimes with rosy tinge on back; distinct black crescent before and over eye; black bar on wings; wings and tail streaked with black; two long, slender, deep red feathers extending from tail, a length of about 18 inches or more; bill yellow or red.

12a shows red-tailed tropic bird in flight using its tail feathers and foot in a characteristic turn.

Young similar but with very short tail feathers.

The white-tailed tropic bird is mainly white with rosy tinge; black crescent in front and over eyes; black feathers on wings; a long tail up to 21 inches in length; yellow, black or red bill; yellow legs and toes; and black feet.

Young, smaller and without long tail feathers.

The red-billed tropic bird is white, with black band through eyes; black bars on upper parts and on wings. Tail feathers are white and up to about 20 inches in length; bill red or orange; legs and toes, yellowish or grayish-white; feet, black.

The young are smaller, but with more black on head and tail and with short tail feathers.

The red-tailed tropic bird is illustrated as representative of the three species which are found around the warm waters in all oceans. The white-tailed tropic bird and the red-billed tropic bird are very similar in appearance to the red-tailed species, the main distinction being that the white-tailed is smaller, and the red-billed has a wavy barred back.

PLATE IV

13. FRIGATE BIRD (white breasted). 13a. *Frigate Bird (dark)*; 13b. *End view*. Adult, black, with very long wings, long forked tail, and short legs. Some adult frigate birds have white areas underneath. Bill, long and slender with sharp hook at end. The young have white heads.

Frigate birds are most easily recognized of all sea birds, but in normal flight the tail is not spread and its forked nature is not always apparent. When the birds are maneuvering in the air they frequently open and close the tail with a scissor-like effect.

14. CORMORANT. 14a. *Swimming*. Plumage, glossy-green, or bluish-black; face and under part of bill, white; bill and naked skin of face, yellow; feet, black.

The common cormorant has black plumage in Europe, Asia and Australia, but some species in tropical and southern Africa have white breasts.

Young, brownish-black with usually lighter color and sometimes white underneath.

The numerous members of the cormorant family vary somewhat in color but are otherwise similar in appearance.

15. JACKASS PENGUIN. 15a. *Swimming*. Bluish-gray or black above and white below. Narrow band of black, in shape of horseshoe, across breast and sides; white spot on tail; bill long and thick, feet black.

Young have upper parts black with white underneath.

The jackass penguin, named for noisy braying sound it makes whether ashore or afloat, is found along the coasts of South Africa as far north as 16° South of Equator. There are sixteen other species of penguins all similar in general appearance to jackass penguin, but differing in size, the arrangement of black and white on face and throat, and color of bill and feet.

16. BROWN PELICAN. Back of head, white; front and top of head, yellow; neck and back, brown; underparts, grayish-brown; wings, black-brown with gray; skin around eyes, blue; bill, grayish; feet, black.

Other species of pelicans are similar in outline and general appearance.

17. GREAT SKUA. Plumage, dark grayish-brown; conspicuous white patches underneath wings; heavy build. Short, square tail, stout curved upper bill.

Young are similar but with slightly different markings.

18. ARCTIC SKUA. Top of head, grayish-brown; rest of head, white; tail and upper parts of wings, grayish-brown; neck and under parts, white. At times the arctic skua is completely sooty-brown except for neck, which is tinged with yellow. Tail long and wedge-shaped, with long, projecting central tail feathers.

The arctic skua is similar to the long-tailed and pomarine skuas.

PLATE V

19. HERRING GULL. 19a. *Swimming.* 19b. *End view.* Large sea gulls with white head and neck in summer; in winter, speckled with gray; white underneath; tail white; black feathers toward outer wing tips; bill yellow, feet flesh color.

Young have grayish-brown heads; streaked with white and light brown; grayer underneath; tail, brownish-black, spotted with white. Young distinguished by their very dark plumage.

The herring gull is closely related to many other species, among them the California gull, the Iceland gull, the lesser black-backed gull and the glaucous-winged gull.

20. SOUTHERN BLACK-BACKED GULL. Adult, back and above wings, black; head, neck and underparts white, except wing tips which are black. Bill, yellow; feet, yellow.

Young, brown, speckled with white; tail blackish; bill, black; feet, brown. Only black-backed gull in Southern Hemisphere with pure white tail.

This gull is similar in appearance and habits to the great black-backed gull, the lesser black-backed gull and others.

21. LAUGHING GULL. Head, black; lower part of neck, white; tail, white; white underneath; back and upper part of wing, dark gray. Top of wing tips, black in winter; head, white mottled with brownish-gray on top and sides; eyes more or less surrounded by dark crescent. Bill, red in summer, blackish in winter; feet, brown. It is similar to many other dark-headed gulls, among them the black-headed gull of western Europe and the Mediterranean black-headed gull.

22. SILVER GULL. Head, dark; tail and under parts, white; wing tips, black with prominent white patch toward end of the tip. Top of wing and back, gray; bill and feet, red.

Young are very similar but upper part of wing and back, speckled with brown. Tail has a narrow brown band; bill, brown; feet, gray.

This gull is similar to several other small gulls.

23, 23a. COMMON KITTIWAKE. Head and neck, white in summer; winter, top and sides of head and back of neck, dark gray, which is also the color of the upper surface of wings and back. Both upper and lower parts of wing tips, black. Tail white; bill, greenish-yellow; feet, blackish.

Young have white heads, some gray on top and lower part, with dark gray bands on back of neck. Underparts of body and wings, white; tail, white with black band. Top of wings and back, gray. Wing tips, black; bill, black; feet, brown.

24. SKIMMER. Top of head and neck, black; forehead and underparts, white; tail, mostly white; bill, bright vermilion red with black tip; legs and feet, orange-vermilion.

Young, similar but with upper parts light brown streaked with grayish-white with black spots; underparts, white; and bill, legs, and feet, dull red.

The skimmer has a unique bill, the lower part being much longer than the upper and both flattened except at the base. Other skimmers similar in appearance differ somewhat in color.

25. WHITE TERN. Head, body, wings and tail, white with black ring around eyes, and long forked tail. Bill, black; feet, black or light blue. Young are similar, but with a black spot behind the eye and black streaks in wing and tail.

26. ARCTIC TERN. 26a. *Sitting.* Top of head, black; throat, breast and underparts, pale neutral gray; tail, very long and dark gray; bill, rich red; feet, coral red.

Young similar but with black-tipped yellow bill.

27. NODDY. Adult, dark brown above; upper main feathers of wing and tail, black; lower part of body, dark brown, with lighter brown under the wings. Head, gray, considerably lighter on forehead, with black band in front of eyes. Bill, black. Feet, brownish-black.

Young, similar but lighter and browner. Top of head, grayish-brown, white line above eyes.

28. SOOTY TERN. Adult, upper part of body, wings and tail, dull black. Forehead and side of head, lower part of neck and underparts of wings and body, pure white. Wings, grayish underneath wing tips. Bill, black; legs and feet, blackish.

Young, upper parts, deep sooty-brown, with upper tail surface tipped with brownish white. Bill, brownish-black or dark brown.

PLATE VI

29. COMMON DIVING PETREL. 29a. *Swimming.* Upper surface, black; wings, glossy black, tinged brown; under wing, tinged gray; sides, mouse gray; under neck and breast, dark gray. Bill, black; legs and feet, bluish.

30. 30a. WILSON'S PETREL. Generally blackish-brown, paler on throat, belly and under wings; darkest on wings and tail; square tail conspicuously white above; legs, long and black; feet, yellow.

31. TRISTAN GREAT SHEARWATER. Head above line from bill, dark sooty-brown; rest of body, sooty-brown; neck, white; underpart, white, with brown patch on belly; under wings, white with brown streaks; bill, dark; feet, flesh color.

32. MANX SHEARWATER. Body, including head, wings and tail, sooty-black; cheeks and behind ears, sides of neck and breast, speckled gray or sooty-brown; under wings and body, white; dark under tail; bill, black; feet, flesh color.

33. SOOTY STORM PETREL. Body, sooty; wings, blackish-brown; tail, forked, upper surface grayish, with white shafts; bill and feet, black.

34. GRAY PHALAROPE. In winter, head, neck and underparts, white; back of head and around eyes, slate; upper parts, light bluish-gray, darker on wings and tail. In summer, female, tip of head and below bill dark gray. In male top of head and back of neck streaked black and buff; cheeks, white; neck and underparts, reddish-brown; back, buff striped with black; under wings, white; bill, yellow; feet, yellowish. Short bill and white-barred wings always identify.

35. RED-NECKED PHALAROPE. In winter, forehead sides of head, neck, underparts, white; sides of chest mixed pale gray; top of head, grayish with blackish spot in front of eye; upper parts, gray. In summer, upper part slate; back striped with light brown, white bar on wing; under parts, white; bill, black; feet, bluish-gray.

36. TUFTED PUFFIN. 36a. *Swimming* (*winter plumage*). Upper parts, sooty-black with yellow on side of head; under wings, brownish-gray; under body, grayish-brown. Forehead and around eyes, white; bill,

very large, salmon red tip, olive green base; skin on side of bill, vermilion; feet, salmon red.

37. HORNED PUFFIN. 37a. *Swimming* (*winter plumage*). Crown, grayish-brown; neck and upper parts, black; sides of face, white in summer, gray in winter. Underparts, white but brownish-gray toward wing tips. Bill, large and brownish-red; feet vermilion. Similar to Atlantic puffin, it breeds and ranges in about same areas as tufted puffin. The Atlantic puffin differs in its large triangular bright beak (grayish-blue base, vermilion tip, crossed with yellow).

38. 38a. COMMON GUILLEMOT. 38b. *Swimming* (*winter plumage*). Head, neck, upper parts, sooty-brown; breast, underparts, white; bill, long, black and pointed; feet, bluish. Arctic murre (or Arctic guillemot) has a stouter bill.

39. PIGEON GUILLEMOT. 39a. *Swimming* (*winter plumage*). In summer, sooty-black, with white under wings barred with black. In winter, wings often all black. Bill, black; feet, vermilion. Called "black guillemot" in Atlantic and Arctic.

40. CRESTED AUKLET. Upper parts, slate-black, black crest on grayish forehead, long white feathers behind eye and across face. Underparts, brownish-gray; bill, short, orange-red, whitish tip; feet, pale violet-gray. Young, no crest or feathers on face.

41. PAROQUET AUKLET. Slate above; white plumes behind eyes and across face in summer; throat, front of neck, sides dull gray in summer, white in winter; grayish-brown under wings; white under body; bill, short and orange-red, lower part curved upward; feet, bluish-gray.

42. LEAST AUKLET. Slate-black above. Shoulders partly white; in summer, white-pointed feathers on forehead, behind eyes and across face. In winter, white and gray; cheeks and under bill, dark slate; mostly white under body; bill, small, dark, with reddish tip; feet, brown.

43. CAPE PIGEON. Black and white petrel with checkered back. General body color black; head, top of wings and feet, sides of face and neck, black, except for speckled throat; rest of back and upper tail surfaces, white. Feathers have black spots at end, giving speckled appearance.

PLATE VII

BIRD PLATE NO.	NAME OF BIRD	HABITAT PAGE NO.	TIME OF YEAR	NUMBER SEEN AT ONE TIME	REASONABLE ASSUMPTION
III	Wandering Albatross, Sooty, and other Southern Albatrosses	179-180	Any month	Any number	May be far from land
III	Black-footed and Laysan Albatross	180	April-October November-March	Any number 12 or more	May be far from land Within 100 miles of breeding place
III	Kermadec Petrel	184	Any month	6 or less Increasing numbers	May be far from land. Show proximity to land. Direction of flight at dawn and dusk shows direction of land
III	Short-tailed Shearwater	184-5	November-March April-October	6 or more Any number	Within 100 miles of breeding places. Direction of flight at dawn and dusk gives direction of land, and increasing numbers show proximity to land. May be far from land
III	Fulmar	182-3	During Northern Summer During Northern Winter—all across Atlantic All year	6 or less Any number Increasing numbers	May be far from land May be far from land Show proximity to land
VII	Cape Pigeon	184	Any month	Any number Increasing numbers	May be far from land Show proximity to land
IV	North Atlantic Gannet Australasian Gannet Cape Gannet	190-3	Any month	Exceptional cases of single birds 3 or more	Up to 300 miles Up to 100 miles
IV	Red-footed Booby	191-2	Any month	3 or more 6 or more 12 or more	Within 75 miles Within 50 miles Within 25 miles
IV	Masked (Blue-faced) Booby	192	Any month	3 or more 6 or more 12 or more	Within 75 miles Within 50 miles Within 25 miles

BIRD PLATE NO.	NAME OF BIRD	HABITAT PAGE NO.	TIME OF YEAR	NUMBER SEEN AT ONE TIME	REASONABLE ASSUMPTION
IV	Brown Booby	191-2	Any month	1 bird (only 1 case recorded— Caribbean Sea) 3 or more 6 or more	120 miles 75 miles Usually within 30 miles
IV	Tropic-Birds Red-tailed Red-billed White-tailed	187	Any month	1 or 2 3 or more	May be far from land 60-80 miles
V	Frigate-Bird	188	Any month	3 or more 6 or more	100 miles Within 75 miles. The direction of flight of *even* 1 bird at dusk generally points to land, as they *never* sleep on the water
V	Cormorants	190	Any month	Any number	25 mile limit
V	Penguins	179	Any month	Any number Increasing numbers	May be far from land throughout the year—except when breeding Show approach to breeding places
V	Brown, or other Pelicans	193	Any month	More than one Increasing numbers	25-mile limit; usually much less. Show approach to land
V	Great Skua	195	Summer months either hemisphere Winter months either hemisphere	Increasing numbers Any number	Show proximity to land May be far from land
V	Other Skuas	195-7	October-May June-September	Any number Any number	Far out Close to land (north of Arctic Circle)
VI	Herring-Gull and all other Gulls except the Kittiwake	197-8	Any month	3 or more Increasing numbers	50 miles (or within the 100-fathom line off coasts) Show approach to land

BIRD PLATE NO.	NAME OF BIRD	HABITAT PAGE NO.	TIME OF YEAR	NUMBER SEEN AT ONE TIME	REASONABLE ASSUMPTION
VI	Kittiwake	198	April-July	6 or more	Close to shore. Within 50 miles
			August-March	Any number	May be far at sea
VI	Black Skimmer	201	Any month	1 or more	Within 25 miles
VI	White Tern	199	Any month	1 or more	Within 40 miles
VI	Arctic Tern	200	May-July	6 or more	(Arctic)—close to shore within 100 miles
			December-February	6 or more	(South and Antarctic) close to shore within 100 miles
			Remainder of year	Any number	May be far at sea
VI	Noddy, Sooty and other Terns, except White, Arctic	200	Any month	Any number	May be far at sea
VII	Diving Petrels	187	July-November Remainder of year	6 or more Any number	Within 75 miles May be far at sea
VII	Storm-Petrels in Southern Hemisphere Storm-Petrels in Northern Hemisphere	181	December-February Remainder of yr. June-August Remainder of yr.	6 or more Any number 6 or more Any number	Within 75 miles May be far at sea Within 75 miles May be far at sea
VII	Tristan Great Shearwater	185	Beginning of October to middle of May Remainder of year	6 or more Any number Greater nos. Smaller nos.	100 miles May be far at sea Inshore Far out
VII	Manx Shearwater	186	April-August	3 or more 12 or more	Within 200 miles Within 100 miles Direction of flight at dawn and dusk gives direction of land
			September-March	Increasing numbers	Show proximity to land

BIRD PLATE NO.	NAME OF BIRD	HABITAT PAGE NO.	TIME OF YEAR	NUMBER SEEN AT ONE TIME	REASONABLE ASSUMPTION
VII	Other Shearwaters, Southern Hemisphere, except Short-tailed Shearwater	184-5	December to February	3 or more 12 or more	Within 200 miles Within 100 miles Direction of flight at dawn and dusk gives direction of land
			Remainder of year	Any number	May be far from land
VII	Sooty Storm Petrel	181	January Remainder of year	6 or more 3 or less	100 miles May be more than 200 miles off shore
VII	Gray Phalarope or Red-necked Plalarope	194-5	June-July August-November February-May December-January	3 or more Any number Any number 3 or more	75 miles May be far from land (migrating) May be far from land (migrating) 75 miles
VII	Tufted Puffin, Horned Puffin, Atlantic Puffin, Common Guillemot	201-2	Any month	3 or more 6 or more	Within 150 miles Direction of flight at dawn and dusk shows direction of land. 70 miles. Direction of flight at dawn and dusk shows direction of land
VII	Arctic or Brünnich's Guillemot or Pallas's Murre (similar to Common Guillemot)	202	May and June Any month	Any number Increasing numbers	Limit of 220 miles in Atlantic, and then off Grand Banks Show proximity to land
VII	Black Guillemots and Auklets	201-2	Any month	1 or more 6 or more	50 miles 25 miles

New crescent moon (waxing) is always close behind the sun

First quarter moon is at highest point (north or south) as sun is setting

When full moon is rising the sun is always setting

Full moon is always at its highest point (north or south) at midnight

When the full moon is setting the sun is always rising

Last quarter moon always rises at midnight

Last quarter moon is at highest point (i.e., directly north or south)
at sunrise

Old crescent moon (waning) rises at dawn just before the sun
PLATE VIII. Positions of the Moon

Chapter 22

What the Moon Can Tell You

MANY PEOPLE travel at night, from fishermen to foresters, from campers to cross-country walkers. All these sportsmen and natural navigators will find that the moon can be an effective guide. For the moon can give direction, the time of night, and light. On all but a few nights in the month anybody can travel at night in reasonably clear weather with confidence in his ability to find his way by the moon.

The moon produces no light itself: it shines only by the reflection of the light of the sun and (to a very minor extent) other heavenly bodies. The illuminated surface of the moon will thus always point towards the sun and will show the sun's position even when it has set. An imaginary line through the horns of the crescent moon will always lie more or less north and south. A perpendicular erected on the midpoint of this line will point through the illuminated side to the sun's position, whether it is above or below the horizon.

Only in certain places, and at certain times of year, does the sun rise in the precise east and set in the precise west. But quite accurate directions can be obtained from the moon by an observer who knows the true direction and time of sunset or sunrise, or who can work them out from the information in the following chapter.

The full moon is always directly opposite the sun: it rises as the sun sets, reaches its highest point at midnight, sets as the sun rises next morning. A waxing half-moon one week old (called "first quarter") rises when the sun is at its highest peak, that is at noon. The first quarter moon will in its turn reach its own highest peak in the heavens at sunset. A waning half-moon three weeks old ("last quarter") rises at midnight and reaches its highest point at sunrise.

It is important to keep in mind that the moon rises and sets an average of approximately fifty minutes later every night.

The "age of the moon" corresponds directly to the shape and size of its illuminated or shining area. The moon takes a little over seven days to grow from the slimmest hairline crescent to a perfect half-moon; a little over seven days more and it is completely full; in yet another seven days and a bit it has waned into an old half-moon; and at the end of the full cycle of about twenty-nine and a half days it has completed the cycle by diminishing into a new moon again. It is worth setting out the moon's ages (correct to the nearest day) in the form of a table:

New Moon is	0 days of age		
First Quarter is	7 " " "
Full Moon is	15 " " "
Last Quarter is	22 " " "
New Moon is	30 " " "

An observer who has become familiar with the face of the moon above his homeland is often surprised when he travels to a different latitude, for he will instantly note that the surface features are tilted. All heavenly bodies appear upside down in the Southern Hemisphere to people who come from the north, and the moon is no exception to this rule.

The natural navigator planning a night journey is not, however, particularly interested in which way up the moon appears to be. But he is often anxious to predict the time at which the moon will rise; how much of a moon there will be; and the period of night in which he can expect to benefit from its light. As we will see, it is quite easy to commit to memory enough information to work the necessary prediction out quite simply.

By way of example, let us suppose that we wish to find the age of the moon for August 16, 1956. We need but one piece only of given information—the age of the moon on a known previous date. We know, then, that the age of the moon on March 1, 1955, was seven days, and can base the whole of our reckoning on this fact.

For each full year of twelve months following March 1, 1955, we add eleven days to this number (seven). If the sum of these two numbers exceeds thirty, we subtract thirty. The age of the moon on March 1, 1956, is therefore 7 + 11, = 18 days.

For each month following March, including the month in question (in this case August), we add one further day. For each day of our required date in the month we also add one day. If the final sum exceeds thirty once more we subtract thirty.

Thus on August 16, 1956, the age of the moon would be:

	18 days	(on March 1, 1956)
Plus	5	(April, May, June, July, August)
Plus	16	(for August 16)
	39	
Less	30	

The moon therefore would be: 9 days old

Now this calculation may appear involved. Anyone who has been through it, however, will see that it is necessary to remember only the age of the moon on a previous first of March and the numbers eleven and thirty.

From our discovery, by this method of calculation, that the moon was nine days old on August 16, 1956, we can predict the amount of light. At nine days the moon is two days past the first quarter. Thus, provided the sky is clear, the light will be considerable. We can also easily work out the period in which the light will be available; for a first quarter moon rises when the sun is overhead and will itself be overhead at sunset. Since the moon rises an average of fifty minutes later each day, at two days past first quarter it will rise approximately at 1:40 P.M. and will be overhead at approximately 7:52 P.M.

Let us suppose then that we wish to find the approximate time at a point during our journey. On studying the moon we note that it has long passed its highest point—and, indeed, is about halfway between this point and its setting point on the horizon. The time must then be about three hours after the time of the moon's highest point. As the moon was at its highest point at 7:52 P.M., the time must be about 11 P.M.

If you are going on a trip at night and you have a choice of dates on which to set out, you would naturally choose the time of full moon because you would get the greatest amount of moonlight and benefit from this light from sunset to sunrise.

When tables are not available and you wish to find the time of high or low tide in your locality, the following method will be generally correct for most practical purposes. Either from your own observation or by inquiry, determine the time difference between moonrise and the high or low tide for your locality. This will be a constant difference for a particular place. Thus by observing the position of the moon in the sky you will note what time has elapsed since moonrise and therefore what the tide is at any moment.

When I was writing this part of the book, I happened to be on my island Katafanga, in the Fiji group. In this part of Fiji high tide happens to coincide with moonrise and moonset and when the moon is at its highest point it is low tide. This is quite a coincidence and I wish to repeat that the opposite will be the case in some other places in the world and there will be constant time differences between the moonrise and high or low tide. Once established, the difference will remain a constant for each locality.

Also at Katafanga at the time was a friend who was very anxious to do some spearfishing at low tide during the daytime and we all wanted to get out on the reef at night to catch crawfish. This crawfish is called spiny lobster in some places, while the French call it *langouste;* and to catch it the hunter needs a moonless night and low tide on the reef.

I therefore needed to know how much of a moon there would be and at what time it would be low tide to go crawfishing, also at what time low tide would be in the daytime for spearfishing.

I should explain here that in most parts of the world there are four tides a day, two high and two low, which are about six hours apart. Actually, they are about six hours and twelve minutes apart because each day the same tide is an average of fifty minutes later than on the previous day, which makes each change of tide during the day about twelve minutes later. For our particular locality it will be high tide at the time of moonrise and moonset and when the moon is at its highest point it will be low tide. In our case the approximate times of high and low water were found as follows:

The date was March 21, 1955.
By our method the moon was 7 days old on March 1, 1955
                    add 21 days for March 21
          The moon is 28 days old on March 21, 1955
This is 2 days before new moon (30 days old)
Because the moon rises an average of 50 minutes later each day, difference in time of moonrise = 2 × 50 = 1 hour 40 minutes.
New moon rises at 6 A.M. (high tide for our locality)
Therefore on March 21 the moon rises 1 hour and 40 minutes earlier, that is 4:20 A.M., which corresponds to high tide.
The morning low tide will be 6 hours and 12 minutes later, or 10:32 A.M. (for spearfishing)
The afternoon high tide will be 4:44 P.M. (remember each change of tide in a day is about 12 minutes later)
The evening low tide (for crawfishing) will be 10:56 P.M.

From these calculations we discovered that we had perfect conditions for our expedition on the reef at night, with a low tide at 11 P.M. and no moon. On a dark night, with the aid of gasoline lamps to momentarily blind the crawfish and with leather gloves to protect our hands, we caught over two dozen averaging about 1½ pounds each, and very delicious they were.

Chapter 23

Directions from the Sun

IF BIRDS and other animals could talk, they would tell us that the sun provides a more ready means of telling direction than almost anything else. The simplest and most fundamental method for the natural navigator is the sun method: the business of relating the direction of the sun (or shadows) to the desired path or to the compass points around the horizon.

For some time after sunset, of course, the western sky near the horizon will be lighter than the rest of the sky, and during the early morning the eastern sky will be brighter. This, however, will give you only a general idea of east and west, because it is only a few times of the year that the sun will rise due east and set due west.

When you are in a latitude where the midday sun is north of you, the sun's rising point is somewhat north of east, and its setting point equally north of west. When the sun at noon is south of you, the rising point is south of east and the setting point south of west. When the sun reaches its highest point at noon, its direction will be either true south or true north.

In the arctic and antarctic regions the sun may be above the horizon all the time, in which case when the sun is at its lowest point or highest point it is in the true north in the Northern Hemisphere and in the true south in the Southern Hemisphere.

Even with an overcast sky, it is often possible to find the direction of the sun by holding a knife blade vertically on your thumbnail or on some light background such as a piece of paper. When the blade is rotated the finest shadow will show the sun's direction.

Shadow of stick is shortest at noon, when it points either
north or south according to your locality and the time of year

In using the sun or shadows as a reference point to enable you
to maintain a straight line while walking, it is useful to know that
in normal latitudes the sun changes in direction an average of
about 15 degrees per hour.

For greater accuracy simple tables of the sun's direction are
given at the back of this book. These tables cover all times of the
years and locations from latitude 60 degrees north of the equator
to latitude 50 degrees south of the equator.

The ordinary tables of directions of the sun, or azimuth tables,
as they are called, are made for navigators and surveyors and are
bulky and complicated. They are compiled for extreme accuracy
and are not practical for the amateur.

The tables that I have provided will be found accurate within
5 degrees, which is all that is required for cross-country trips on
foot. It is as well to keep in mind that the resultant error of one
degree will be one mile in a 60-mile walk, so that a 5-degree
deviation to one side of your desired track would amount to an
error of 5 miles to one side of your objective in that distance.

It is suggested that before setting out on a journey the reader copy the table of the sun's direction made for his locality, and carry it with him. To show how to use the tables, I shall give an example:

Suppose that we are located near Bangor, Maine. From a map or atlas we find that the nearest parallel of latitude (which lines run east and west on the map) is 45 degrees north latitude. The date is August 10. The time is 10 A.M. We wish to know the direction of the sun.

We turn to the table for latitude 45 degrees north, a copy of which is reproduced on the opposite page. The left-hand column in each table is headed "Hours from Noon." This applies equally to hours before noon and hours after noon. The tables are so arranged in order to reduce their bulk by half. The angle of the sun is the same number of degrees at any particular time before noon as it is the same length of time after noon, the only difference being that the angle is measured in a different direction.

Since 10 A.M. is two hours from noon, from 2 in the left-hand column we look horizontally to the column for the nearest date, which is August 12. This is close enough for our purposes. We see that the direction of the sun for this date and time is 130 degrees. We note from the information at the top of the table that for the morning hours we measure this from north towards east.

A method of finding the north and south points commonly used and trusted, especially by youthful explorers, but which cannot be recommended, is by means of a pocket watch. Just in case you have not heard of it, you are supposed to hold your watch horizontally, set on local time and with the hour hand turned to the sun. If you are in the Northern Hemisphere, a line midway between the hour hand and twelve is then supposedly taken as pointing south. In the Southern Hemisphere, this line is to be taken as indicating north.

It is a great pity to destroy illusions, but in this case it is necessary to do so, because the apparent simplicity of this method may give a very wrong impression as to its accuracy. There are times and places where such use of the watch will be reasonably cor-

LATITUDE 45° NORTH

Before noon read all angles from North to East.
After noon read all angles from North to West.

Hours from Noon	MAR 21 SEP 23	MAR 31 SEP 13	APR 11 SEP 2	APR 22 AUG 22	MAY 1 AUG 12	MAY 12 AUG 2	MAY 26 JUL 19	JUN 10 JUL 3
0	180	180	180	180	180	180	180	180
1	159	158	156	154	152	150	148	146
2	141	138	136	133	130	127	124	122
3	125	122	120	116	114	111	108	106
4	112	109	106	103	101	98	95	94
5	101	98	95	92	90	87	85	83
6	90	87	84	81	79	77	75	73
7					69	67	65	63
Rises & Sets	90°	84°	79°	73°	69°	64°	60°	56°

Specimen table of the sun's direction
(See page 226)

rect, but there are others where serious errors will result from it.
It is hard to understand how a rule which may be as much as 24
degrees in error has become so universally accepted as reliable.
In latitudes between 40 degrees and 60 degrees north or south of
the equator at certain times of the year, the results gotten by this
method will be somewhat close to the truth. But the corrections
necessary, even for these latitudes, make the method too complicated to be of any practical use. The only times when no
correction is necessary are at sunrise and sunset on March 21 and
September 23, and at noon on any day, at any place where the

sun is directly north or south, but then only if your watch happens to be running on *accurate local time*. The watch method is, of course, entirely impractical anywhere near the North or South Poles, as the change in local time with distance east and west increases steadily the closer one approaches the pole.

Chapter 24

Directions from the Stars

ON A CLEAR NIGHT the stars provide a most useful means of maintaining a desired direction. If we, like the Polynesians, consider the overhead night sky as the inside of a huge half shell on which are strewn multitudes of bright points, we see that these points, or stars, are carried around as if they were revolving on a fixed axis. The stars stay in the same relation to one another, pass over the same places on the earth night after night, but rise four minutes earlier each night.

We see the stars rise at the same points each night on the eastern horizon and set at the same points on the western horizon. If we are in the Northern Hemisphere and turn to the south, we notice that the groups of stars which pass above the horizon somewhat to the east of south, attain but a slight elevation when at their highest in the south, and when descending set as far to the west of the south as they had risen to the east of it.

Turning to the north, we see that there are groups of stars which remain visible the whole night, wheeling around a fixed point, the Pole Star, and describing circles of greater or less magnitude according to whether they are at a greater or less distance from that point.

Unlike the sun and the moon, which fluctuate in a north and south direction each day, the star sphere has such a uniform motion as to provide excellent reference points as long as we take into consideration their westward movement in terms of time.

In order to recognize the principal stars visible in the night sky, the ancients divided them into groups, which, with a little imagination, suggested designs of people, animals, birds, fish, etc. They named these groups or constellations accordingly. It takes quite a stretch of the imagination to see some of the designs as they pictured them.

So that you will not be lost in a maze of stars, which at first sight look so much alike, it will be helpful to recognize the patterns of the principal constellations—those which include the brightest stars in all parts of the heavens. Thus you will be able to identify any other star by taking its direction and position from stars in nearby constellations.

In the diagrams on pages 231 to 237, the principal constellations are shown in such a way that if you will follow the dotted lines and form these pictures in your mind, the imaginary connection between certain of the principal stars will enable you to recognize them in the heavens.

In addition to recognizing the stars from their patterns, it is useful to know that the color of certain stars will identify them even if the rest of the sky is clouded over. This is particularly so if the star's position in the sky is also taken into consideration. The distinguishing colors of certain stars are as follows:

Antares, Aldebaran and Betelgeux—reddish
Arcturus, Procyon and Pollux—yellowish
Vega and Altair—bluish white
Capella, Canopus and Sirius, and a number of other stars, are
brilliantly white.

The eight diagrams include constellations covering all parts of the sky and two of stars around the Poles. The stars making a complete revolution around either pole, above the horizon, are called circumpolar stars. Which ones completely revolve above your horizon depends on how far you are from the equator. The diagrams of the stars around the poles in Plates IX and X will be valuable for directional purposes.

In observing the heavens you will see in various parts of the sky very bright starlike bodies which must not be confused with the stars. These are the planets, four of which are bright—Venus,

PLATE IX

Stars in the North Polar Area

PLATE X

Stars in the South Polar Area

Mars, Jupiter and Saturn. Unless you recognize these as planets you may become confused in trying to find them on the star diagrams. They are not shown on these plates, because their movement is different from that of the stars. It is very difficult to keep track of the position of the planets in the heavens without complicated tables.

To avoid confusing planets with any of the bright stars, the following points may be useful:

At sea level stars usually twinkle, but planets shine with a steady luster.

Planets are all overhead at points on the earth within 30 degrees north and south of the equator.

Venus, a brilliant planet, is always near the sun, either ahead of it or behind it, and never more than 47 degrees, or 3 hours from the sun. This means that Venus is always seen before or after sunrise or before or after sunset. Venus may frequently be seen throughout the daylight hours if you know where to look for it.

Mars may be recognized by its color, which is ruddy.

These wanderers in the heavens can best be identified by watching their position each night, when they will be seen to have moved in relation to the stars around them.

In the Northern Hemisphere on a clear night, the easiest way of finding your north point is by the Pole Star. The star diagram in Plate IX will assist in locating this star. If the Pole Star is not visible, or you cannot identify it, look for the point in the heavens around which the stars are pivoting in small circles; this will be true north.

The following are four ways of finding the North Pole in the heavens:

Refer to the star diagram of the north polar area (Plate IX). Look for the two pointers in the Big Dipper. From a point midway between Merak and Dubhe, measure through Dubhe two thumb and middle finger spans of 15 degrees, and this will be the position of the Pole Star. With the arm outstretched as far as possible the average person's span between the thumb and middle

PLATE XI

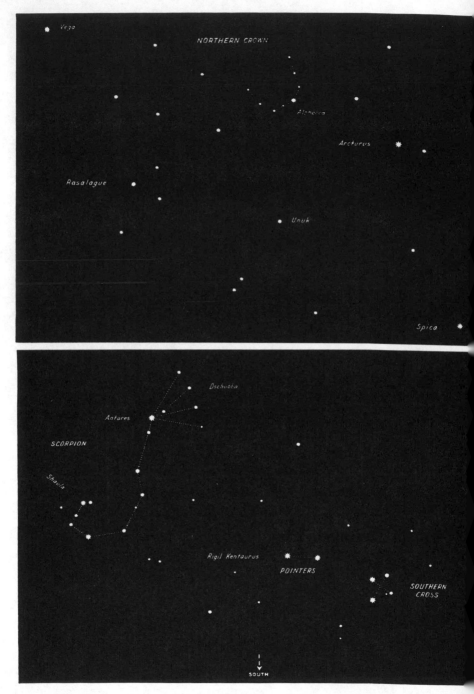

The Heavens around the Northern Crown, the Scorpion, and Southern
Cross

PLATE XII

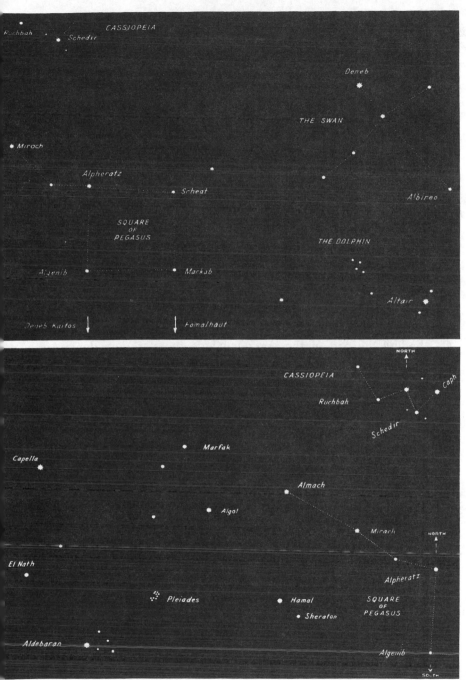

The Heavens around the Square of Pegasus and Cassiopeia

finger—the fingers extended just comfortably—will measure an angle of about 15 degrees.

On a continuation of a line from Arcturus through Benetnasch (Plate XIII) measure three similar spans from Benetnasch, and this will give you the position of the North Pole of the heavens.

The Pole Star can also be found two spans of 15 degrees each from Ruchbah, in the constellation of Cassiopeia (Plate XII) toward Mizar, which is in the handle of the Big Dipper. The constellation of Cassiopeia appears as a "W," the top center of which points towards, and is two spans of 15 degrees each away from, the Pole Star.

With a clear sky you can roughly distinguish the eastern horizon by watching where the stars suddenly appear above it; and the western horizon by the point where the stars are sinking below it. In these parts of the horizon the movement of the stars is most easily noticed.

If you are in the Northern Hemisphere you can determine true south from the stars, even if you cannot identify any of them, by finding the part of the horizon where the stars low down are moving almost directly horizontally to the right. You will not have to look very long to recognize which way the stars are moving, and you can take the central point of these low stars moving in a short, flat arc, as true south.

Similarly in the Southern Hemisphere, stars low down on the northern horizon move fairly horizontally, and provided it is a clear night you should have no difficulty in finding the north point in this manner.

Near the Southern Cross (Plate X) you will note two bright stars known as "the Pointers." Two middle finger to thumb spans, which will be equal to one-half the distance along a line towards Achenar, from the designated point between the Southern Cross and the near Pointer, will give the position of the South Pole of the heavens. The Southern Cross is visible anywhere in the Southern Hemisphere and as far as about 25 degrees north of the equator.

When you are near the equator, the best indication of true directions will be from the east and west points of the horizon,

PLATE XIII

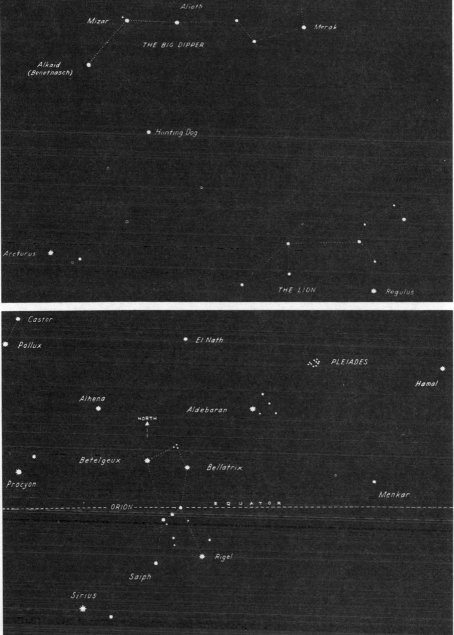

The Heavens around the Big Dipper and Orion

where stars rising exactly east of you will ascend vertically, and after passing overhead will set directly on the western horizon. At all other points of the horizon they appear to the observer to arch away from the vertical.

If the brightest and most beautiful of all constellations, Orion, is visible, you will see from the diagram in Plate XIII that a continuation from Saiph through Betelgeux will give you an approximate north and south line. It is also important to remember that the northern one of the three stars of Orion's belt is practically over the equator. Orion rises, on its side, due east, irrespective of the observer's latitude, reaches its highest point in the heavens over the equator, and sets due west. Seven hours after Orion has passed overhead the Southern Cross will be seen far to the south in its highest position, and can be used as previously described.

Remember that stars rise and set at the same points on the horizon as long as the observer remains in the same latitude, but that they rise and set approximately four minutes earlier each night. A star rising due east of you does not pass directly overhead unless you are at the equator.

To an observer standing at either pole, stars will revolve in small circles above him and in gradually widening circles parallel to the horizon. The Pole Star is at no time visible at sea level more than one degree south of the equator. In the southern sky, unfortunately, there is no Pole Star by which to orient yourself.

In the absence of a compass, or even as a means of checking a compass, a convenient method of determining true south is by observing the Southern Cross. This well-known constellation appears nearly upright when it reaches its highest point, and an observer facing it at that time is looking very nearly directly south, with his right hand to the west, his left hand to the east and his back to the north.

Chapter 25

Telling the Time by the Stars

THE STARS which appear to revolve around the North and South Poles of the heavens provide a natural clock to tell the local time. In the Northern Hemisphere the two bright stars in the Big Dipper, which are known as the Pointers to the Pole Star, can be used as the hour hand; and the position of the Pole Star can be taken as the imaginary center around which the hand rotates.

In order to tell the time by the stars, it is necessary for us to determine Local Star Time—which is significant only to a navigator or astronomer; and from this, to obtain our Local Sun Time —which is what is shown on our everyday clocks and watches.

The steps to be taken to arrive at the local time can be seen in the following example:

The date is August 28 and the Pointers of the Big Dipper are at seven o'clock on the imaginary Star Clock (12-hour clock; see diagram on page 240).

To find first of all the Local Star Time:

Subtract the time on the Star Clock,
7 hours, from 12 = 5
Multiply by   2 = 10
Add 11 (always) = 21 hours = Local Star Time.

Local Star Time is faster than sun time (civil time), which is the time usually kept on our clocks, by one day a year; which equals two hours a month, or four minutes a day.

So in order to find the Local Sun Time we must convert the Local Star Time in the following manner:

Star Clock, using the Pole Star and Big Dipper

Subtract two hours for each full month since March 23 and four minutes for each day of the remaining part of the month.

Our date is August 28.
March 23 to August 23 = 5 (months) × 2 hours = 10 hours
August 23 to August 28 = 5 (days) × 4 minutes a day =
$$20 \text{ minutes}$$
Total: 10 hours 20 minutes
Subtract this from the Local Star Time—21 hours
minus 10 hours 20 minutes
= Local Civil Time: 10:40 P.M.

If the Big Dipper is below the horizon or not visible because of clouds, we can use another conspicuous group of stars, Cassiopeia, to tell the time. This constellation has the shape of a straggly W, and revolves around the Pole Star.

As Cassiopeia is on the opposite side of the Pole Star from the Big Dipper, there will be many occasions when you can use it if the Big Dipper is below the horizon.

The numbers around the accompanying diagram are not dates or hours of your day but are figures to facilitate the conversion of the position of the stars to your local time.

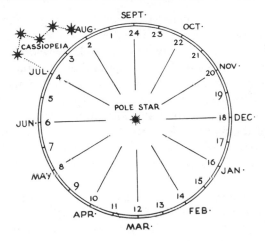

Star Clock, using Cassiopeia

One particular star of Cassiopeia is used—the right hand star of the group forming the W when it is upright, named Caph (Plate XII).

To tell the time from this star proceed as follows:

> The imaginary clock dial has the Pole Star at the center, and is divided into 24 parts, with 24 on top and numbered counterclockwise.
>
> Read the number on this circle which corresponds with the imaginary hand connecting the Pole Star with Caph.
>
> In this case it is 4.
>
> To this add the number corresponding to your approximate date, which in this example is February 1. The number is 14.
>
> $$4 + 14 = 18 \text{ hours} = 6 \text{ P.M.}$$
>
> If the addition comes to more than 24, subtract 24.

This does not take into account any error resulting from Daylight Saving Time, which we may have in our locality; or a Zone Time used for convenience. Any local difference can be found by inquiry.

It is not always realized that the Big Dipper and Cassiopeia are visible well south of the equator on their upward revolution around the Pole Star. They can be used, therefore, by most people in southern latitudes for telling the time at night.

Those too far south to observe these constellations, or who find them clouded over, can obtain time from the position of the Southern Cross. (Incidentally, although there is no star in the position of the South Pole in the heavens, the place in the southern sky of the focal point of movement can be found by extending the long axis of the cross 4½ times from the bottom of the cross.)

Taking the long axis of the cross as the hand of the clock, and the foot of the cross as the center of the dial, we can make an imaginary division of the dial into twenty-four hours instead of the conventional twelve (see diagram below).

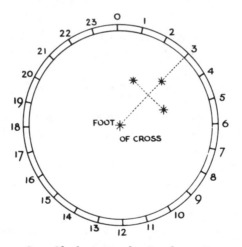

Star Clock, using the Southern Cross

Reading the "time" from the position of the long axis of the cross, we subtract 2 hours for every month and 4 minutes for each day since the last March 29. The result will be the time after midnight on the 24-hour clock.

Example:

Date: May 31
Time on star clock: 3 hours
Borrow 24 hours
3 hours + 24 hours = 27 hours
March 29 to May 29 = 2 (months) × 2 hours = 4 hours
May 29 to May 31 = 2 (days) × 4 minutes = 8 minutes
Subtract 4 hours, 8 minutes from 24 hours = 22 hours, 52 minutes
Subtract 12 hours − local time· 10:52 P.M.

Selective Bibliography

ALEXANDER, W. B. *Birds of the Ocean,* 2nd ed. London, Putnam, 1955.

ARCTOWSKI, HENRYK. "Exploration of Antarctic Lands," *Geographical Journal,* Vol. XVII (1901), pp. 150-180.

AUFRÈRE, L. "L'Orientation des dunes continentales," *Report of Proceedings of* (12th) *International Geographic Congress,* 1928 (Cambridge, 1930), pp. 220-231.

BAER, K. E. VON. *Why Are the Right Banks of Our Rivers Flowing Northwards High, and the Left Depressed?* (in Russian). Moscow, 1857.

BAGNOLD, R. A. "Navigating Ashore," *Journal of the Institute of Navigation,* Vol. VI (April, 1953), pp. 184-193.

BIERVLIET, J. J. VAN. *L'Homme droit et l'homme gauche.* Paris, 1901.

BONNIER, PIERRE. "La Question de l'orientation lointaine," *Revue Scientifique,* Sér. 5, Vol. II, Paris, 1910, pp. 837-839.

BOUGAINVILLE, LOUIS ANTOINE DE. *A Voyage Round the World in the Years 1766, 1767, 1768 and 1769.* London, 1772.

BYRD, RICHARD E. *Little America: Aerial Exploration in the Antarctic: the Flight to the South Pole.* New York and London, 1930.

CABOT, THOMAS D. "Finding the Way," *Handbook of Travel,* Cambridge, Mass., 1935, pp. 180-182.

CAMPBELL, D. "Notes on Scouting," *Royal United Services Institute Journal,* Vol. LXI, London, 1916, pp. 375-391.

CANNON, HELEN L. "Botanical Methods of Prospecting for Uranium," *Mining Engineer* (February, 1954), pp. 217-220.
"The Effects of Uranium-Vanadium Deposits on the Vegetation of the Colorado Plateau," *American Journal of Science,* Vol. CCL (October, 1952), pp. 735-770.

CHAPMAN, F. SPENCER. "On Not Getting Lost," *The Boys' Country Book* (ed. John Moore). London, Collins, 1955, pp. 39-48.

CHARLEVOIX, PÈRE FRANCOIS-XAVIER DE. "Journal d'un voyage dans l'Amérique septentrionale," *Histoire et description générales de la Nouvelle-France*, Vol. III, Paris, 1744, p. 304.

CLIFFE, EDWARD. "The Voyage of Mr. John Winter into the South Sea by the Streight of Magellan, in consort with Francis Drake, Begun in the Yeere 1577," *Hakluyt*, Vol. VIII, p. 91.

CRICHTON, A. *History of Arabia*, Vol. I, Edinburgh, 1833, p. 111.

CUILLANDRE, JOSEPH. *La droite et la gauche dans les poèmes homériques en concordance avec la doctrine pythagoricienne et avec la tradition celtique*, Paris, 1944, pp. 460-81.

DARWIN, CHARLES, letter published in *Nature*, Vol. VIII, London, 1873, p. 396.

DIDEROT, D. (transl. and ed. M. Jourdain) "Letter on the Blind," *Early Philosophical Works*, Chicago, 1916, pp. 68-141.

DODGE, RICHARD I. *Our Wild Indians*. Hartford, Conn., 1890.

DRESCO, ÉDOUARD. *L'Orientation en randonnée*, Paris, 1945, p. 66.

DRESSLAR, F. B. "On the Pressure Sense of the Drum of the Ear and Facial Vision," *American Journal of Psychology*, Vol. V, 1893, pp. 344-350.

DUMAS, J. B. *L'Homme à la main heureuse. La droite et la gauche*. Unpublished MS in Bibliothèque Nationale, Paris, 1938.

Explorer Scout Manual, New York, 1946, p. 382.

FALGER, DR. F. *Das Orientierungsvermögen. Deutscher und Österreichischen Alpenverein Mitteilungen*. Munich, 1924, pp. 201-2.

FARROW, EDWARD S. *Mountain Scouting*. New York, 1881, pp. 100-106.

FISCHER, M. H. "Die Orientierung im Raume bei Wirbeltieren und beim Menschen," *Handbuch der norm. und path. Physiol.* Vol. XV, part 2. Berlin, 1931.

FISHER, JAMES. *The Fulmar*, Collins' *New Naturalist Series*. London, 1952.

FISHER, JAMES and LOCKLEY, R. M. *Sea Birds*, Collins' *New Naturalist Series*. London, 1954.

FREE, MONTAGUE. "Who Says Plants Follow the Sun?" *Home Garden*, November, 1953, Vol. XXII, pp. 62-65.

FRERE, H. BARTLE E. "Notes on the Runn of Cutch and Neighboring Region," *Journal of the Royal Geographical Society,* Vol. XL, London, 1870, pp. 181-207.

GATTY, HAROLD, co-author with WILEY POST. *Around the World in Eight Days.* Chicago, 1931.

GATTY, HAROLD. *The Raft Book.* New York, 1943.

GULDBERG, F. O. "Die Circularbewegung als thierische Grundbewegung, ihre Ursache, Phänomenalität und Bedeutung," *Zeitschrift für Biologie,* Vol, XXXV, 1897, pp. 419-458.

GULDBERG, G. A. "Über die morphologische und functionelle Asymmetrie der Gliedmassen beim Menschen und bei den höheren Vertebraten," *Biol. Centralbl.,* Vol. XVI, 1896, pp. 806-813.

HEINE-GELDERN, ROBERT. "Heyerdahl's Hypothesis of Polynesian Origins: a Criticism," *Geographical Journal,* Vol. CXVI, 1950, pp. 183-192.

HELLER, TH. *Studien zur Blindenpsychologie.* Leipzig, 1904.

HENSHAW, HENRY W. *The Book of Birds,* National Geographic Society, Washington, 1918, pp. 187-190.

HERTZ, R. "La Préeminence de la main droite," *Revue Philosophique,* Vol. II, 1909, p. 553.

HORNELL, JAMES. "The Role of Birds in Early Navigation," *Antiquity,* Vol. LXXIX, 1946, pp. 142-149.

HOUZEAU, J. C. *Études sur les facultés mentales des animaux comparées à celles de l'homme.* Leipzig, 1872.

HOWITT, A. W. "A Letter," *Nature,* August 21, 1873, Vol. VIII, p. 323.

IDRIESS, ION L. *The Scout.* Sydney, 1943, p. 123.

JACCARD, PIERRE. "Une enquête sur la désorientation en montagne," *Bull. Soc. Vaud. Sci. Nat.,* Vol. LVI, No. 217, 1926, pp. 151-159.

JACCARD, PIERRE. *Le sens de la direction et l'orientation lointaine chez l'homme.* Paris, 1932, p. 354.

JARVAL, EMILE. "The Sixth Sense," *On Becoming Blind,* 1905, pp. 152-169.

JESPERSEN, P. "On the Frequency of Birds over the High Atlantic Ocean," *Verhandl. VI Internat. Ornith. Kongress, Copenhagen* (1926), 1929, pp. 163-172.

KELLY, WILLIAM. "On the Stationary Clouds of the St. Lawrence," *Nautical Magazine,* 1845, pp. 303-309.

KING, W. J. H. "Pioneer Desert Exploration," *Geographical Journal*, June, 1931, Vol. LXXVII, pp. 541-547.

KLEBELSBERG, R. VON. *Handbuch der Gletscherkunde und Glatialgeologie.* Vol. I, Vienna, Springer, 1948, pp. 127-131.

LAFITAU, PÈRE JOSEPH-FRANÇOIS. *Les moeurs des sauvages Amériquains comparées aux moeurs des premiers temps*, Vol. II, Paris, 1724, pp. 240-241.

LANE, FRANK W. "Have Animals a Time-Sense?" *Animal Wonderland*, London, 1948, pp. 93-110.

LEECHMAN, DOUGLAS. *The Hiker's Handbook.* New York, 1944, p. 220.

LINDER, CH. "Observations sur les Fourmilières-Boussoles," *Bulletin de la Société Vaudoise des Sciences Naturelles*, Vol. XLIV, No. 164, 1938, pp. 303-310.

LINDSAY, H. A. *The Bushman's Handbook.* Sydney, 1950.

LINSCHOTEN, J. H. VAN. *Voyages.* London, 1598.

LOCKLEY, R. M. *Shearwaters.* London, Dent, 1942.

LOCKLEY, R. M. *Puffins.* London, Dent, 1953.

LUND, F. H. "Physical Asymmetries and Disorientation," *American Journal of Psychology*, January, 1930, Vol. XLII, pp. 51-62.

MACH, E. "Über Orientierungsempfindungen," *Schr. Ver. Verbr. Naturw. Kenntnisse in Wien*, 37, 1897.

MADIGAN, C. T. "The Australian Sand-Ridge Deserts," *Geographical Review*, Vol. XXVI, 1936, pp. 205-227.

MAGAREY, A. T. "Tracking by the Australian Aborigine," *Proceedings of the Royal Geographical Society of Australasia*, Vol. III, 1899, p. 120.

MANCIOT, ANDRÉ. *Orientation manuel pratique*, Collection de la revue "Camping." Paris, 1943.

MARLOTH, R. *The Flora of South Africa.* London, 1932.

MAWSON, DOUGLAS. *The Home of the Blizzard*, 2 vols. London, 1915.

MILLS, ENOS ABICAIL. *The Adventures of a Nature Guide.* New York, 1920.

MURPHY, ROBERT CUSHMAN. *Oceanic Birds of South America*, 2 vols. New York, 1936.

MACLEOD, R. B. and ROFF, M. F. "An Experiment in Temporal Disorientation," *Acta Psychol. Hague*, Vol. I, 1936, pp. 381-423.

248   SELECTIVE BIBLIOGRAPHY

Post, Wiley and Gatty Harold, *Around the World in Eight Days*. Chicago, 1931.

Prinsep, James. "Note on the Nautical Instruments of the Arabs," *Introduction à l'astronomie nautique Arabe* by Gabriel Ferrand. Paris, 1928.

Rankama, Kalervo. "Some Recent Trends in Prospecting Chemical, Biogeochemical and Geobotanical Methods," *Mining and Metallurgy*, June, 1947, pp. 282-284.

Ratcliffe, F. N., Gay, F. J. and Greaves, T. *Australian Termites*, Melbourne, 1952.

Rockie, W. A. "Snowdrift Erosion in the Palouse," *Geographical Review*, July, 1951, pp. 457-463.

Ryan, T. A. and M. S. "Geographical Orientation," *American Journal of Psychology*, Vol. LIII, Ithaca, 1940, pp. 204-215.

Salt (periodical), "Living off the Land, a Manual of Bushcraft," Melbourne, 1944.

Sandstrom, Carl Ivar. *Orientation in the Present Space*. Stockholm, 1951, pp. 128-191.

Saussure, Léopold de. "L'origine de la rose des vents et l'invention de la boussole," *Introduction à l'astronomie nautique Arabe* by Gabriel Ferrand. Paris, 1928.

Schaeffer, A. A. "Spiral Movement in Man," *Journal of Morphology and Physiology*, June, 1928, Vol. XLV, pp. 293-398.

Scott, Robert Falcon. (ed. Leonard Huxley), *The Journals of Captain R. F. Scott*. Vol. I of *Scott's Last Expedition*, 2 vols. London, 1913.

Seton, Ernest Thompson, *The Book of Woodcraft*. New York, 1921.

Shackleton, Ernest H. *The Heart of the Antarctic*, 2 vols. London, 1910.

Sommerfelt, Carl Jacob. *Orienteringsboka, händbök i tur og kongurransorientering*. Oslo, J. Dybwad, 1946.

Speiss, F. *Die "Meteor" Fahrt*. Berlin, 1928.

Supa, Michael, Cotzin, Milton and Dallenbach, Karl M. "Facial Vision: the Perception of Obstacles by the Blind," *American Journal of Psychology*, April, 1944, Vol. LVII, No. 2, pp. 133-183.

Szymanski, J. S. "Versuche über den Richtungsinn beim Menschen," *Arch. für die grs. Physiologie*. Bonn, 1913, pp. 158-170.

TROWBRIDGE, C. C. "On Fundamental Methods of Orientation and Imaginary Maps," *Science*. New Series, Vol. XXXVIII (July-December, 1913), New York, pp. 888-897.

TRUSCHEL, L. "Der sechste Sinn der Blinden," *Zeitschrift für Exper. Pädagogik*, Vol. III, 1906, pp. 109-142, Vol. IV, 1907, pp. 129-155, Vol. V, 1907, pp. 66-77.

VILLEY, PIERRE. *The World of the Blind: a Psychological Study.* London, 1930, pp. 101-131.

WIDMER, CHARLES. "Die Desorientierung in den Bergen," *Die Alpen*, Bern, January, 1927, Vol. III, pp. 218-223.

WIESNER, JULIUS VON. *Der Lichtgenuss der Pflanzen, photometrische und physiologische Untersuchungen.* Vol. VII(1), Leipzig, 1907, p. 322.

WRANGELL [or WRANGEL], FERDINAND VON. *Narrative of an Expedition to the Polar Sea in 1820-1823.* London, 1840.

WRIGHT, JOHN KIRTLAND. "Primitive Cartography," *Geographical Review*, July, 1932, Vol. XXII, No. 3, pp. 491-492.

YOSHIOKA, JOSEPH. "A Direction-Orientation Study with Visitors at the New York World's Fair," *Journal of General Psychology*, Vol. XXVII, 1942, pp. 3-33.

SIMPLE TABLES OF DIRECTIONS OF THE SUN

(For procedure in using these tables for orientation refer to Chapter 23, "Directions from the Sun")

LATITUDE 2½° NORTH

Hours from Noon	MAR 21 → SEP 23	MAR 31 SEP 13	APR 11 SEP 2	APR 22 AUG 22	MAY 1 AUG 12	MAY 12 AUG 2	MAY 26 JUL 19	JUN 10 JUL 3 ↓
0	180	x	0	0	0	0	0	0
1	99	84	69	57	49	42	37	34
2	94	86	78	71	65	60	55	52
3	92	87	81	76	71	67	63	61
4	91	87	82	78	74	71	67	65
5	91	87	82	78	75	72	69	67
6	90	86	82	78	75	72	69	67
Rises & Sets	90°	86°	82°	78°	75°	72°	69°	67°

Hours from Noon	SEP 23 → MAR 21	OCT 4 MAR 11	OCT 14 MAR 1	OCT 25 FEB 18	NOV 3 FEB 9	NOV 14 JAN 29	NOV 27 JAN 16	DEC 11 JAN 2 ↓
0	180	180	180	180	180	180	180	180
1	99	113	125	134	140	145	149	151
2	94	102	110	116	121	126	130	132
3	92	98	104	109	113	117	120	122
4	91	96	101	105	108	112	115	117
5	91	95	99	103	106	109	112	114
Rises & Sets	90°	94°	98°	102°	105°	108°	111°	113°

LATITUDE 0° (EQUATOR)

Hours from Noon	MAR 21 → SEP 23	MAR 31 SEP 13	APR 11 SEP 2	APR 22 AUG 22	MAY 1 AUG 12	MAY 12 AUG 2	MAY 26 JUL 19	JUN 10 JUL 3 ↓
0	x	x	x	0	0	0	0	0
1	90	75	61	51	44	39	34	31
2	90	82	74	67	62	57	52	50
3	90	84	79	73	69	65	61	59
4	90	85	81	76	73	69	66	64
5	90	86	82	78	74	71	68	66
6	90	86	82	78	75	72	69	67
Rises & Sets	90°	86°	82°	78°	75°	72°	69°	67°

Hours from Noon	SEP 23 → MAR 21	OCT 4 MAR 11	OCT 14 MAR 1	OCT 25 FEB 18	NOV 3 FEB 9	NOV 14 JAN 29	NOV 27 JAN 16	DEC 11 JAN 2 ↓
0	x	x	x	180	180	180	180	180
1	90	105	119	129	136	141	146	149
2	90	98	106	113	118	123	128	130
3	90	96	101	107	111	115	119	121
4	90	95	99	104	107	111	114	116
5	90	94	98	102	106	109	112	114
6	90	94	98	102	105	108	111	113
Rises & Sets	90°	94°	98°	102°	105°	108°	111°	113°

Before noon read all angles from North to East. *After* noon read all angles from North to West. Where an X appears the sun's direction is changing too rapidly to be of any practical value.

LATITUDE 7½° NORTH

Hours from Noon	MAR → 21	MAR 31	APR 11	APR 22	MAY 1	MAY 12	MAY 26	JUN 10 ↓
	SEP 23	SEP 13	SEP 2	AUG 22	AUG 12	AUG 2	JUL 19	JUL 3
0	180	180	x	x	0	0	0	0
1	116	103	87	72	62	53	44	41
2	103	95	87	79	73	67	62	58
3	97	92	86	80	76	72	68	65
4	94	89	85	80	77	73	70	68
5	92	88	84	80	76	73	70	68
6	90	86	82	78	75	72	69	67
Rises & Sets	90°	86°	82°	78°	75°	72°	69°	67°

Hours from Noon	SEP → 23	OCT 4	OCT 14	OCT 25	NOV 3	NOV 14	NOV 27	DEC 11 ↓
	MAR 21	MAR 11	MAR 1	FEB 18	FEB 9	JAN 29	JAN 16	JAN 2
0	180	180	180	180	180	180	180	180
1	116	127	136	142	147	150	153	155
2	103	110	116	123	127	131	135	137
3	97	103	108	113	117	120	124	126
4	94	99	103	108	111	114	117	119
5	92	96	100	104	107	110	113	115
6	90							
Rises & Sets	90°	94°	98°	102°	105°	108°	111°	113°

LATITUDE 5° NORTH

Hours from Noon	MAR → 21	MAR 31	APR 11	APR 22	MAY 1	MAY 12	MAY 26	JUN 10 ↓
	SEP 23	SEP 13	SEP 2	AUG 22	AUG 12	AUG 2	JUL 19	JUL 3
0	180	180	x	0	0	0	0	0
1	108	93	78	64	55	47	41	37
2	99	91	83	75	69	64	58	55
3	95	89	84	78	74	70	66	63
4	93	88	84	79	76	72	69	66
5	91	87	83	78	76	73	70	67
6	90	86	82	78	75	72	69	67
Rises & Sets	90°	86°	82°	78°	75°	72°	69°	67°

Hours from Noon	SEP → 23	OCT 4	OCT 14	OCT 25	NOV 3	NOV 14	NOV 27	DEC 11 ↓
	MAR 21	MAR 11	MAR 1	FEB 18	FEB 9	JAN 29	JAN 16	JAN 2
0	180	180	180	180	180	180	180	180
1	108	121	131	139	144	148	151	153
2	99	106	113	120	124	129	132	135
3	95	101	106	111	115	119	122	124
4	93	97	102	106	110	113	116	118
5	91	95	100	104	107	110	113	115
6	90							
Rises & Sets	90°	94°	98°	102°	105°	108°	111°	113°

Before noon read all angles from North to East. *After* noon read all angles from North to West. Where an X appears the sun's direction is changing too rapidly to be of any practical value.

LATITUDE 12½° NORTH

Hours from Noon	MAR ↑ 21	MAR 31	APR 11	APR 22	MAY 1	MAY 12	MAY 26	JUN 10
	SEP 23	SEP 13	AUG 2	AUG 22	AUG 12	AUG 2	JUL 19	JUL 3 ↓
0	180	180	x	x	x	x	x	x
1	129	119	105	90	79	67	57	52
2	111	103	96	88	82	75	69	66
3	102	97	91	86	81	77	72	70
4	97	93	88	83	80	76	73	71
5	93	89	85	81	78	75	72	70
6	90	86	82	78	75	72	69	67
Rises & Sets	90°	86°	82°	78°	75°	72°	68°	66°

Hours from Noon	SEP ↑ 23	OCT 4	OCT 14	OCT 25	NOV 3	NOV 14	NOV 27	DEC 11
	MAR 21	MAR 11	MAR 1	FEB 18	FEB 9	JAN 29	JAN 16	JAN 2 ↓
0	180	180	180	180	180	180	180	180
1	129	137	143	148	151	154	156	157
2	111	117	123	128	131	135	138	140
3	102	107	112	117	120	124	127	128
4	97	102	106	110	113	116	119	121
5	93	97	101	105	108	111	114	116
6	90							
Rises & Sets	90°	94°	98°	102°	105°	108°	111°	114°

LATITUDE 10° NORTH

Hours from Noon	MAR ↑ 21	MAR 31	APR 11	APR 22	MAY 1	MAY 12	MAY 26	JUN 10
	SEP 23	SEP 13	SEP 2	AUG 22	AUG 12	AUG 2	JUL 19	JUL 3 ↓
0	180	180	180	x	x	x	x	x
1	123	111	96	81	70	60	51	46
2	107	99	91	83	77	71	66	62
3	100	94	89	83	79	74	70	67
4	96	91	87	82	78	75	71	69
5	93	89	84	80	77	74	71	69
6	90	86	82	78	75	72	69	67
Rises & Sets	90°	86°	82°	78°	75°	72°	69°	67°

Hours from Noon	SEP ↑ 23	OCT 4	OCT 14	OCT 25	NOV 3	NOV 14	NOV 27	DEC 11
	MAR 21	MAR 11	MAR 1	FEB 18	FEB 9	JAN 29	JAN 16	JAN 2 ↓
0	180	180	180	180	180	180	180	180
1	123	132	140	146	149	152	155	156
2	107	114	120	126	130	133	137	139
3	100	105	110	115	119	122	125	127
4	96	100	105	109	112	115	118	120
5	93	97	101	105	108	111	114	116
6	90							
Rises & Sets	90°	94°	98°	102°	105°	108°	111°	113°

Before noon read all angles from North to East. *After* noon read all angles from North to West. Where an X appears the sun's direction is changing too rapidly to be of any practical value.

LATITUDE 17½° NORTH

Hours from Noon	MAR 21 / SEP 23 →	MAR 31 / SEP 13	APR 11 / SEP 2	APR 22 / AUG 22	MAY 1 / AUG 12	MAY 12 / AUG 2	MAY 26 / JUL 19	JUN 10 / JUL 3 ↓
0	180	180	180	180	x	x	x	x
1	138	131	121	109	98	86	74	66
2	117	111	104	97	91	84	78	74
3	107	102	96	91	87	82	78	75
4	100	95	91	87	83	80	76	74
5	95	91	87	83	80	76	73	71
6	90	86	82	79	76	73	70	68
Rises & Sets	90°	86°	82°	77°	74°	71°	68°	66°

Hours from Noon	SEP 23 / MAR 21 →	OCT 4 / MAR 11	OCT 14 / MAR 1	OCT 25 / FEB 18	NOV 3 / FEB 9	NOV 14 / JAN 29	NOV 27 / JAN 16	DEC 11 / JAN 2 ↓
0	180	180	180	180	180	180	180	180
1	138	144	149	152	155	157	158	160
2	117	123	128	133	136	139	141	143
3	107	112	116	120	123	126	129	131
4	100	104	108	112	115	118	121	123
5	95	98	102	106	109	112	115	117
Rises & Sets	90°	94°	98°	103°	106°	109°	112°	114°

LATITUDE 15° NORTH

Hours from Noon	MAR 21 / SEP 23 →	MAR 31 / SEP 13	APR 11 / SEP 2	APR 22 / AUG 22	MAY 1 / AUG 12	MAY 12 / AUG 2	MAY 26 / JUL 19	JUN 10 / JUL 3 ↓
0	180	180	180	180	x	x	x	x
1	134	125	114	100	88	76	65	58
2	114	107	100	92	86	80	74	70
3	105	99	94	88	84	81	75	72
4	98	94	90	85	81	78	74	72
5	94	90	86	82	79	76	73	70
6	90	86	82	78	75	73	70	68
Rises & Sets	90°	86°	82°	78°	74°	71°	68°	66°

Hours from Noon	SEP 23 / MAR 21 →	OCT 4 / MAR 11	OCT 14 / MAR 1	OCT 25 / FEB 18	NOV 3 / FEB 9	NOV 14 / JAN 29	NOV 27 / JAN 16	DEC 11 / JAN 2 ↓
0	180	180	180	180	180	180	180	180
1	134	141	146	150	153	155	157	159
2	114	120	126	131	134	137	140	142
3	105	110	114	119	122	125	128	130
4	98	103	107	111	114	117	120	122
5	94	98	102	106	109	112	114	116
6	90							
Rises & Sets	90°	94°	98°	102°	106°	109°	112°	114°

Before noon read all angles from North to East. *After* noon read all angles from North to West. Where an X appears the sun's direction is changing too rapidly to be of any practical value.

LATITUDE 22½° NORTH

Hours from Noon	MAR 21 → SEP 23	MAR 31 SEP 13	APR 11 SEP 2	APR 22 AUG 22	MAY 1 AUG 12	MAY 12 AUG 2	MAY 26 JUL 19	JUN 10 JUL 3 ↓
0	180	180	180	180	180	180	180	0
1	145	140	133	124	115	105	93	85
2	124	118	112	105	100	94	87	83
3	111	106	101	96	92	88	83	80
4	102	98	94	90	86	83	79	77
5	96	92	88	84	81	78	75	73
6	90	86	83	79	76	73	70	69
Rises & Sets	90°	86°	81°	77°	74°	70°	67°	65°

Hours from Noon	SEP 23 → MAR 21	OCT 4 MAR 11	OCT 14 MAR 1	OCT 25 FEB 18	NOV 3 FEB 9	NOV 14 JAN 29	NOV 27 JAN 16	DEC 11 JAN 2 ↓
0	180	180	180	180	180	180	180	180
1	145	149	153	155	157	159	160	161
2	124	128	133	137	139	142	144	145
3	111	115	120	123	126	129	131	133
4	102	106	110	114	117	120	122	124
5	96	100	103	107	110	112	115	117
6	90							
Rises & Sets	90°	94°	99°	103°	106°	110°	113°	115°

LATITUDE 20° NORTH

Hours from Noon	MAR 21 → SEP 23	MAR 31 SEP 13	APR 11 SEP 2	APR 22 AUG 22	MAY 1 AUG 12	MAY 12 AUG 2	MAY 26 JUL 19	JUN 10 JUL 3 ↓
0	180	180	180	180	180	180	180	x
1	142	136	127	117	107	95	83	75
2	121	115	108	101	95	89	83	78
3	109	104	99	93	89	85	80	77
4	101	97	93	88	85	81	78	75
5	95	91	87	83	80	77	74	72
6	90	86	82	79	76	73	70	68
Rises & Sets	90°	86°	82°	79°	76°	73°	70°	68°

Hours from Noon	SEP 23 → MAR 21	OCT 4 MAR 11	OCT 14 MAR 1	OCT 25 FEB 18	NOV 3 FEB 9	NOV 14 JAN 29	NOV 27 JAN 16	DEC 11 JAN 2 ↓
0	180	180	180	180	180	180	180	180
1	142	147	151	154	156	158	159	160
2	121	126	131	135	138	140	143	144
3	109	113	118	122	125	128	130	132
4	101	105	109	113	116	119	122	123
5	95	99	103	107	109	112	115	117
6	90							
Rises & Sets	90°	94°	99°	103°	106°	109°	112°	115°

Before noon read all angles from North to East. *After* noon read all angles from North to West. Where an X appears the sun's direction is changing too rapidly to be of any practical value.

LATITUDE 27½° NORTH

Hours from Noon	MAR 21 / SEP 23 →	MAR 31 / SEP 13	APR 11 / SEP 2	APR 22 / AUG 22	MAY 1 / AUG 12	MAY 12 / AUG 2	MAY 26 / JUL 19	JUN 10 / JUL 3 ↓
0	180	180	180	180	180	180	180	180
1	150	146	141	135	129	121	112	105
2	129	124	119	113	108	103	97	93
3	115	110	106	101	97	93	89	86
4	105	101	97	93	90	86	83	80
5	97	93	90	86	83	80	77	75
6	90	86	83	79	77	74	71	69
Rises & Sets	90°	85°	81°	76°	73°	70°	66°	64°

Hours from Noon	SEP 23 / MAR 21 →	OCT 4 / MAR 11	OCT 14 / MAR 1	OCT 25 / FEB 18	NOV 3 / FEB 9	NOV 14 / JAN 29	NOV 27 / JAN 16	DEC 11 / JAN 2 ↓
0	180	180	180	180	180	180	180	180
1	150	153	156	158	159	161	162	163
2	129	133	136	140	142	144	146	147
3	115	119	123	126	129	131	133	135
4	105	109	112	116	118	121	123	125
5	97	101	104	108	110	113	115	117
Rises & Sets	90°	94°	99°	104°	107°	110°	114°	116°

Before noon read all angles from North to East. *After* noon read all angles from North to West.

LATITUDE 25° NORTH

Hours from Noon	MAR 21 / SEP 23 →	MAR 31 / SEP 13	APR 11 / SEP 2	APR 22 / AUG 22	MAY 1 / AUG 12	MAY 12 / AUG 2	MAY 26 / JUL 19	JUN 10 / JUL 3 ↓
0	180	180	180	180	180	180	180	180
1	148	143	137	130	123	114	103	95
2	126	121	116	109	104	98	92	88
3	113	108	104	99	95	90	86	83
4	104	100	96	91	88	85	81	79
5	96	93	89	85	82	79	76	74
6	90	86	83	79	76	74	71	69
Rises & Sets	90°	86°	81°	77°	73°	70°	67°	64°

Hours from Noon	SEP 23 / MAR 21 →	OCT 4 / MAR 11	OCT 14 / MAR 1	OCT 25 / FEB 18	NOV 3 / FEB 9	NOV 14 / JAN 29	NOV 27 / JAN 16	DEC 11 / JAN 2 ↓
0	180	180	180	180	180	180	180	180
1	148	151	154	157	158	160	161	162
2	126	131	135	138	141	143	145	146
3	113	117	121	125	127	130	132	134
4	104	108	111	115	118	120	123	125
5	96	100	104	107	110	113	115	117
6	90							
Rises & Sets	90°	94°	99°	103°	107°	110°	113°	116°

Before noon read all angles from North to East. *After* noon read all angles from North to West.

LATITUDE 32½° NORTH

Hours from Noon	MAR →21 SEP 23	MAR 31 SEP 13	APR 11 SEP 2	APR 22 AUG 22	MAY 1 AUG 12	MAY 12 AUG 2	MAY 26 JUL 19	JUN 10 JUL 3 ↓
0	180	180	180	180	180	180	180	180
1	153	151	147	143	139	133	127	122
2	133	129	125	120	116	111	106	102
3	118	114	110	106	102	99	95	92
4	107	104	100	96	93	90	86	84
5	98	95	91	88	85	82	79	77
6	90	87	83	80	77	75	72	70
7								63
Rises & Sets	90°	85°	80°	76°	72°	68°	65°	62°

Hours from Noon	SEP →23 MAR 21	OCT 4 MAR 11	OCT 14 MAR 1	OCT 25 FEB 18	NOV 3 FEB 9	NOV 14 JAN 29	NOV 27 JAN 16	DEC 11 JAN 2 ↓
0	180	180	180	180	180	180	180	180
1	153	156	158	160	161	162	163	164
2	133	136	139	142	144	146	148	149
3	118	122	125	128	131	133	135	136
4	107	111	114	117	120	122	124	126
5	98	102	105	108	111	113	116	118°
Rises & Sets	90°	95°	99°	104°	108°	111°	116°	118°

LATITUDE 30° NORTH

Hours from Noon	MAR →21 SEP 23	MAR 31 SEP 13	APR 11 SEP 2	APR 22 AUG 22	MAY 1 AUG 12	MAY 12 AUG 2	MAY 26 JUL 19	JUN 10 JUL 3 ↓
0	180	180	180	180	180	180	180	180
1	152	149	144	139	134	128	120	114
2	131	127	122	116	112	107	101	97
3	117	112	108	103	100	96	92	89
4	106	102	98	94	91	88	85	82
5	98	94	90	87	84	81	78	76
6	90	87	83	80	77	74	72	70
Rises & Sets	90°	85°	81°	76°	73°	69°	66°	63°

Hours from Noon	SEP →23 MAR 21	OCT 4 MAR 11	OCT 14 MAR 1	OCT 25 FEB 18	NOV 3 FEB 9	NOV 14 JAN 29	NOV 27 JAN 16	DEC 11 JAN 2 ↓
0	180	180	180	180	180	180	180	180
1	152	155	157	159	160	161	162	163
2	131	135	138	141	143	145	147	148
3	117	120	124	127	130	132	134	136
4	106	110	113	117	119	122	124	125
5	98	101	105	108	111	113	116	117
6	90							
Rises & Sets	90°	95°	99°	104°	107°	111°	114°	117°

Before noon read all angles from North to East. After noon read all angles from North to West.

LATITUDE 37½° NORTH

Hours from Noon	MAR ↗21 / SEP 23	MAR 31 / SEP 13	APR 11 / SEP 2	APR 22 / AUG 22	MAY 1 / AUG 12	MAY 12 / AUG 2	MAY 26 / JUL 19	JUN 10 / JUL 3 ↓
0	180	180	180	180	180	180	180	180
1	156	154	151	148	145	143	138	134
2	136	133	130	126	122	118	114	111
3	121	118	114	110	107	104	100	98
4	109	106	103	99	96	93	90	88
5	99	96	93	89	87	84	81	79
6	90	87	84	80	78	76	73	71
7							64	63
Rises & Sets	90°	85°	78°	75°	71°	67°	63°	60°

Hours from Noon	SEP ↗23 / MAR 21	OCT 4 / MAR 11	OCT 14 / MAR 1	OCT 25 / FEB 18	NOV 3 / FEB 9	NOV 14 / JAN 29	NOV 27 / JAN 16	DEC 11 / JAN 2 ↓
0	180	180	180	180	180	180	180	180
1	156	158	160	161	162	163	164	164
2	136	139	142	144	146	147	149	150
3	121	124	127	130	132	134	136	137
4	109	113	116	119	121	123	125	127
5	99	102	106	109	111	113		
6	90							
Rises & Sets	90°	95°	100°	105°	109°	113°	117°	119°

After noon read all angles from North to West.

LATITUDE 35° NORTH

Hours from Noon	MAR ↗21 / SEP 23	MAR 31 / SEP 13	APR 11 / SEP 2	APR 22 / AUG 22	MAY 1 / AUG 12	MAY 12 / AUG 2	MAY 26 / JUL 19	JUN 10 / JUL 3 ↓
0	180	180	180	180	180	180	180	180
1	155	152	149	146	142	138	133	129
2	135	131	127	123	119	115	110	107
3	120	116	112	108	105	101	97	95
4	108	105	101	97	94	91	88	86
5	99	95	92	88	86	83	80	78
6	90	87	83	80	78	75	73	71
7							64	63
Rises & Sets	90°	85°	80°	75°	72°	68°	64°	62°

Hours from Noon	SEP ↗23 / MAR 21	OCT 4 / MAR 11	OCT 14 / MAR 1	OCT 25 / FEB 18	NOV 3 / FEB 9	NOV 14 / JAN 29	NOV 27 / JAN 16	DEC 11 / JAN 2 ↓
0	180	180	180	180	180	180	180	180
1	155	157	159	160	161	162	163	164
2	135	138	141	143	145	147	148	149
3	120	123	126	129	131	134	136	137
4	108	112	115	118	120	123	125	126
5	99	102	105	108	111	113		
6	90							
Rises & Sets	90°	95°	100°	105°	108°	112°	116°	118°

Before noon read all angles from North to East.

LATITUDE 40° NORTH

Hours from Noon	MAR →21 SEP 23	MAR 31 SEP 13	APR 11 SEP 2	APR 22 AUG 22	MAY 1 AUG 12	MAY 12 AUG 2	MAY 26 JUL 19	JUN 10 JUL 3 ↓
0	180	180	180	180	180	180	180	180
1	157	155	153	151	148	145	142	139
2	138	135	132	128	125	122	118	115
3	123	120	116	112	109	106	103	100
4	110	107	104	100	98	95	92	90
5	100	97	93	90	88	85	82	81
6	90	87	84	81	78	76	74	72
7							67	65
Rises & Sets	90°	85°	80°	74°	70°	66°	62°	59°

Hours from Noon	SEP →23 MAR 21	OCT 4 MAR 11	OCT 14 MAR 1	OCT 25 FEB 18	NOV 3 FEB 9	NOV 14 JAN 29	NOV 27 JAN 16	DEC 11 JAN 2 ↓
0	180	180	180	180	180	180	180	180
1	157	159	160	162	163	163	164	165
2	138	141	143	145	147	148	150	150
3	123	126	128	131	133	135	137	138
4	110	113	116	119	121	123	125	127
5	100	103	106	109	111			
6	90							
Rises & Sets	90°	95°	100°	106°	110°	114°	118°	121°

LATITUDE 42½° NORTH

Hours from Noon	MAR →21 SEP 23	MAR 31 SEP 13	APR 11 SEP 2	APR 22 AUG 22	MAY 1 AUG 12	MAY 12 AUG 2	MAY 26 JUL 19	JUN 10 JUL 3 ↓
0	180	180	180	180	180	180	180	180
1	158	157	155	152	150	148	145	143
2	139	137	134	131	128	125	121	119
3	124	121	118	114	112	109	105	103
4	111	108	105	102	99	96	94	92
5	100	97	94	91	89	86	84	82
6	90	87	84	81	79	77	74	73
7							67	65
Rises & Sets	90°	85°	79°	74°	69°	65°	61°	58°

Hours from Noon	SEP →23 MAR 21	OCT 4 MAR 11	OCT 14 MAR 1	OCT 25 FEB 18	NOV 3 FEB 9	NOV 14 JAN 29	NOV 27 JAN 16	DEC 11 JAN 2 ↓
0	180	180	180	180	180	180	180	180
1	158	160	161	162	163	164	165	165
2	139	142	144	146	147	149	150	151
3	124	127	129	132	134	135	137	138
4	111	114	117	120	122	124	126	127
5	100	103	106	109	111			
6	90							
Rises & Sets	90°	95°	101°	106°	111°	115°	119°	122°

Before noon read all angles from North to East. *After* noon read all angles from North to West.

LATITUDE 45° NORTH

Hours from Noon	MAR 21 / SEP 23	MAR 31 / SEP 13	APR 11 / SEP 2	APR 22 / AUG 22	MAY 1 / AUG 12	MAY 12 / AUG 2	MAY 26 / JUL 19	JUN 10 / JUL 3
0	180	180	180	180	180	180	180	180
1	159	158	156	154	152	150	148	146
2	141	138	136	133	130	127	124	122
3	125	122	120	116	114	111	108	106
4	112	109	106	103	101	98	95	94
5	101	98	95	92	90	87	85	83
6	90	87	84	81	79	77	75	73
7					69	67	65	63
Rises & Sets	90°	84°	79°	73°	69°	64°	60°	56°

Hours from Noon	SEP 23 / MAR 21	OCT 4 / MAR 11	OCT 14 / MAR 1	OCT 25 / FEB 18	NOV 3 / FEB 9	NOV 14 / JAN 29	NOV 27 / JAN 16	DEC 11 / JAN 2
0	180	180	180	180	180	180	180	180
1	159	161	162	163	164	164	165	165
2	141	143	145	147	148	149	150	151
3	125	128	130	133	134	136	137	139
4	112	115	118	120	122	124	126	127
5	101	104	106	109				
6	90							
Rises & Sets	90°	96°	101°	107°	111°	116°	120°	124°

LATITUDE 47½° NORTH

Hours from Noon	MAR 21 / SEP 23	MAR 31 / SEP 13	APR 11 / SEP 2	APR 22 / AUG 22	MAY 1 / AUG 12	MAY 12 / AUG 2	MAY 26 / JUL 19	JUN 10 / JUL 3
0	180	180	180	180	180	180	180	180
1	160	159	157	156	154	152	150	149
2	142	140	137	135	132	130	127	125
3	126	124	121	118	116	113	110	108
4	113	110	108	105	102	100	97	95
5	101	98	96	93	91	88	86	84
6	90	87	85	82	80	78	75	74
7					69	67	65	64
Rises & Sets	90°	84°	78°	72°	67°	63°	58°	55°

Hours from Noon	SEP 23 / MAR 21	OCT 4 / MAR 11	OCT 14 / MAR 1	OCT 25 / FEB 18	NOV 3 / FEB 9	NOV 14 / JAN 29	NOV 27 / JAN 16	DEC 11 / JAN 2
0	180	180	180	180	180	180	180	180
1	160	161	162	163	164	164	165	165
2	142	144	146	147	149	150	151	152
3	126	129	131	133	135	136	138	139
4	113	116	118	121	122	124	126	127
5	101	104	106	109				
6	90							
Rises & Sets	90°	96°	102°	108°	113°	117°	122°	125°

Before noon read all angles from North to East. After noon read all angles from North to West.

LATITUDE 52½° NORTH

Hours from Noon	MAR 21 / SEP 23 →	MAR 31 / SEP 13	APR 11 / SEP 2	APR 22 / AUG 22	MAY 1 / AUG 12	MAY 12 / AUG 2	MAY 26 / JUL 19	JUN 10 / JUL 3 ↓
0	180	180	180	180	180	180	180	180
1	161	160	159	158	157	155	154	153
2	144	142	140	138	136	134	132	131
3	128	126	124	121	119	117	115	113
4	115	112	110	107	105	103	101	99
5	102	99	97	94	92	90	88	87
6	90	88	85	83	81	79	77	75
7				71	69	67	66	64
8						54	54	53
Rises & Sets	90°	83°	77°	70°	65°	59°	54°	50°

Hours from Noon	SEP 23 / MAR 21 →	OCT 4 / MAR 11	OCT 14 / MAR 1	OCT 25 / FEB 18	NOV 3 / FEB 9	NOV 14 / JAN 29	NOV 27 / JAN 16	DEC 11 / JAN 2 ↓
0	180	180	180	180	180	180	180	180
1	161	162	163	164	164	165	165	166
2	144	146	147	149	150	151	151	152
3	128	130	132	134	136	137	138	139
4	115	117	119	121	123	124	126	
5	102	104	107					
6	90							
Rises & Sets	90°	97°	103°	110°	115°	121°	126°	130°

LATITUDE 50° NORTH

Hours from Noon	MAR 21 / SEP 23 →	MAR 31 / SEP 13	APR 11 / SEP 2	APR 22 / AUG 22	MAY 1 / AUG 12	MAY 12 / AUG 2	MAY 26 / JUL 19	JUN 10 / JUL 3 ↓
0	180	180	180	180	180	180	180	180
1	161	160	158	157	155	154	152	151
2	143	141	139	136	134	132	130	128
3	127	125	123	120	118	115	113	111
4	114	111	109	106	104	101	99	97
5	102	99	96	94	92	89	87	86
6	90	87	85	82	80	78	76	75
7					69	67	65	64
Rises & Sets	90°	84°	77°	71°	66°	61°	56°	53°

Hours from Noon	SEP 23 / MAR 21 →	OCT 4 / MAR 11	OCT 14 / MAR 1	OCT 25 / FEB 18	NOV 3 / FEB 9	NOV 14 / JAN 29	NOV 27 / JAN 16	DEC 11 / JAN 2 ↓
0	180	180	180	180	180	180	180	180
1	161	162	163	164	164	165	165	166
2	143	145	146	148	149	150	151	152
3	127	130	132	134	135	137	138	139
4	114	116	119	121	123	124	126	
5	102	104	107	109				
6	90							
Rises & Sets	90°	96°	102°	109°	114°	119°	124°	127°

Before noon read all angles from North to East. After noon read all angles from North to West.

LATITUDE 57½° NORTH

Hours from Noon	MAR 21 / SEP 23	MAR 31 / SEP 13	APR 11 / SEP 2	APR 22 / AUG 22	MAY 1 / AUG 12	MAY 12 / AUG 2	MAY 26 / JUL 19	JUN 10 / JUL 3 ↓
0	180	180	180	180	180	180	180	180
1	162	161	160	159	158	157	156	156
2	146	144	142	141	140	138	136	135
3	130	128	126	124	123	121	119	117
4	116	114	112	110	108	106	104	103
5	103	101	98	96	94	93	91	89
6	90	88	86	83	82	80	78	77
7				71	69	68	66	65
8						55	54	53
Rises & Sets	90°	82°	75°	67°	61°	55°	48°	43°

Hours from Noon	SEP 23 / MAR 21	OCT 4 / MAR 1	OCT 14 / FEB 18	OCT 25 / FEB 9	NOV 3 / JAN 29	NOV 14 / JAN 16	NOV 27 / JAN 2	DEC 11 ↓
0	180	180	180	180	180	180	180	180
1	162	163	164	164	165	165	166	166
2	145	147	148	149	150	151	152	152
3	130	132	134	135	136	137	139	139
4	116	118	120	122	123			
5	103	105	107					
6	90							
Rises & Sets	90°	97°	105°	113°	119°	125°	132°	137°

Before noon read all angles from North to East. After noon read all angles from North to West.

LATITUDE 55° NORTH

Hours from Noon	MAR 21 / SEP 23	MAR 31 / SEP 13	APR 11 / SEP 2	APR 22 / AUG 22	MAY 1 / AUG 12	MAY 12 / AUG 2	MAY 26 / JUL 19	JUN 10 / JUL 3 ↓
0	180	180	180	180	180	180	180	180
1	162	161	160	159	158	157	156	155
2	145	143	141	140	138	136	134	133
3	129	127	125	123	121	119	117	115
4	115	113	111	108	106	104	102	101
5	102	100	98	95	93	92	90	88
6	90	88	85	83	81	79	78	76
7				71	69	68	66	65
8							54	53
Rises & Sets	90°	83°	76°	69°	63°	57°	51°	47°

Hours from Noon	SEP 23 / MAR 21	OCT 4 / MAR 11	OCT 14 / MAR 1	OCT 25 / FEB 18	NOV 3 / FEB 9	NOV 14 / JAN 29	NOV 27 / JAN 16	DEC 11 / JAN 2 ↓
0	180	180	180	180	180	180	180	180
1	162	163	163	164	165	165	166	166
2	145	146	148	149	150	151	152	152
3	129	131	133	135	136	137	138	139
4	115	117	120	122	123	125		
5	102	105	107					
6	90							
Rises & Sets	90°	97°	104°	111°	117°	123°	129°	133°

Before noon read all angles from North to East.

LATITUDE 2½° SOUTH

Hours from Noon	MAR 21 ↑ / SEP 23	MAR 31 / SEP 13	APR 11 / SEP 2	APR 22 / AUG 22	MAY 1 / AUG 12	MAY 12 / AUG 2	MAY 26 / JUL 19	JUN 10 ↓ / JUL 3
0	180	180	180	180	180	180	180	180
1	99	113	125	135	140	145	149	151
2	94	102	110	117	121	126	130	133
3	93	98	104	109	113	117	120	123
4	91	96	101	105	108	112	115	117
5	91	95	101	103	106	109	112	114
6	90	94	98	102	105	108	111	113
Rises & Sets	90°	94°	98°	102°	105°	108°	111°	113°

Hours from Noon	SEP 23 ↑ / MAR 21	OCT 4 / MAR 11	OCT 14 / MAR 1	OCT 25 / FEB 18	NOV 3 / FEB 9	NOV 14 / JAN 29	NOV 27 / JAN 16	DEC 11 ↓ / JAN 2
0	180	0	0	0	0	0	0	0
1	99	84	69	57	49	43	37	34
2	94	86	78	71	65	60	55	52
3	93	87	81	76	71	67	63	61
4	92	87	82	78	75	72	69	67
5	91	87	82	78	75	72	69	67
6	90	86	82	78	75	72	69	67
Rises & Sets	90°	86°	82°	78°	75°	72°	69°	67°

Before noon read all angles from South to East.
After noon read all angles from South to West.

LATITUDE 60° NORTH

Hours from Noon	MAR 21 ↑ / SEP 23	MAR 31 / SEP 13	APR 11 / SEP 2	APR 22 / AUG 22	MAY 1 / AUG 12	MAY 12 / AUG 2	MAY 26 / JUL 19	JUN 10 ↓ / JUL 3
0	180	180	180	180	180	180	180	180
1	163	162	161	160	159	158	157	
2	146	145	144	142	141	140	138	137
3	131	129	127	126	124	122	121	119
4	117	115	113	111	109	107	106	104
5	103	101	99	97	95	94	92	91
6	90	88	86	84	82	81	79	78
7				71	70	68	67	66
8						55	54	53
9								41
Rises & Sets	90°	82°	74°	65°	59°	52°	44°	39°

Hours from Noon	SEP 23 ↑ / MAR 21	OCT 4 / MAR 11	OCT 14 / MAR 1	OCT 25 / FEB 18	NOV 3 / FEB 9	NOV 14 / JAN 29	NOV 27 / JAN 16	DEC 11 ↓ / JAN 2
0	180	180	180	180	180	180	180	180
1	163	163	164	165	165	165	166	166
2	146	147	149	150	150	151	152	153
3	131	132	134	135	137	138	139	
4	117	118	120	122	123			
5	103	105	107					
Rises & Sets	90°	98°	106°	115°	121°	128°	136°	141°

Before noon read all angles from North to East.
After noon read all angles from North to West.

LATITUDE 7½° SOUTH

Hours from Noon	MAR →21 / SEP 23	MAR 31 / SEP 13	APR 11 / SEP 2	APR 22 / AUG 22	MAY 1 / AUG 12	MAY 12 / AUG 2	MAY 26 / JUL 19	JUN 10 / JUL 3 ↓
0	180	180	180	180	180	180	180	180
1	116	127	136	142	147	150	153	155
2	103	110	117	123	127	131	135	137
3	97	103	108	113	117	120	124	126
4	94	99	103	108	111	114	117	119
5	92	96	100	104	107	110	113	115
6	90							
Rises & Sets	90°	94°	98°	102°	105°	108°	111°	113°

Hours from Noon	SEP →23 / MAR 21	OCT 4 / MAR 11	OCT 14 / MAR 1	OCT 25 / FEB 18	NOV 3 / FEB 9	NOV 14 / JAN 29	NOV 27 / JAN 16	DEC 11 / JAN 2 ↓
0	180	180	0	0	0	0	0	0
1	116	102	87	72	62	53	45	41
2	103	95	87	79	73	67	62	58
3	97	92	86	80	76	72	68	65
4	94	90	85	80	77	73	70	68
5	92	88	84	78	75	72	69	67
6	90	86	82	78	75	72	69	67
Rises & Sets	90°	86°	82°	78°	75°	72°	69°	67°

LATITUDE 5° SOUTH

Hours from Noon	MAR →21 / SEP 23	MAR 31 / SEP 13	APR 11 / SEP 2	APR 22 / AUG 22	MAY 1 / AUG 12	MAY 12 / AUG 2	MAY 26 / JUL 19	JUN 10 / JUL 3 ↓
0	180	180	180	180	180	180	180	180
1	108	121	131	139	144	148	151	153
2	99	106	113	120	124	129	132	135
3	95	101	106	111	115	119	122	124
4	93	97	102	106	110	113	116	118
5	91	95	100	104	107	110	113	115
6	90	94	98					
Rises & Sets	90°	94°	98°	102°	105°	108°	111°	113°

Hours from Noon	SEP →23 / MAR 21	OCT 4 / MAR 11	OCT 14 / MAR 1	OCT 25 / FEB 18	NOV 3 / FEB 9	NOV 14 / JAN 29	NOV 27 / JAN 16	DEC 11 / JAN 2 ↓
0	180	180	0	0	0	0	0	0
1	108	93	78	64	55	47	41	37
2	99	91	83	75	69	64	58	55
3	95	89	84	75	74	70	66	63
4	93	88	84	79	76	72	69	66
5	91	87	83	78	76	73	70	67
6	90	86	82	78	75	72	69	67
Rises & Sets	90°	86°	82°	78°	75°	72°	69°	67°

Before noon read all angles from South to East. *After* noon read all angles from South to West.

LATITUDE 10° SOUTH

Hours from Noon	MAR 21 ↑	MAR 31	APR 11	APR 22	MAY 1	MAY 12	MAY 26	JUN 10 ↓
	SEP 23	SEP 13	SEP 2	AUG 22	AUG 12	AUG 2	JUL 19	JUL 3
0	180	180	180	180	180	180	180	180
1	123	132	140	146	149	152	155	156
2	107	114	120	126	130	133	137	139
3	100	105	110	115	119	122	125	127
4	96	100	105	109	112	115	118	120
5	93	97	101	105	108	111	114	116
6	90							
Rises & Sets	90°	94°	98°	102°	105°	108°	111°	113°

Hours from Noon	SEP 23 ↑	OCT 4	OCT 14	OCT 25	NOV 3	NOV 14	NOV 27	DEC 11 ↓
	MAR 21 ↑	MAR 11	MAR 1	FEB 18	FEB 9	JAN 29	JAN 16	JAN 2 ↓
0	180	180	180	0	0	0	0	0
1	123	111	96	81	70	60	51	46
2	107	99	91	83	77	71	66	62
3	100	94	89	83	79	74	70	67
4	96	91	87	82	78	75	71	69
5	93	89	84	80	77	74	71	69
6	90	86	82	78	75	72	69	67
Rises & Sets	90°	86°	82°	78°	75°	72°	69°	67°

LATITUDE 12½° SOUTH

Hours from Noon	MAR 21 ↑	MAR 31	APR 11	APR 22	MAY 1	MAY 12	MAY 26	JUN 10 ↓
	SEP 23	SEP 13	SEP 2	AUG 22	AUG 12	AUG 2	JUL 19	JUL 3
0	180	180	180	180	180	180	180	180
1	129	137	143	148	151	154	156	157
2	111	117	123	128	132	135	138	140
3	102	107	112	117	120	124	127	129
4	97	102	106	110	113	116	119	121
5	93	97	101	105	108	111	114	116
6	90							
Rises & Sets	90°	94°	98°	102°	105°	108°	112°	114°

Hours from Noon	SEP 23 ↑	OCT 4	OCT 14	OCT 25	NOV 3	NOV 14	NOV 27	DEC 11 ↓
	MAR 21 ↑	MAR 11	MAR 1	FEB 18	FEB 9	JAN 29	JAN 16	JAN 2 ↓
0	180	180	180	0	0	0	0	0
1	129	119	105	90	79	67	57	52
2	111	103	96	88	82	75	69	66
3	102	97	91	86	81	77	73	70
4	97	93	88	83	80	76	73	71
5	93	89	85	81	78	75	72	70
6	90	86	82	78	75	72	69	67
Rises & Sets	90°	86°	82°	78°	75°	72°	68°	66°

Before noon read all angles from South to East. *After* noon read all angles from South to West.

LATITUDE 15° SOUTH

Hours from Noon	MAR 21 ↑ / SEP 23	MAR 31 / SEP 13	APR 11 / SEP 2	APR 22 / AUG 22	MAY 1 / AUG 12	MAY 12 / AUG 2	MAY 26 / JUL 19	JUN 10 / JUL 3 ↓
0	180	180	180	180	180	180	180	180
1	134	141	146	150	153	155	157	159
2	114	120	126	131	134	137	140	142
3	105	110	114	119	122	125	128	130
4	98	103	107	111	114	117	120	122
5	94	98	102	106	109	112	114	116
6	90							
Rises & Sets	90°	94°	98°	102°	106°	109°	112°	114°

Hours from Noon	SEP 23 ↑ / MAR 21	OCT 4 / MAR 11	OCT 14 / MAR 1	OCT 25 / FEB 18	NOV 3 / FEB 9	NOV 14 / JAN 29	NOV 27 / JAN 16	DEC 11 / JAN 2 ↓
0	180	180	180	180	180	0	0	0
1	134	125	114	100	88	76	65	58
2	114	107	100	92	86	80	74	70
3	105	99	94	88	84	80	75	72
4	98	94	90	85	81	78	74	72
5	94	90	86	82	79	76	73	70
6	90	86	82	78	75	73	70	68
Rises & Sets	90°	86°	82°	78°	74°	71°	68°	66°

LATITUDE 17½° SOUTH

Hours from Noon	MAR 21 ↑ / SEP 23	MAR 31 / SEP 13	APR 11 / SEP 2	APR 22 / AUG 22	MAY 1 / AUG 12	MAY 12 / AUG 2	MAY 26 / JUL 19	JUN 10 / JUL 3 ↓
0	180	180	180	180	180	180	180	180
1	138	144	149	152	155	157	158	160
2	117	123	128	133	136	139	141	143
3	107	112	116	120	123	126	129	131
4	100	104	108	112	115	118	121	123
5	95	98	102	106	109	112	115	117
6	90							
Rises & Sets	90°	94°	98°	103°	106°	109°	112°	114°

Hours from Noon	SEP 23 ↑ / MAR 21	OCT 4 / MAR 11	OCT 14 / MAR 1	OCT 25 / FEB 18	NOV 3 / FEB 9	NOV 14 / JAN 29	NOV 27 / JAN 16	DEC 11 / JAN 2 ↓
0	180	180	180	180	180	180	0	0
1	138	131	121	109	98	86	74	66
2	117	111	104	97	91	84	78	74
3	107	102	96	91	87	82	78	75
4	100	96	91	87	83	80	76	74
5	95	91	87	83	80	76	73	71
6	90	86	82	79	76	73	70	68
Rises & Sets	90°	86°	82°	77°	74°	71°	68°	66°

Before noon read all angles from South to East. *After* noon read all angles from South to West.

LATITUDE 22½° SOUTH

Hours from Noon	MAR 21 / SEP 23 ↑	MAR 31 / SEP 13	APR 11 / SEP 2	APR 22 / AUG 22	MAY 1 / AUG 12	MAY 12 / AUG 2	MAY 26 / JUL 19	JUN 10 / JUL 3 ↓
0	180	180	180	180	180	180	180	180
1	145	149	153	155	157	159	160	161
2	124	128	133	137	139	142	144	145
3	111	115	120	123	126	129	131	133
4	102	106	110	114	117	120	122	124
5	96	100	107	110	112	115	117	
6	90							
Rises & Sets	90°	94°	99°	103°	106°	110°	113°	115°

Hours from Noon	SEP 23 / MAR 21 ↑	OCT 4 / MAR 11	OCT 14 / MAR 1	OCT 25 / FEB 18	NOV 3 / FEB 9	NOV 14 / JAN 29	NOV 27 / JAN 16	DEC 11 / JAN 2 ↓
0	180	180	180	180	180	180	180	0
1	145	140	133	124	115	105	93	85
2	124	118	112	105	100	94	87	83
3	111	106	101	96	92	88	83	80
4	102	98	94	90	86	83	79	77
5	96	92	88	84	81	78	75	73
6	90	86	83	79	76	73	70	69
Rises & Sets	90°	86°	81°	77°	74°	74°	70°	67° 65°

LATITUDE 20° SOUTH

Hours from Noon	MAR 21 / SEP 23 ↑	MAR 31 / SEP 13	APR 11 / SEP 2	APR 22 / AUG 22	MAY 1 / AUG 12	MAY 12 / AUG 2	MAY 26 / JUL 19	JUN 10 / JUL 3 ↓
0	180	180	180	180	180	180	180	180
1	142	147	151	154	156	158	159	160
2	121	126	131	135	138	140	143	144
3	109	113	118	122	125	128	130	132
4	101	105	109	113	116	119	122	123
5	95	99	103	107	109	112	115	117
6	90							
Rises & Sets	90°	94°	99°	103°	106°	109°	112°	115°

Hours from Noon	SEP 23 / MAR 21 ↑	OCT 4 / MAR 11	OCT 14 / MAR 1	OCT 25 / FEB 18	NOV 3 / FEB 9	NOV 14 / JAN 29	NOV 27 / JAN 16	DEC 11 / JAN 2 ↓
0	180	180	180	180	180	180	180	180
1	142	136	127	117	107	94	83	75
2	121	115	108	101	94	89	83	78
3	109	104	99	93	89	85	80	77
4	101	97	93	88	85	81	78	75
5	94	91	87	83	80	77	74	72
6	90	90	86	82	79	76	70	68
Rises & Sets	90°	86°	81°	77°	74°	71°	68°	65°

Before noon read all angles from South to East. *After* noon read all angles from South to West.

LATITUDE 25° SOUTH

Hours from Noon	MAR→21 / SEP 23	MAR 31 / SEP 13	APR 11 / SEP 2	APR 22 / AUG 22	MAY 1 / AUG 12	MAY 12 / AUG 2	MAY 26 / JUL 19	JUN 10 / JUL 3 ↓
0	180	180	180	180	180	180	180	180
1	148	151	154	157	158	160	161	162
2	126	131	135	138	141	143	145	146
3	113	117	121	125	127	130	132	134
4	104	108	111	115	118	120	123	125
5	96	100	104	107	110	113	115	117
Rises & Sets	90°	94°	99°	103°	107°	110°	113°	116°

Hours from Noon	SEP→23 / MAR 21	OCT 4 / MAR 11	OCT 14 / MAR 1	OCT 25 / FEB 18	NOV 3 / FEB 9	NOV 14 / JAN 29	NOV 27 / JAN 16	DEC 11 / JAN 2 ↓
0	180	180	180	180	180	180	180	180
1	148	143	137	130	123	114	103	95
2	126	121	116	109	104	98	92	88
3	113	108	104	99	95	90	86	83
4	104	100	96	91	88	85	81	79
5	96	93	89	85	82	79	76	74
6	90	86	83	79	76	74	71	69
Rises & Sets	90°	86°	81°	77°	73°	70°	67°	64°

LATITUDE 27½° SOUTH

Hours from Noon	MAR→21 / SEP 23	MAR 31 / SEP 13	APR 11 / SEP 2	APR 22 / AUG 22	MAY 1 / AUG 12	MAY 12 / AUG 2	MAY 26 / JUL 19	JUN 10 / JUL 3 ↓
0	180	180	180	180	180	180	180	180
1	150	153	156	158	159	161	162	163
2	129	133	136	140	142	144	146	147
3	115	119	123	126	128	131	133	135
4	105	109	112	116	118	121	123	125
5	97	101	105	109	110	113	115	117
6	90							
Rises & Sets	90°	94°	99°	104°	107°	110°	114°	116°

Hours from Noon	SEP→23 / MAR 21	OCT 4 / MAR 11	OCT 14 / MAR 1	OCT 25 / FEB 18	NOV 3 / FEB 9	NOV 14 / JAN 29	NOV 27 / JAN 16	DEC 11 / JAN 2 ↓
0	180	180	180	180	180	180	180	180
1	150	146	141	135	129	121	112	105
2	129	124	119	113	108	103	97	93
3	115	110	106	101	97	93	89	86
4	105	101	97	93	90	86	83	80
5	97	93	90	86	83	80	77	75
6	90	86	83	79	77	74	71	69
Rises & Sets	90°	85°	81°	76°	73°	70°	66°	64°

Before noon read all angles from South to East. *After* noon read all angles from South to West.

LATITUDE 32¼° SOUTH

Hours from Noon	MAR 21 / SEP 23	MAR 31 / SEP 13	APR 11 / SEP 2	APR 22 / AUG 22	MAY 1 / AUG 12	MAY 12 / AUG 2	MAY 26 / JUL 19	JUN 10 / JUL 3 ↓
0	180	180	180	180	180	180	180	180
1	153	156	158	160	161	162	163	164
2	133	136	139	142	144	146	148	149
3	118	122	125	128	131	133	135	136
4	107	111	114	117	120	122	124	126
5	98	102	105	108	111	113	116	
6	90							
Rises & Sets	90°	95°	99°	104°	108°	111°	115°	118°

Hours from Noon	SEP 23 / MAR 21	OCT 4 / MAR 11	OCT 14 / MAR 1	NOV 25 / FEB 18	NOV 3 / FEB 9	NOV 14 / JAN 29	NOV 27 / JAN 16	DEC 11 / JAN 2 ↓
0	180	180	180	180	180	180	180	180
1	153	151	147	143	139	133	127	122
2	133	129	125	120	116	111	106	102
3	118	114	110	106	102	99	95	92
4	107	104	100	96	93	90	86	84
5	98	95	91	88	85	82	79	77
6	90	87	83	80	77	75	72	70
7								63
Rises & Sets	90°	85°	80°	76°	72°	68°	65°	62°

LATITUDE 30° SOUTH

Hours from Noon	MAR 21 / SEP 23	MAR 31 / SEP 13	APR 11 / SEP 2	APR 22 / AUG 22	MAY 1 / AUG 12	MAY 12 / AUG 2	MAY 26 / JUL 19	JUN 10 / JUL 3 ↓
0	180	180	180	180	180	180	180	180
1	152	155	157	159	160	161	162	163
2	131	135	138	141	143	145	147	148
3	117	120	124	127	130	132	134	136
4	106	110	113	117	119	122	124	125
5	98	101	105	108	111	113	116	117
6	90							
Rises & Sets	90°	95°	99°	104°	107°	111°	114°	117°

Hours from Noon	SEP 23 / MAR 21	OCT 4 / MAR 11	OCT 14 / MAR 1	NOV 25 / FEB 18	NOV 3 / FEB 9	NOV 14 / JAN 29	NOV 27 / JAN 16	DEC 11 / JAN 2 ↓
0	180	180	180	180	180	180	180	180
1	152	149	144	139	134	128	120	114
2	131	127	122	116	112	107	101	97
3	117	112	108	103	100	96	92	89
4	106	102	98	94	91	88	85	82
5	98	94	90	87	84	81	78	76
6	90	87	83	80	77	74	72	70
Rises & Sets	90°	85°	81°	76°	73°	69°	66°	63°

Before noon read all angles from South to East. *After* noon read all angles from South to West.

LATITUDE 37½° SOUTH

Hours from Noon	MAR →21 / SEP 23	MAR 3- / SEP 13	APR 11 / SEP 2	APR 22 / AUG 22	MAY 1 / AUG 12	MAY 12 / AUG 2	MAY 26 / JUL 19	JUN 10 / JUL 3 ↓
0	180	180	180	180	180	180	180	180
1	156	158	160	161	162	163	164	164
2	136	159	142	144	146	147	149	150
3	121	124	127	130	132	134	136	137
4	109	113	116	119	120	123	125	127
5	99	102	106	109	111	113		
6	90							
Rises & Sets	90°	95°	100°	105°	109°	113°	117°	119°

Hours from Noon	SEP →23 / MAR 21	OCT 4 / MAR 11	OCT 14 / MAR 1	OCT 25 / FEB 18	NOV 3 / FEB 9	NOV 14 / JAN 29	NOV 27 / JAN 16	DEC 11 / JAN 2 ↓
0	180	180	180	180	180	180	180	180
1	156	154	151	148	145	142	138	134
2	136	133	130	126	122	118	114	111
3	121	118	114	110	107	104	100	98
4	109	106	103	99	96	93	90	88
5	99	96	93	89	87	84	81	79
6	90	37	84	80	78	76	73	71
7							64	63
Rises & Sets	90°	85°	80°	75°	71°	67°	63°	60°

After noon read all angles from South to West.

LATITUDE 35° SOUTH

Hours from Noon	MAR →21 / SEP 23	MAR 31 / SEP 13	APR 11 / SEP 2	APR 22 / AUG 22	MAY 1 / AUG 12	MAY 12 / AUG 2	MAY 26 / JUL 19	JUN 10 / JUL 3 ↓
0	180	180	180	180	180	180	180	180
1	155	157	159	160	161	162	163	164
2	135	138	141	143	145	147	148	149
3	110	123	126	129	131	134	136	137
4	108	112	115	118	120	123	125	126
5	99	102	105	108	111	113		
6	90							
Rises & Sets	90°	95°	100°	105°	108°	112°	116°	118°

Hours from Noon	SEP →23 / MAR 21	OCT 4 / MAR 11	OCT 14 / MAR 1	OCT 25 / FEB 18	NOV 3 / FEB 9	NOV 14 / JAN 29	NOV 27 / JAN 16	DEC 11 / JAN 2 ↓
0	180	180	180	180	180	180	180	180
1	155	152	149	146	142	138	133	129
2	135	131	127	123	119	115	110	107
3	120	116	112	108	105	101	97	95
4	108	105	101	97	94	91	88	86
5	99	95	92	88	86	83	80	78
6	90	87	83	80	78	75	73	71
7							64	63
Rises & Sets	90°	85°	80°	75°	72°	68°	64°	62°

Before noon read all angles from South to East.

LATITUDE 42½° SOUTH

Hours from Noon	MAR 21 (→) / SEP 23	MAR 31 / SEP 13	APR 11 / SEP 2	APR 22 / AUG 22	MAY 1 / AUG 12	MAY 12 / AUG 2	MAY 26 / JUL 19	JUN 10 / JUL 3 (↓)
0	180	180	180	180	180	180	180	180
1	158	160	161	162	163	164	165	165
2	139	142	144	146	147	149	150	151
3	124	127	129	132	134	135	137	138
4	111	114	117	120	122	124	126	127
5	100	103	106	109	111			
6	90							
Rises & Sets	90°	95°	101°	106°	111°	115°	119°	122°

Hours from Noon	SEP 23 (→) / MAR 21	OCT 4 / MAR 11	OCT 14 / MAR 1	OCT 25 / FEB 18	NOV 3 / FEB 9	NOV 14 / FEB 29	NOV 27 / JAN 16	DEC 11 / JAN 2 (↓)
0	180	180	180	180	180	180	180	180
1	158	157	155	152	150	148	145	143
2	139	137	134	131	128	125	121	119
3	124	121	118	114	112	109	105	103
4	111	108	105	102	99	96	94	92
5	100	97	94	91	89	86	84	82
6	90	87	84	81	79	77	74	73
7						67	65	63
Rises & Sets	90°	85°	79°	74°	69°	65°	61°	58°

LATITUDE 40° SOUTH

Hours from Noon	MAR 21 (→) / SEP 23	MAR 31 / SEP 13	APR 11 / SEP 2	APR 22 / AUG 22	MAY 1 / AUG 12	MAY 12 / AUG 2	MAY 26 / JUL 19	JUN 10 / JUL 3 (↓)
0	180	180	180	180	180	180	180	180
1	157	159	160	162	163	164	165	165
2	138	141	143	145	147	148	150	150
3	123	126	128	131	133	135	137	138
4	110	113	116	119	121	123	125	127
5	100	103	106	109	111			
6	90							
Rises & Sets	90°	95°	100°	106°	110°	114°	118°	121°

Hours from Noon	SEP 23 (→) / MAR 21	OCT 4 / MAR 11	OCT 14 / MAR 1	OCT 25 / FEB 18	NOV 3 / FEB 9	NOV 14 / FEB 29	NOV 27 / JAN 16	DEC 11 / JAN 2 (↓)
0	180	180	180	180	180	180	180	180
1	157	155	153	151	148	145	142	139
2	138	135	132	128	125	122	118	115
3	123	120	116	112	109	106	103	100
4	110	107	104	100	98	95	92	90
5	100	97	93	90	88	85	82	81
6	90	87	84	81	78	76	74	72
7						67	65	63
Rises & Sets	90°	85°	80°	74°	70°	66°	62°	59°

Before noon read all angles from South to East. *After* noon read all angles from South to West.

LATITUDE 47½° SOUTH

Hours from Noon	MAR 21 / SEP 23	MAR 31 / SEP 13	APR 11 / SEP 2	APR 22 / AUG 22	MAY 1 / AUG 12	MAY 12 / AUG 2	MAY 26 / JUL 19	JUN 10 / JUL 3 ↓
0	180	180	180	180	180	180	180	180
1	160	161	162	163	164	164	165	165
2	142	144	146	147	149	150	151	152
3	126	129	131	133	135	136	138	139
4	113	115	118	121	122	124	126	127
5	101	104	106	109				
6	90							
Rises & Sets	90°	96°	102°	108°	113°	117°	122°	125°

Hours from Noon	SEP 23 / MAR 21	OCT 4 / MAR 11	OCT 14 / MAR 1	OCT 25 / FEB 18	NOV 3 / FEB 9	NOV 14 / JAN 29	NOV 27 / JAN 16	DEC 11 / JAN 2 ↓
0	180	180	180	180	180	180	180	180
1	160	159	157	156	154	152	150	149
2	142	140	137	135	132	130	127	125
3	126	124	121	118	116	113	110	108
4	113	110	108	105	102	100	97	95
5	101	98	96	93	91	88	86	84
6	90	87	85	82	80	78	75	74
7					69	67	65	64
Rises & Sets	90°	84°	78°	72°	67°	63°	58°	55°

After noon read all angles from South to West.

LATITUDE 45° SOUTH

Hours from Noon	MAR 21 / SEP 23	MAR 31 / SEP 13	APR 11 / SEP 2	APR 22 / AUG 22	MAY 1 / AUG 12	MAY 12 / AUG 2	MAY 26 / JUL 19	JUN 10 / JUL 3 ↓
0	180	180	180	180	180	180	180	180
1	159	161	162	163	163	164	165	165
2	141	143	145	147	148	149	150	151
3	125	128	130	133	134	136	137	139
4	112	115	118	120	122	124	126	127
5	101	104	106	109				
6	90							
Rises & Sets	90°	96°	101°	107°	111°	116°	120°	124°

Hours from Noon	SEP 23 / MAR 21	OCT 4 / MAR 11	OCT 14 / MAR 1	OCT 25 / FEB 18	NOV 3 / FEB 9	NOV 14 / JAN 29	NOV 27 / JAN 16	DEC 11 / JAN 2 ↓
0	180	180	180	180	180	180	180	180
1	159	158	156	154	152	150	148	146
2	141	138	136	133	130	127	124	122
3	125	122	120	116	114	111	108	106
4	112	109	106	103	101	98	95	94
5	101	98	95	92	90	87	85	83
6	90	87	84	81	79	77	75	73
7					69	67	65	63
Rises & Sets	90°	84°	79°	73°	69°	64°	60°	56°

Before noon read all angles from South to East. *After* noon read all angles from South to West.

LATITUDE 50° SOUTH

Hours from Noon	MAR →21	MAR 31	APR 11	APR 22	MAY 1	MAY 12	MAY 26	JUN 10
	SEP 23	SEP 13	SEP 2	AUG 22	AUG 12	AUG 2	JUL 19	JUL 3 ↓
0	180	180	180	180	180	180	180	180
1	161	162	163	164	164	165	165	166
2	143	145	146	148	149	150	151	152
3	127	130	132	134	135	137	138	139
4	114	116	119	121	123	124	126	
5	102	104	107	109				
6	90							
Rises & Sets	90°	84°	77°	71°	66°	61°	56°	53°

Hours from Noon	SEP →23	OCT 4	OCT 14	OCT 25	NOV 3	NOV 14	NOV 27	DEC 11
	MAR 21	MAR 11	MAR 1	FEB 18	FEB 9	JAN 29	JAN 16	JAN 2 ↓
0	180	180	180	180	180	180	180	180
1	161	160	158	157	155	154	152	151
2	143	141	139	136	134	132	130	128
3	127	125	123	120	118	115	113	111
4	114	111	109	106	104	101	99	97
5	102	99	96	94	92	89	87	86
6	90	87	85	82	80	78	76	75
7					69	67	65	64
8								53
Rises & Sets	90°	84°	77°	71°	66°	61°	56°	53°

Before noon read all angles from South to East. *After* noon read all angles from South to West.

Index

References to illustration pages are in italic type

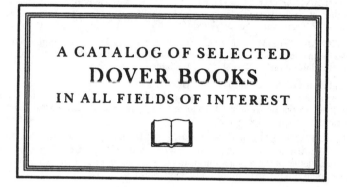

A CATALOG OF SELECTED

DOVER BOOKS

IN ALL FIELDS OF INTEREST

A CATALOG OF SELECTED DOVER
BOOKS IN ALL FIELDS OF INTEREST

CONCERNING THE SPIRITUAL IN ART, Wassily Kandinsky. Pioneering work by father of abstract art. Thoughts on color theory, nature of art. Analysis of earlier masters. 12 illustrations. 80pp. of text. 5⅜ x 8½. 0-486-23411-8

CELTIC ART: The Methods of Construction, George Bain. Simple geometric techniques for making Celtic interlacements, spirals, Kells-type initials, animals, humans, etc. Over 500 illustrations. 160pp. 9 x 12. (Available in U.S. only.) 0-486-22923-8

AN ATLAS OF ANATOMY FOR ARTISTS, Fritz Schider. Most thorough reference work on art anatomy in the world. Hundreds of illustrations, including selections from works by Vesalius, Leonardo, Goya, Ingres, Michelangelo, others. 593 illustrations. 192pp. 7⅛ x 10¼. 0-486-20241-0

CELTIC HAND STROKE-BY-STROKE (Irish Half-Uncial from "The Book of Kells"): An Arthur Baker Calligraphy Manual, Arthur Baker. Complete guide to creating each letter of the alphabet in distinctive Celtic manner. Covers hand position, strokes, pens, inks, paper, more. Illustrated. 48pp. 8¼ x 11. 0-486-24336-2

EASY ORIGAMI, John Montroll. Charming collection of 32 projects (hat, cup, pelican, piano, swan, many more) specially designed for the novice origami hobbyist. Clearly illustrated easy-to-follow instructions insure that even beginning papercrafters will achieve successful results. 48pp. 8¼ x 11. 0-486-27298-2

BLOOMINGDALE'S ILLUSTRATED 1886 CATALOG: Fashions, Dry Goods and Housewares, Bloomingdale Brothers. Famed merchants' extremely rare catalog depicting about 1,700 products: clothing, housewares, firearms, dry goods, jewelry, more. Invaluable for dating, identifying vintage items. Also, copyright-free graphics for artists, designers. Co-published with Henry Ford Museum & Greenfield Village. 160pp. 8¼ x 11. 0-486-25780-0

THE ART OF WORLDLY WISDOM, Baltasar Gracian. "Think with the few and speak with the many," "Friends are a second existence," and "Be able to forget" are among this 1637 volume's 300 pithy maxims. A perfect source of mental and spiritual refreshment, it can be opened at random and appreciated either in brief or at length. 128pp. 5⅜ x 8½. 0-486-44034-6

JOHNSON'S DICTIONARY: A Modern Selection, Samuel Johnson (E. L. McAdam and George Milne, eds.). This modern version reduces the original 1755 edition's 2,300 pages of definitions and literary examples to a more manageable length, retaining the verbal pleasure and historical curiosity of the original. 480pp. 5⁵⁄₁₆ x 8¼. 0-486-44089-3

ADVENTURES OF HUCKLEBERRY FINN, Mark Twain, Illustrated by E. W. Kemble. A work of eternal richness and complexity, a source of ongoing critical debate, and a literary landmark, Twain's 1885 masterpiece about a barefoot boy's journey of self-discovery has enthralled readers around the world. This handsome clothbound reproduction of the first edition features all 174 of the original black-and-white illustrations. 368pp. 5⅜ x 8½. 0-486-44322-1

CATALOG OF DOVER BOOKS

STICKLEY CRAFTSMAN FURNITURE CATALOGS, Gustav Stickley and L. & J. G. Stickley. Beautiful, functional furniture in two authentic catalogs from 1910. 594 illustrations, including 277 photos, show settles, rockers, armchairs, reclining chairs, bookcases, desks, tables. 183pp. 6½ x 9¼. 0-486-23838-5

AMERICAN LOCOMOTIVES IN HISTORIC PHOTOGRAPHS: 1858 to 1949, Ron Ziel (ed.). A rare collection of 126 meticulously detailed official photographs, called "builder portraits," of American locomotives that majestically chronicle the rise of steam locomotive power in America. Introduction. Detailed captions. xi+ 129pp. 9 x 12. 0-486-27393-8

AMERICA'S LIGHTHOUSES: An Illustrated History, Francis Ross Holland, Jr. Delightfully written, profusely illustrated fact-filled survey of over 200 American lighthouses since 1716. History, anecdotes, technological advances, more. 240pp. 8 x 10¾. 0-486-25576-X

TOWARDS A NEW ARCHITECTURE, Le Corbusier. Pioneering manifesto by founder of "International School." Technical and aesthetic theories, views of industry, economics, relation of form to function, "mass-production split" and much more. Profusely illustrated. 320pp. 6⅛ x 9¼. (Available in U.S. only.) 0-486-25023-7

HOW THE OTHER HALF LIVES, Jacob Riis. Famous journalistic record, exposing poverty and degradation of New York slums around 1900, by major social reformer. 100 striking and influential photographs. 233pp. 10 x 7⅞. 0-486-22012-5

FRUIT KEY AND TWIG KEY TO TREES AND SHRUBS, William M. Harlow. One of the handiest and most widely used identification aids. Fruit key covers 120 deciduous and evergreen species; twig key 160 deciduous species. Easily used. Over 300 photographs. 126pp. 5⅜ x 8½. 0-486-20511-8

COMMON BIRD SONGS, Dr. Donald J. Borror. Songs of 60 most common U.S. birds: robins, sparrows, cardinals, bluejays, finches, more—arranged in order of increasing complexity. Up to 9 variations of songs of each species.
Cassette and manual 0-486-99911-4

ORCHIDS AS HOUSE PLANTS, Rebecca Tyson Northen. Grow cattleyas and many other kinds of orchids—in a window, in a case, or under artificial light. 63 illustrations. 148pp. 5⅜ x 8½. 0-486-23261-1

MONSTER MAZES, Dave Phillips. Masterful mazes at four levels of difficulty. Avoid deadly perils and evil creatures to find magical treasures. Solutions for all 32 exciting illustrated puzzles. 48pp. 8¼ x 11. 0-486-26005-4

MOZART'S DON GIOVANNI (DOVER OPERA LIBRETTO SERIES), Wolfgang Amadeus Mozart. Introduced and translated by Ellen H. Bleiler. Standard Italian libretto, with complete English translation. Convenient and thoroughly portable—an ideal companion for reading along with a recording or the performance itself. Introduction. List of characters. Plot summary. 121pp. 5¼ x 8½. 0-486-24944-1

FRANK LLOYD WRIGHT'S DANA HOUSE, Donald Hoffmann. Pictorial essay of residential masterpiece with over 160 interior and exterior photos, plans, elevations, sketches and studies. 128pp. 9¼ x 10¾. 0-486-29120-0

THE CLARINET AND CLARINET PLAYING, David Pino. Lively, comprehensive work features suggestions about technique, musicianship, and musical interpretation, as well as guidelines for teaching, making your own reeds, and preparing for public performance. Includes an intriguing look at clarinet history. "A godsend," *The Clarinet,* Journal of the International Clarinet Society. Appendixes. 7 illus. 320pp. 5⅜ x 8½. 0-486-40270-3

HOLLYWOOD GLAMOR PORTRAITS, John Kobal (ed.). 145 photos from 1926-49. Harlow, Gable, Bogart, Bacall; 94 stars in all. Full background on photographers, technical aspects. 160pp. 8⅜ x 11¼. 0-486-23352-9

THE RAVEN AND OTHER FAVORITE POEMS, Edgar Allan Poe. Over 40 of the author's most memorable poems: "The Bells," "Ulalume," "Israfel," "To Helen," "The Conqueror Worm," "Eldorado," "Annabel Lee," many more. Alphabetic lists of titles and first lines. 64pp. 5³⁄₁₆ x 8¼. 0-486-26685-0

PERSONAL MEMOIRS OF U. S. GRANT, Ulysses Simpson Grant. Intelligent, deeply moving firsthand account of Civil War campaigns, considered by many the finest military memoirs ever written. Includes letters, historic photographs, maps and more. 528pp. 6⅛ x 9¼. 0-486-28587-1

ANCIENT EGYPTIAN MATERIALS AND INDUSTRIES, A. Lucas and J. Harris. Fascinating, comprehensive, thoroughly documented text describes this ancient civilization's vast resources and the processes that incorporated them in daily life, including the use of animal products, building materials, cosmetics, perfumes and incense, fibers, glazed ware, glass and its manufacture, materials used in the mummification process, and much more. 544pp. 6¹⁄₈ x 9¹⁄₄. (Available in U.S. only.) 0-486-40446-3

RUSSIAN STORIES/RUSSKIE RASSKAZY: A Dual-Language Book, edited by Gleb Struve. Twelve tales by such masters as Chekhov, Tolstoy, Dostoevsky, Pushkin, others. Excellent word-for-word English translations on facing pages, plus teaching and study aids, Russian/English vocabulary, biographical/critical introductions, more. 416pp. 5⅜ x 8½. 0-486-26244-8

PHILADELPHIA THEN AND NOW: 60 Sites Photographed in the Past and Present, Kenneth Finkel and Susan Oyama. Rare photographs of City Hall, Logan Square, Independence Hall, Betsy Ross House, other landmarks juxtaposed with contemporary views. Captures changing face of historic city. Introduction. Captions. 128pp. 8¼ x 11. 0-486-25790-8

NORTH AMERICAN INDIAN LIFE: Customs and Traditions of 23 Tribes, Elsie Clews Parsons (ed.). 27 fictionalized essays by noted anthropologists examine religion, customs, government, additional facets of life among the Winnebago, Crow, Zuni, Eskimo, other tribes. 480pp. 6⅛ x 9¼. 0-486-27377-6

TECHNICAL MANUAL AND DICTIONARY OF CLASSICAL BALLET, Gail Grant. Defines, explains, comments on steps, movements, poses and concepts. 15-page pictorial section. Basic book for student, viewer. 127pp. 5⅜ x 8½. 0-486-21843-0

THE MALE AND FEMALE FIGURE IN MOTION: 60 Classic Photographic Sequences, Eadweard Muybridge. 60 true-action photographs of men and women walking, running, climbing, bending, turning, etc., reproduced from rare 19th-century masterpiece. vi + 121pp. 9 x 12. 0-486-24745-7

CATALOG OF DOVER BOOKS

ANIMALS: 1,419 Copyright-Free Illustrations of Mammals, Birds, Fish, Insects, etc.,
Jim Harter (ed.). Clear wood engravings present, in extremely lifelike poses, over
1,000 species of animals. One of the most extensive pictorial sourcebooks of its kind.
Captions. Index. 284pp. 9 x 12. 0-486-23766-4

1001 QUESTIONS ANSWERED ABOUT THE SEASHORE, N. J. Berrill and
Jacquelyn Berrill. Queries answered about dolphins, sea snails, sponges, starfish, fishes, shore birds, many others. Covers appearance, breeding, growth, feeding, much
more. 305pp. 5¼ x 8¼. 0-486-23366-9

ATTRACTING BIRDS TO YOUR YARD, William J. Weber. Easy-to-follow guide
offers advice on how to attract the greatest diversity of birds: birdhouses, feeders,
water and waterers, much more. 96pp. 5³⁄₁₆ x 8¼. 0-486-28927-3

MEDICINAL AND OTHER USES OF NORTH AMERICAN PLANTS: A
Historical Survey with Special Reference to the Eastern Indian Tribes, Charlotte
Erichsen-Brown. Chronological historical citations document 500 years of usage of
plants, trees, shrubs native to eastern Canada, northeastern U.S. Also complete identifying information. 343 illustrations. 544pp. 6½ x 9¼. 0-486-25951-X

STORYBOOK MAZES, Dave Phillips. 23 stories and mazes on two-page spreads:
Wizard of Oz, Treasure Island, Robin Hood, etc. Solutions. 64pp. 8¼ x 11.
0-486-23628-5

AMERICAN NEGRO SONGS: 230 Folk Songs and Spirituals, Religious and
Secular, John W. Work. This authoritative study traces the African influences of songs
sung and played by black Americans at work, in church, and as entertainment. The
author discusses the lyric significance of such songs as "Swing Low, Sweet Chariot,"
"John Henry," and others and offers the words and music for 230 songs.
Bibliography. Index of Song Titles. 272pp. 6½ x 9¼. 0-486-40271-1

MOVIE-STAR PORTRAITS OF THE FORTIES, John Kobal (ed.). 163 glamor,
studio photos of 106 stars of the 1940s: Rita Hayworth, Ava Gardner, Marlon
Brando, Clark Gable, many more. 176pp. 8⅜ x 11¼. 0-486-23546-7

YEKL and THE IMPORTED BRIDEGROOM AND OTHER STORIES OF
YIDDISH NEW YORK, Abraham Cahan. Film Hester Street based on Yekl (1896).
Novel, other stories among first about Jewish immigrants on N.Y.'s East Side. 240pp.
5⅜ x 8½. 0-486-22427-9

SELECTED POEMS, Walt Whitman. Generous sampling from Leaves of Grass.
Twenty-four poems include "I Hear America Singing," "Song of the Open Road," "I
Sing the Body Electric," "When Lilacs Last in the Dooryard Bloom'd," "O Captain!
My Captain!"–all reprinted from an authoritative edition. Lists of titles and first lines.
128pp. 5³⁄₁₆ x 8¼. 0-486-26878-0

SONGS OF EXPERIENCE: Facsimile Reproduction with 26 Plates in Full Color,
William Blake. 26 full-color plates from a rare 1826 edition. Includes "The Tyger,"
"London," "Holy Thursday," and other poems. Printed text of poems. 48pp. 5¼ x 7.
0 486 24636 1

THE BEST TALES OF HOFFMANN, E. T. A. Hoffmann. 10 of Hoffmann's most
important stories: "Nutcracker and the King of Mice," "The Golden Flowerpot," etc.
458pp. 5⅜ x 8½. 0-486-21793-0

THE BOOK OF TEA, Kakuzo Okakura. Minor classic of the Orient: entertaining,
charming explanation, interpretation of traditional Japanese culture in terms of tea
ceremony. 94pp. 5⅜ x 8½. 0-486-20070-1

FRENCH STORIES/CONTES FRANÇAIS: A Dual-Language Book, Wallace Fowlie. Ten stories by French masters, Voltaire to Camus: "Micromegas" by Voltaire; "The Atheist's Mass" by Balzac; "Minuet" by de Maupassant; "The Guest" by Camus, six more. Excellent English translations on facing pages. Also French-English vocabulary list, exercises, more. 352pp. 5⅜ x 8½. 0-486-26443-2

CHICAGO AT THE TURN OF THE CENTURY IN PHOTOGRAPHS: 122 Historic Views from the Collections of the Chicago Historical Society, Larry A. Viskochil. Rare large-format prints offer detailed views of City Hall, State Street, the Loop, Hull House, Union Station, many other landmarks, circa 1904-1913. Introduction. Captions. Maps. 144pp. 9⅜ x 12¼. 0-486-24656-6

OLD BROOKLYN IN EARLY PHOTOGRAPHS, 1865-1929, William Lee Younger. Luna Park, Gravesend race track, construction of Grand Army Plaza, moving of Hotel Brighton, etc. 157 previously unpublished photographs. 165pp. 8⅜ x 11¾. 0-486-23587-4

THE MYTHS OF THE NORTH AMERICAN INDIANS, Lewis Spence. Rich anthology of the myths and legends of the Algonquins, Iroquois, Pawnees and Sioux, prefaced by an extensive historical and ethnological commentary. 36 illustrations. 480pp. 5⅜ x 8½. 0-486-25967-6

AN ENCYCLOPEDIA OF BATTLES: Accounts of Over 1,560 Battles from 1479 B.C. to the Present, David Eggenberger. Essential details of every major battle in recorded history from the first battle of Megiddo in 1479 B.C. to Grenada in 1984. List of Battle Maps. New Appendix covering the years 1967-1984. Index. 99 illustrations. 544pp. 6½ x 9¼. 0-486-24913-1

SAILING ALONE AROUND THE WORLD, Captain Joshua Slocum. First man to sail around the world, alone, in small boat. One of great feats of seamanship told in delightful manner. 67 illustrations. 294pp. 5⅜ x 8½. 0-486-20326-3

ANARCHISM AND OTHER ESSAYS, Emma Goldman. Powerful, penetrating, prophetic essays on direct action, role of minorities, prison reform, puritan hypocrisy, violence, etc. 271pp. 5⅜ x 8½. 0-486-22484-8

MYTHS OF THE HINDUS AND BUDDHISTS, Ananda K. Coomaraswamy and Sister Nivedita. Great stories of the epics; deeds of Krishna, Shiva, taken from puranas, Vedas, folk tales; etc. 32 illustrations. 400pp. 5⅜ x 8½. 0-486-21759-0

MY BONDAGE AND MY FREEDOM, Frederick Douglass. Born a slave, Douglass became outspoken force in antislavery movement. The best of Douglass' autobiographies. Graphic description of slave life. 464pp. 5⅜ x 8½. 0-486-22457-0

FOLLOWING THE EQUATOR: A Journey Around the World, Mark Twain. Fascinating humorous account of 1897 voyage to Hawaii, Australia, India, New Zealand, etc. Ironic, bemused reports on peoples, customs, climate, flora and fauna, politics, much more. 197 illustrations. 720pp. 5⅜ x 8½. 0-486-26113-1

THE PEOPLE CALLED SHAKERS, Edward D. Andrews. Definitive study of Shakers: origins, beliefs, practices, dances, social organization, furniture and crafts, etc. 33 illustrations. 351pp. 5⅜ x 8½. 0-486-21081-2

THE MYTHS OF GREECE AND ROME, H. A. Guerber. A classic of mythology, generously illustrated, long prized for its simple, graphic, accurate retelling of the principal myths of Greece and Rome, and for its commentary on their origins and significance. With 64 illustrations by Michelangelo, Raphael, Titian, Rubens, Canova, Bernini and others. 480pp. 5⅜ x 8½. 0-486-27584-1

PSYCHOLOGY OF MUSIC, Carl E. Seashore. Classic work discusses music as a medium from psychological viewpoint. Clear treatment of physical acoustics, auditory apparatus, sound perception, development of musical skills, nature of musical feeling, host of other topics. 88 figures. 408pp. 5⅜ x 8½.   0-486-21851-1

LIFE IN ANCIENT EGYPT, Adolf Erman. Fullest, most thorough, detailed older account with much not in more recent books, domestic life, religion, magic, medicine, commerce, much more. Many illustrations reproduce tomb paintings, carvings, hieroglyphs, etc. 597pp. 5⅜ x 8½.   0-486-22632-8

SUNDIALS, Their Theory and Construction, Albert Waugh. Far and away the best, most thorough coverage of ideas, mathematics concerned, types, construction, adjusting anywhere. Simple, nontechnical treatment allows even children to build several of these dials. Over 100 illustrations. 230pp. 5⅜ x 8½.   0-486-22947-5

THEORETICAL HYDRODYNAMICS, L. M. Milne-Thomson. Classic exposition of the mathematical theory of fluid motion, applicable to both hydrodynamics and aerodynamics. Over 600 exercises. 768pp. 6⅛ x 9¼.   0-486-68970-0

OLD-TIME VIGNETTES IN FULL COLOR, Carol Belanger Grafton (ed.). Over 390 charming, often sentimental illustrations, selected from archives of Victorian graphics—pretty women posing, children playing, food, flowers, kittens and puppies, smiling cherubs, birds and butterflies, much more. All copyright-free. 48pp. 9¼ x 12¼.   0-486-27269-9

PERSPECTIVE FOR ARTISTS, Rex Vicat Cole. Depth, perspective of sky and sea, shadows, much more, not usually covered. 391 diagrams, 81 reproductions of drawings and paintings. 279pp. 5⅜ x 8½.   0-486-22487-2

DRAWING THE LIVING FIGURE, Joseph Sheppard. Innovative approach to artistic anatomy focuses on specifics of surface anatomy, rather than muscles and bones. Over 170 drawings of live models in front, back and side views, and in widely varying poses. Accompanying diagrams. 177 illustrations. Introduction. Index. 144pp. 8⅜ x11¼.   0-486-26723-7

GOTHIC AND OLD ENGLISH ALPHABETS: 100 Complete Fonts, Dan X. Solo. Add power, elegance to posters, signs, other graphics with 100 stunning copyright-free alphabets: Blackstone, Dolbey, Germania, 97 more—including many lower-case, numerals, punctuation marks. 104pp. 8⅛ x 11.   0-486-24695-7

THE BOOK OF WOOD CARVING, Charles Marshall Sayers. Finest book for beginners discusses fundamentals and offers 34 designs. "Absolutely first rate . . . well thought out and well executed."–E. J. Tangerman. 118pp. 7¾ x 10⅜.   0-486-23654-4

ILLUSTRATED CATALOG OF CIVIL WAR MILITARY GOODS: Union Army Weapons, Insignia, Uniform Accessories, and Other Equipment, Schuyler, Hartley, and Graham. Rare, profusely illustrated 1846 catalog includes Union Army uniform and dress regulations, arms and ammunition, coats, insignia, flags, swords, rifles, etc. 226 illustrations. 160pp. 9 x 12.   0-486-24939-5

WOMEN'S FASHIONS OF THE EARLY 1900s: An Unabridged Republication of "New York Fashions, 1909," National Cloak & Suit Co. Rare catalog of mail-order fashions documents women's and children's clothing styles shortly after the turn of the century. Captions offer full descriptions, prices. Invaluable resource for fashion, costume historians. Approximately 725 illustrations. 128pp. 8⅜ x 11¼.
           0-486-27276-1

HOW TO DO BEADWORK, Mary White. Fundamental book on craft from simple projects to five-bead chains and woven works. 106 illustrations. 142pp. 5⅜ x 8.
0-486-20697-1

THE 1912 AND 1915 GUSTAV STICKLEY FURNITURE CATALOGS, Gustav Stickley. With over 200 detailed illustrations and descriptions, these two catalogs are essential reading and reference materials and identification guides for Stickley furniture. Captions cite materials, dimensions and prices. 112pp. 6½ x 9¼. 0-486-26676-1

EARLY AMERICAN LOCOMOTIVES, John H. White, Jr. Finest locomotive engravings from early 19th century: historical (1804–74), main-line (after 1870), special, foreign, etc. 147 plates. 142pp. 11⅜ x 8¼. 0-486-22772-3

LITTLE BOOK OF EARLY AMERICAN CRAFTS AND TRADES, Peter Stockham (ed.). 1807 children's book explains crafts and trades: baker, hatter, cooper, potter, and many others. 23 copperplate illustrations. 140pp. 4⁵/₈ x 6.
0-486-23336-7

VICTORIAN FASHIONS AND COSTUMES FROM HARPER'S BAZAR, 1867–1898, Stella Blum (ed.). Day costumes, evening wear, sports clothes, shoes, hats, other accessories in over 1,000 detailed engravings. 320pp. 9⅜ x 12¼.
0-486-22990-4

THE LONG ISLAND RAIL ROAD IN EARLY PHOTOGRAPHS, Ron Ziel. Over 220 rare photos, informative text document origin (1844) and development of rail service on Long Island. Vintage views of early trains, locomotives, stations, passengers, crews, much more. Captions. 8⅞ x 11¾. 0-486-26301-0

VOYAGE OF THE LIBERDADE, Joshua Slocum. Great 19th-century mariner's thrilling, first-hand account of the wreck of his ship off South America, the 35-foot boat he built from the wreckage, and its remarkable voyage home. 128pp. 5⅜ x 8½.
0-486-40022-0

TEN BOOKS ON ARCHITECTURE, Vitruvius. The most important book ever written on architecture. Early Roman aesthetics, technology, classical orders, site selection, all other aspects. Morgan translation. 331pp. 5⅜ x 8½. 0-486-20645-9

THE HUMAN FIGURE IN MOTION, Eadweard Muybridge. More than 4,500 stopped-action photos, in action series, showing undraped men, women, children jumping, lying down, throwing, sitting, wrestling, carrying, etc. 390pp. 7⅞ x 10⅝.
0-486-20204-6 Clothbd.

TREES OF THE EASTERN AND CENTRAL UNITED STATES AND CANADA, William M. Harlow. Best one-volume guide to 140 trees. Full descriptions, woodlore, range, etc. Over 600 illustrations. Handy size. 288pp. 4½ x 6⅜. 0-486-20395-6

GROWING AND USING HERBS AND SPICES, Milo Miloradovich. Versatile handbook provides all the information needed for cultivation and use of all the herbs and spices available in North America. 4 illustrations. Index. Glossary. 236pp. 5⅜ x 8½.
0-486-25058-X

BIG BOOK OF MAZES AND LABYRINTHS, Walter Shepherd. 50 mazes and labyrinths in all–classical, solid, ripple, and more–in one great volume. Perfect inexpensive puzzler for clever youngsters. Full solutions. 112pp. 8⅛ x 11. 0-486-22951-3

PIANO TUNING, J. Cree Fischer. Clearest, best book for beginner, amateur. Simple repairs, raising dropped notes, tuning by easy method of flattened fifths. No previous skills needed. 4 illustrations. 201pp. 5⅜ x 8½. 0-486-23267-0

HINTS TO SINGERS, Lillian Nordica. Selecting the right teacher, developing confidence, overcoming stage fright, and many other important skills receive thoughtful discussion in this indispensible guide, written by a world-famous diva of four decades' experience. 96pp. 5⅜ x 8½. 0-486-40094-8

THE COMPLETE NONSENSE OF EDWARD LEAR, Edward Lear. All nonsense limericks, zany alphabets, Owl and Pussycat, songs, nonsense botany, etc., illustrated by Lear. Total of 320pp. 5⅜ x 8½. (Available in U.S. only.) 0-486-20167-8

VICTORIAN PARLOUR POETRY: An Annotated Anthology, Michael R. Turner. 117 gems by Longfellow, Tennyson, Browning, many lesser-known poets. "The Village Blacksmith," "Curfew Must Not Ring Tonight," "Only a Baby Small," dozens more, often difficult to find elsewhere. Index of poets, titles, first lines. xxiii + 325pp. 5⅜ x 8¼. 0-486-27044-0

DUBLINERS, James Joyce. Fifteen stories offer vivid, tightly focused observations of the lives of Dublin's poorer classes. At least one, "The Dead," is considered a masterpiece. Reprinted complete and unabridged from standard edition. 160pp. 5³⁄₁₆ x 8¼. 0-486-26870-5

GREAT WEIRD TALES: 14 Stories by Lovecraft, Blackwood, Machen and Others, S. T. Joshi (ed.). 14 spellbinding tales, including "The Sin Eater," by Fiona McLeod, "The Eye Above the Mantel," by Frank Belknap Long, as well as renowned works by R. H. Barlow, Lord Dunsany, Arthur Machen, W. C. Morrow and eight other masters of the genre. 256pp. 5⅜ x 8½. (Available in U.S. only.) 0-486-40436-6

THE BOOK OF THE SACRED MAGIC OF ABRAMELIN THE MAGE, translated by S. MacGregor Mathers. Medieval manuscript of ceremonial magic. Basic document in Aleister Crowley, Golden Dawn groups. 268pp. 5⅜ x 8½. 0-486-23211-5

THE BATTLES THAT CHANGED HISTORY, Fletcher Pratt. Eminent historian profiles 16 crucial conflicts, ancient to modern, that changed the course of civilization. 352pp. 5⅜ x 8½. 0-486-41129-X

NEW RUSSIAN-ENGLISH AND ENGLISH-RUSSIAN DICTIONARY, M. A. O'Brien. This is a remarkably handy Russian dictionary, containing a surprising amount of information, including over 70,000 entries. 366pp. 4½ x 6⅛. 0-486-20208-9

NEW YORK IN THE FORTIES, Andreas Feininger. 162 brilliant photographs by the well-known photographer, formerly with *Life* magazine. Commuters, shoppers, Times Square at night, much else from city at its peak. Captions by John von Hartz. 181pp. 9¼ x 10¾. 0-486-23585-8

INDIAN SIGN LANGUAGE, William Tomkins. Over 525 signs developed by Sioux and other tribes. Written instructions and diagrams. Also 290 pictographs. 111pp. 6⅛ x 9¼. 0-486-22029-X

ANATOMY: A Complete Guide for Artists, Joseph Sheppard. A master of figure drawing shows artists how to render human anatomy convincingly. Over 460 illustrations. 224pp. 8⅜ x 11¼. 0-486-27279-6

MEDIEVAL CALLIGRAPHY: Its History and Technique, Marc Drogin. Spirited history, comprehensive instruction manual covers 13 styles (ca. 4th century through 15th). Excellent photographs; directions for duplicating medieval techniques with modern tools. 224pp. 8⅜ x 11¼. 0-486-26142-5

DRIED FLOWERS: How to Prepare Them, Sarah Whitlock and Martha Rankin. Complete instructions on how to use silica gel, meal and borax, perlite aggregate, sand and borax, glycerine and water to create attractive permanent flower arrangements. 12 illustrations. 32pp. 5⅜ x 8½.　　　　　　　　　0-486-21802-3

EASY-TO-MAKE BIRD FEEDERS FOR WOODWORKERS, Scott D. Campbell. Detailed, simple-to-use guide for designing, constructing, caring for and using feeders. Text, illustrations for 12 classic and contemporary designs. 96pp. 5⅜ x 8½.
　　　　　　　　　　　　　　　　　　　　　　　　0-486-25847-5

THE COMPLETE BOOK OF BIRDHOUSE CONSTRUCTION FOR WOOD-WORKERS, Scott D. Campbell. Detailed instructions, illustrations, tables. Also data on bird habitat and instinct patterns. Bibliography. 3 tables. 63 illustrations in 15 figures. 48pp. 5¼ x 8½.　　　　　　　　　　　　　　　0-486-24407-5

SCOTTISH WONDER TALES FROM MYTH AND LEGEND, Donald A. Mackenzie. 16 lively tales tell of giants rumbling down mountainsides, of a magic wand that turns stone pillars into warriors, of gods and goddesses, evil hags, powerful forces and more. 240pp. 5⅜ x 8½.　　　　　　　0-486-29677-6

THE HISTORY OF UNDERCLOTHES, C. Willett Cunnington and Phyllis Cunnington. Fascinating, well-documented survey covering six centuries of English undergarments, enhanced with over 100 illustrations: 12th-century laced-up bodice, footed long drawers (1795), 19th-century bustles, 19th-century corsets for men, Victorian "bust improvers," much more. 272pp. 5⅜ x 8¼.　　0-486-27124-2

ARTS AND CRAFTS FURNITURE: The Complete Brooks Catalog of 1912, Brooks Manufacturing Co. Photos and detailed descriptions of more than 150 now very collectible furniture designs from the Arts and Crafts movement depict davenports, settees, buffets, desks, tables, chairs, bedsteads, dressers and more, all built of solid, quarter-sawed oak. Invaluable for students and enthusiasts of antiques, Americana and the decorative arts. 80pp. 6½ x 9¼.　　　0-486-27471-3

WILBUR AND ORVILLE: A Biography of the Wright Brothers, Fred Howard. Definitive, crisply written study tells the full story of the brothers' lives and work. A vividly written biography, unparalleled in scope and color, that also captures the spirit of an extraordinary era. 560pp. 6⅛ x 9¼.　　　0-486-40297-5

THE ARTS OF THE SAILOR: Knotting, Splicing and Ropework, Hervey Garrett Smith. Indispensable shipboard reference covers tools, basic knots and useful hitches; handsewing and canvas work, more. Over 100 illustrations. Delightful reading for sea lovers. 256pp. 5⅜ x 8½.　　　　　　　　　　　0-486-26440-8

FRANK LLOYD WRIGHT'S FALLINGWATER: The House and Its History, Second, Revised Edition, Donald Hoffmann. A total revision–both in text and illustrations–of the standard document on Fallingwater, the boldest, most personal architectural statement of Wright's mature years, updated with valuable new material from the recently opened Frank Lloyd Wright Archives. "Fascinating"–*The New York Times*. 116 illustrations. 128pp. 9¼ x 10¾.　　　0-486-27430-6

PHOTOGRAPHIC SKETCHBOOK OF THE CIVIL WAR, Alexander Gardner. 100 photos taken on field during the Civil War. Famous shots of Manassas Harper's Ferry, Lincoln, Richmond, slave pens, etc. 244pp. 10⅝ x 8¼.　0-486-22731-6

FIVE ACRES AND INDEPENDENCE, Maurice G. Kains. Great back-to-the-land classic explains basics of self-sufficient farming. The one book to get. 95 illustrations. 397pp. 5⅜ x 8½.　　　　　　　　　　　　　　　0-486-20974-1

A MODERN HERBAL, Margaret Grieve. Much the fullest, most exact, most useful compilation of herbal material. Gigantic alphabetical encyclopedia, from aconite to zedoary, gives botanical information, medical properties, folklore, economic uses, much else. Indispensable to serious reader. 161 illustrations. 888pp. 6½ x 9¼. 2-vol. set. (Available in U.S. only.)   Vol. I: 0-486-22798-7   Vol. II: 0-486-22799-5

HIDDEN TREASURE MAZE BOOK, Dave Phillips. Solve 34 challenging mazes accompanied by heroic tales of adventure. Evil dragons, people-eating plants, blood-thirsty giants, many more dangerous adversaries lurk at every twist and turn. 34 mazes, stories, solutions. 48pp. 8¼ x 11.   0-486-24566-7

LETTERS OF W. A. MOZART, Wolfgang A. Mozart. Remarkable letters show bawdy wit, humor, imagination, musical insights, contemporary musical world; includes some letters from Leopold Mozart. 276pp. 5⅜ x 8½.   0-486-22859-2

BASIC PRINCIPLES OF CLASSICAL BALLET, Agrippina Vaganova. Great Russian theoretician, teacher explains methods for teaching classical ballet. 118 illustrations. 175pp. 5⅜ x 8½.   0-486-22036-2

THE JUMPING FROG, Mark Twain. Revenge edition. The original story of The Celebrated Jumping Frog of Calaveras County, a hapless French translation, and Twain's hilarious "retranslation" from the French. 12 illustrations. 66pp. 5⅜ x 8½.
0-486-22686-7

BEST REMEMBERED POEMS, Martin Gardner (ed.). The 126 poems in this superb collection of 19th- and 20th-century British and American verse range from Shelley's "To a Skylark" to the impassioned "Renascence" of Edna St. Vincent Millay and to Edward Lear's whimsical "The Owl and the Pussycat." 224pp. 5⅜ x 8½.
0-486-27165-X

COMPLETE SONNETS, William Shakespeare. Over 150 exquisite poems deal with love, friendship, the tyranny of time, beauty's evanescence, death and other themes in language of remarkable power, precision and beauty. Glossary of archaic terms. 80pp. 5³⁄₁₆ x 8¼.   0-486-26686-9

HISTORIC HOMES OF THE AMERICAN PRESIDENTS, Second, Revised Edition, Irvin Haas. A traveler's guide to American Presidential homes, most open to the public, depicting and describing homes occupied by every American President from George Washington to George Bush. With visiting hours, admission charges, travel routes. 175 photographs. Index. 160pp. 8¼ x 11.   0-486-26751-2

THE WIT AND HUMOR OF OSCAR WILDE, Alvin Redman (ed.). More than 1,000 ripostes, paradoxes, wisecracks: Work is the curse of the drinking classes; I can resist everything except temptation; etc. 258pp. 5⅜ x 8½.   0-486-20602-5

SHAKESPEARE LEXICON AND QUOTATION DICTIONARY, Alexander Schmidt. Full definitions, locations, shades of meaning in every word in plays and poems. More than 50,000 exact quotations. 1,485pp. 6½ x 9¼. 2-vol. set.
Vol. 1: 0-486-22726-X   Vol. 2: 0-486-22727-8

SELECTED POEMS, Emily Dickinson. Over 100 best-known, best-loved poems by one of America's foremost poets, reprinted from authoritative early editions. No comparable edition at this price. Index of first lines. 64pp. 5³⁄₁₆ x 8¼. 0-486-26466-1

THE INSIDIOUS DR. FU-MANCHU, Sax Rohmer. The first of the popular mystery series introduces a pair of English detectives to their archnemesis, the diabolical Dr. Fu-Manchu. Flavorful atmosphere, fast-paced action, and colorful characters enliven this classic of the genre. 208pp. 5³⁄₁₆ x 8¼.   0-486-29898-1

THE MALLEUS MALEFICARUM OF KRAMER AND SPRENGER, translated by Montague Summers. Full text of most important witchhunter's "bible," used by both Catholics and Protestants. 278pp. 6⅝ x 10.   0-486-22802-9

SPANISH STORIES/CUENTOS ESPAÑOLES: A Dual-Language Book, Angel Flores (ed.). Unique format offers 13 great stories in Spanish by Cervantes, Borges, others. Faithful English translations on facing pages. 352pp. 5⅜ x 8½.

0-486-25399-6

GARDEN CITY, LONG ISLAND, IN EARLY PHOTOGRAPHS, 1869–1919, Mildred H. Smith. Handsome treasury of 118 vintage pictures, accompanied by carefully researched captions, document the Garden City Hotel fire (1899), the Vanderbilt Cup Race (1908), the first airmail flight departing from the Nassau Boulevard Aerodrome (1911), and much more. 96pp. 8⅞ x 11¾.   0-486-40669-5

OLD QUEENS, N.Y., IN EARLY PHOTOGRAPHS, Vincent F. Seyfried and William Asadorian. Over 160 rare photographs of Maspeth, Jamaica, Jackson Heights, and other areas. Vintage views of DeWitt Clinton mansion, 1939 World's Fair and more. Captions. 192pp. 8⅞ x 11.   0-486-26358-4

CAPTURED BY THE INDIANS: 15 Firsthand Accounts, 1750-1870, Frederick Drimmer. Astounding true historical accounts of grisly torture, bloody conflicts, relentless pursuits, miraculous escapes and more, by people who lived to tell the tale. 384pp. 5⅜ x 8½.   0-486-24901-8

THE WORLD'S GREAT SPEECHES (Fourth Enlarged Edition), Lewis Copeland, Lawrence W. Lamm, and Stephen J. McKenna. Nearly 300 speeches provide public speakers with a wealth of updated quotes and inspiration–from Pericles' funeral oration and William Jennings Bryan's "Cross of Gold Speech" to Malcolm X's powerful words on the Black Revolution and Earl of Spenser's tribute to his sister, Diana, Princess of Wales. 944pp. 5⅜ x 8⅜.   0-486-40903-1

THE BOOK OF THE SWORD, Sir Richard F. Burton. Great Victorian scholar/adventurer's eloquent, erudite history of the "queen of weapons"–from prehistory to early Roman Empire. Evolution and development of early swords, variations (sabre, broadsword, cutlass, scimitar, etc.), much more. 336pp. 6⅛ x 9¼.

0-486-25434-8

AUTOBIOGRAPHY: The Story of My Experiments with Truth, Mohandas K. Gandhi. Boyhood, legal studies, purification, the growth of the Satyagraha (nonviolent protest) movement. Critical, inspiring work of the man responsible for the freedom of India. 480pp. 5⅜ x 8½. (Available in U.S. only.)   0-486-24593-4

CELTIC MYTHS AND LEGENDS, T. W. Rolleston. Masterful retelling of Irish and Welsh stories and tales. Cuchulain, King Arthur, Deirdre, the Grail, many more. First paperback edition. 58 full-page illustrations. 512pp. 5⅜ x 8½.   0-486-26507-2

THE PRINCIPLES OF PSYCHOLOGY, William James. Famous long course complete, unabridged. Stream of thought, time perception, memory, experimental methods; great work decades ahead of its time. 94 figures. 1,391pp. 5⅜ x 8½. 2-vol. set.
Vol. I: 0-486-20381-6   Vol. II: 0-486-20382-4

THE WORLD AS WILL AND REPRESENTATION, Arthur Schopenhauer. Definitive English translation of Schopenhauer's life work, correcting more than 1,000 errors, omissions in earlier translations. Translated by E. F. J. Payne. Total of 1,269pp. 5⅜ x 8½. 2-vol. set.   Vol. 1: 0-486-21761-2   Vol. 2: 0-486-21762-0

CATALOG OF DOVER BOOKS

MAGIC AND MYSTERY IN TIBET, Madame Alexandra David-Neel. Experiences among lamas, magicians, sages, sorcerers, Bonpa wizards. A true psychic discovery. 32 illustrations. 321pp. 5⅜ x 8½. (Available in U.S. only.)　　0-486-22682-4

THE EGYPTIAN BOOK OF THE DEAD, E. A. Wallis Budge. Complete reproduction of Ani's papyrus, finest ever found. Full hieroglyphic text, interlinear transliteration, word-for-word translation, smooth translation. 533pp. 6½ x 9¼.
　　0 486 21866 X

HISTORIC COSTUME IN PICTURES, Braun & Schneider. Over 1,450 costumed figures in clearly detailed engravings–from dawn of civilization to end of 19th century. Captions. Many folk costumes. 256pp. 8⅜ x 11¾.　　0-486-23150-X

MATHEMATICS FOR THE NONMATHEMATICIAN, Morris Kline. Detailed, college-level treatment of mathematics in cultural and historical context, with numerous exercises. Recommended Reading Lists. Tables. Numerous figures. 641pp. 5⅜ x 8½.
　　0-486-24823-2

PROBABILISTIC METHODS IN THE THEORY OF STRUCTURES, Isaac Elishakoff. Well-written introduction covers the elements of the theory of probability from two or more random variables, the reliability of such multivariable structures, the theory of random function, Monte Carlo methods of treating problems incapable of exact solution, and more. Examples. 502pp. 5⅜ x 8½.　　0-486-40691-1

THE RIME OF THE ANCIENT MARINER, Gustave Doré, S. T. Coleridge. Doré's finest work; 34 plates capture moods, subtleties of poem. Flawless full-size reproductions printed on facing pages with authoritative text of poem. "Beautiful. Simply beautiful."–Publisher's Weekly. 77pp. 9¼ x 12.　　0-486-22305-1

SCULPTURE: Principles and Practice, Louis Slobodkin. Step-by-step approach to clay, plaster, metals, stone; classical and modern. 253 drawings, photos. 255pp. 8⅜ x 11.
　　0-486-22960-2

THE INFLUENCE OF SEA POWER UPON HISTORY, 1660-1783, A. T. Mahan. Influential classic of naval history and tactics still used as text in war colleges. First paperback edition. 4 maps. 24 battle plans. 640pp. 5⅜ x 8½.　　0-486-25509-3

THE STORY OF THE TITANIC AS TOLD BY ITS SURVIVORS, Jack Winocour (ed.). What it was really like. Panic, despair, shocking inefficiency, and a little heroism. More thrilling than any fictional account. 26 illustrations. 320pp. 5⅜ x 8½.
　　0-486-20610-6

ONE TWO THREE . . . INFINITY: Facts and Speculations of Science, George Gamow. Great physicist's fascinating, readable overview of contemporary science: number theory, relativity, fourth dimension, entropy, genes, atomic structure, much more. 128 illustrations. Index. 352pp. 5⅜ x 8½.　　0-486-25664-2

DALÍ ON MODERN ART: The Cuckolds of Antiquated Modern Art, Salvador Dalí. Influential painter skewers modern art and its practitioners. Outrageous evaluations of Picasso, Cézanne, Turner, more. 15 renderings of paintings discussed. 44 calligraphic decorations by Dalí. 96pp. 5⅜ x 8½. (Available in U.S. only.)　　0-486-29220-7

ANTIQUE PLAYING CARDS: A Pictorial History, Henry René D'Allemagne. Over 900 elaborate, decorative images from rare playing cards (14th–20th centuries): Bacchus, death, dancing dogs, hunting scenes, royal coats of arms, players cheating, much more. 96pp. 9¼ x 12¼.　　0-486-29265-7

MAKING FURNITURE MASTERPIECES: 30 Projects with Measured Drawings, Franklin H. Gottshall. Step-by-step instructions, illustrations for constructing handsome, useful pieces, among them a Sheraton desk, Chippendale chair, Spanish desk, Queen Anne table and a William and Mary dressing mirror. 224pp. 8⅛ x 11¼.
0-486-29338-6

NORTH AMERICAN INDIAN DESIGNS FOR ARTISTS AND CRAFTSPEOPLE, Eva Wilson. Over 360 authentic copyright-free designs adapted from Navajo blankets, Hopi pottery, Sioux buffalo hides, more. Geometrics, symbolic figures, plant and animal motifs, etc. 128pp. 8⅜ x 11. (Not for sale in the United Kingdom.)   0-486-25341-4

THE FOSSIL BOOK: A Record of Prehistoric Life, Patricia V. Rich et al. Profusely illustrated definitive guide covers everything from single-celled organisms and dinosaurs to birds and mammals and the interplay between climate and man. Over 1,500 illustrations. 760pp. 7½ x 10¼.   0-486-29371-8

VICTORIAN ARCHITECTURAL DETAILS: Designs for Over 700 Stairs, Mantels, Doors, Windows, Cornices, Porches, and Other Decorative Elements, A. J. Bicknell & Company. Everything from dormer windows and piazzas to balconies and gable ornaments. Also includes elevations and floor plans for handsome, private residences and commercial structures. 80pp. 9⅜ x 12¼.   0-486-44015-X

WESTERN ISLAMIC ARCHITECTURE: A Concise Introduction, John D. Hoag. Profusely illustrated critical appraisal compares and contrasts Islamic mosques and palaces—from Spain and Egypt to other areas in the Middle East. 139 illustrations. 128pp. 6 x 9.   0-486-43760-4

CHINESE ARCHITECTURE: A Pictorial History, Liang Ssu-ch'eng. More than 240 rare photographs and drawings depict temples, pagodas, tombs, bridges, and imperial palaces comprising much of China's architectural heritage. 152 halftones, 94 diagrams. 232pp. 10¾ x 9⅞.   0-486-43999-2

THE RENAISSANCE: Studies in Art and Poetry, Walter Pater. One of the most talked-about books of the 19th century, *The Renaissance* combines scholarship and philosophy in an innovative work of cultural criticism that examines the achievements of Botticelli, Leonardo, Michelangelo, and other artists. "The holy writ of beauty."–Oscar Wilde. 160pp. 5⅜ x 8½.   0-486-44025-7

A TREATISE ON PAINTING, Leonardo da Vinci. The great Renaissance artist's practical advice on drawing and painting techniques covers anatomy, perspective, composition, light and shadow, and color. A classic of art instruction, it features 48 drawings by Nicholas Poussin and Leon Battista Alberti. 192pp. 5⅜ x 8½.
0-486-44155-5

THE MIND OF LEONARDO DA VINCI, Edward McCurdy. More than just a biography, this classic study by a distinguished historian draws upon Leonardo's extensive writings to offer numerous demonstrations of the Renaissance master's achievements, not only in sculpture and painting, but also in music, engineering, and even experimental aviation. 384pp. 5⅜ x 8½.   0-486-44142-3

WASHINGTON IRVING'S RIP VAN WINKLE, Illustrated by Arthur Rackham. Lovely prints that established artist as a leading illustrator of the time and forever etched into the popular imagination a classic of Catskill lore. 51 full-color plates. 80pp. 8⅜ x 11.   0-486-44242-X

HENSCHE ON PAINTING, John W. Robichaux. Basic painting philosophy and methodology of a great teacher, as expounded in his famous classes and workshops on Cape Cod. 7 illustrations in color on covers. 80pp. 5⅜ x 8½.   0-486-43728-0

LIGHT AND SHADE: A Classic Approach to Three-Dimensional Drawing, Mrs. Mary P. Merrifield. Handy reference clearly demonstrates principles of light and shade by revealing effects of common daylight, sunshine, and candle or artificial light on geometrical solids. 13 plates. 64pp. 5⅜ x 8½. 0-486-44143-1

ASTROLOGY AND ASTRONOMY: A Pictorial Archive of Signs and Symbols, Ernst and Johanna Lehner. Treasure trove of stories, lore, and myth, accompanied by more than 300 rare illustrations of planets, the Milky Way, signs of the zodiac, comets, meteors, and other astronomical phenomena. 192pp. 8⅜ x 11. 0-486-43981-X

JEWELRY MAKING: Techniques for Metal, Tim McCreight. Easy-to-follow instructions and carefully executed illustrations describe tools and techniques, use of gems and enamels, wire inlay, casting, and other topics. 72 line illustrations and diagrams. 176pp. 8¼ x 10⅞. 0-486-44043-5

MAKING BIRDHOUSES: Easy and Advanced Projects, Gladstone Califf. Easy-to-follow instructions include diagrams for everything from a one-room house for bluebirds to a forty-two-room structure for purple martins. 56 plates; 4 figures. 80pp. 8¼ x 6⅝. 0-486-44183-0

LITTLE BOOK OF LOG CABINS: How to Build and Furnish Them, William S. Wicks. Handy how-to manual, with instructions and illustrations for building cabins in the Adirondack style, fireplaces, stairways, furniture, beamed ceilings, and more. 102 line drawings. 96pp. 8¼ x 6⅝. 0-486-44259-4

THE SEASONS OF AMERICA PAST, Eric Sloane. From "sugaring time" and strawberry picking to Indian summer and fall harvest, a whole year's activities described in charming prose and enhanced with 79 of the author's own illustrations. 160pp. 8¼ x 11. 0-486-44220-9

THE METROPOLIS OF TOMORROW, Hugh Ferriss. Generous, prophetic vision of the metropolis of the future, as perceived in 1929. Powerful illustrations of towering structures, wide avenues, and rooftop parks—all features in many of today's modern cities. 59 illustrations. 144pp. 8¼ x 11. 0-486-43727-2

THE PATH TO ROME, Hilaire Belloc. This 1902 memoir abounds in lively vignettes from a vanished time, recounting a pilgrimage on foot across the Alps and Apennines in order to "see all Europe which the Christian Faith has saved." 77 of the author's original line drawings complement his sparkling prose. 272pp. 5⅜ x 8½. 0-486-44001-X

THE HISTORY OF RASSELAS: Prince of Abissinia, Samuel Johnson. Distinguished English writer attacks eighteenth-century optimism and man's unrealistic estimates of what life has to offer. 112pp. 5⅜ x 8½. 0-486-44094-X

A VOYAGE TO ARCTURUS, David Lindsay. A brilliant flight of pure fancy, where wild creatures crowd the fantastic landscape and demented torturers dominate victims with their bizarre mental powers. 272pp. 5⅜ x 8½. 0-486-44198-9